SELECTED CONTEMPORARY NATIVE ISSUES IN CANADA

SELECTED CONTEMPORARY NATIVE ISSUES IN CANADA

OBSERVATIONS MADE IN THE FIELD

By Eric John Large

Former Councilor and Chief of a Cree Nation in Western Canada

Copyright © 2012 by Eric John Large.

Library of Congress Control Number:		2012907559
ISBN:	Hardcover	978-1-4771-0301-2
	Softcover	978-1-4771-0300-5
	Ebook	978-1-4771-0302-9

All rights reserved. No part of this book may be reproduced or transmitted in any form or by any means, electronic or mechanical, including photocopying, recording, or by any information storage and retrieval system, without permission in writing from the copyright owner.

All errors, commissions, and omissions are the author's. The author's commentaries, opinions, and extracts are not intended to harm anyone one living, dead, or to exist in the future.

This book was printed in the United States of America.

To order additional copies of this book, contact:
Xlibris Corporation
1-888-795-4274
www.Xlibris.com
Orders@Xlibris.com

TABLE OF CONTENTS

Preface ix

Chapter 1   International Definition of a Nation—Contrast
              Northern Plains Cree Definition with the Standard
              Definition of a Nation 1

Chapter 2   Law, Legislation, and Court Decisions - Control and
              Impact on First Nations 5

Chapter 3   Government of Canada and First Nations—Contrasting
              Views of Land, Unresolved Treaties and their
              Enforcement in Relation to Health, Education, and
              Other Development Benefits 9

Chapter 4   Indian Residential Schools, Policy, Impact, and the
              Challenge of Reconciliation 13

Chapter 5   Future Trends—Dealing with Ruptured Canada
              and First Nations Relations, Increasing First Nation
              Youth Population, Diminishing Indigenous Languages
              and Culture, Alienation, Marginalization, Anomie,
              Despair, and Depression in First Nations Peoples;
              Responsibility of the Government of Canada, Second
              Level Governments (Provincial and Municipal), and
              First Nations Governments to Work in True Partnership 19

References 25

Appendix A   Health Care as a Treaty Right Position Paper Read at a
              Rally in Calgary, Alberta—September 19, 1995 27

Appendix B   News Advisory—September 11, 1995 29

Appendix C News Advisory in Regard to Dalton Halfe-Arcand—
            December 6, 1995 31

Appendix D Unrepresented Nations and Peoples Organization
            (UNPO) Monitor Working Group on Indigenous
            Populations Seventeenth Session, July 26–30, 1999
            [Partial Excerpt from UNPO Transcript] 33

Appendix E News Release Re: Sixth Session Working Group on
            Indigenous Populations November 20–December 1,
            2000, Geneva, Switzerland 39

Appendix F Report of Conference Hosted by the Indigenous Bar
            Association – Ottawa, Ontario October 20–22, 2000 43

Appendix G Report on the Indigenous Bar Association
            Conference—October 19–20, 2001, Vancouver, BC—
            Theme of Building Treaties and Restoring Relationships 47

Appendix H A Brief Analysis of Bill C-7 (2002) The First Nations
            Governance Act 67

Appendix I Report on the AFN Confederacy of Nations Meeting—
            December 10, 11, and 12, 2002, the Crown Plaza Hotel,
            Ottawa, Ontario 69

Appendix J New Duties for the Crown and Aboriginal Peoples
            Forum, April 26–27, 2005, Fairmont Chateau Laurier,
            Ottawa, Ontario — A Report 83

Appendix K Keynote Address National Cree Gathering 2005 at
            Saddle Lake Cree Nation 103

References and Acknowledgments 113

Appendix L 7th World Indigenous Peoples Conference on Education
            (WIPCE), November 27–December 1, 2005 117

Appendix M 2006 World Indigenous Higher Education Consortium
[WINHEC] Conference, Fond du Lac Tribal
Community College [FDLTCC], Cloquet, Minnesota,
USA, August 7, 8, and 9, 2006—A Report 139

Appendix N Indian Residential Schools Hearing—October 12–13,
2006, Alberta Court of Queen's Bench, Court House,
611—4th Sw, Calgary—A Partial Report.............................. 155

Appendix O First Nations Confederacy of Cultural Education
Centers Annual General Assembly, October 20–21,
2006—Radisson Hotel, Winnipeg, Manitoba—A Report 171

Appendix P United Nations Expert Seminar on Treaties,
Agreements, and Other Constructive Arrangements
Between States and Indigenous Peoples—Hobbema,
Alberta, November 14–17, 2006—A Partial Report............179

Appendix Q Assembly of First Nations Special Chiefs Assembly,
December 5, 6, and 7, 2006, Westin Ottawa Hotel/
Ottawa Congress Centre—A Partial Report 189

Appendix R "Breaking the Silence: International Conference of the
Indian Residential Schools Truth and Reconciliation
Commission of Canada" at L'Université de Montréal,
September 26–27, 2008, a Brief Report................................ 205

Appendix S Truth and Reconciliation Commission—Sharing
Truth: Creating a National Research Centre on
Residential Schools Conference, March 1–3, 2011,
Vancouver, British Columbia—A Summary Report........... 221

Appendix T "Delgamuukw: One Year After" Conference, February
18–19, 1999, Victoria Conference Centre, Victoria,
British Columbia—A Report.. 245

Appendix U Preparing for the Truth Commission: Sharing the Truth About Residential Schools—A Conference on Truth and Reconciliation as Restorative Justice June 14–17, 2007, at the University of Calgary—A Partial Report........ 259

Appendix V United Nations Inauguration Ceremony for the Year of Indigenous Peoples, December 10, 1992 New York City, New York—A Brief Report... 279

Resume 285

PREFACE

> Do I disturb the universe?
> In a minute there is time
> For decisions and revisions which a minute
> will reverse.
> —*The Love Song of J. Alfred Prufrock*,
> T. S. Eliot (1888–1965)

THIS BOOK IS an attempt to summarize, paraphrase, and provide commentary on contemporary Native issues in Canada I have observed prior to my public life in Native politics and in eighteen consecutive years in elected office, for a total of about thirty-five years. These issues are contrasting views of nationhood of the larger society and of Native people in general and, in particular, my Cree people; the role of law in controlling Native peoples; government views and Native peoples' views of land, treaties, health, education, and other benefits; the Indian residential school experiment and impact; and the future of Canada and Native peoples' relations. I include also twenty-two appendices composed of reports, summaries, and news releases most of which I have written and that relate to aspects of the topics covered in the five chapters of this brief book.

I provide my personal views from my life in Native politics and in my engagements with representatives of the federal and provincial governments or their agencies. These views do not necessarily reflect the current leadership of my Native Cree nation of Saddle Lake. I extract or paraphrase the views of other Canadian politicians, Native politicians, legal representatives, institutional representatives, and Native peoples (elders and women) and Canadian citizens. I also comment on the challenges, risks, and benefits that are inherent in engaging, meeting, mitigating, or highlighting these issues. Lastly, I offer suggestions on how the Native peoples of Canada may coexist with all Canadians in a spirit of peace, friendship, honour, and respect through understanding our histories and contributions and venturing together into the future.

I wish to acknowledge the verbal support and suggestions of Ms. Paulette Regan, author of *Unsettling the Settler within Indian Residential Schools, Truth Telling, and Reconciliation in Canada*, in how to handle the more controversial topics of my book and in dealing with content derived from comments of public persons, organizations, and institutions. I would also like to thank Miss Jennifer Jackson of the Saddle Lake Cree Nation for the valuable assistance she provided me by applying her knowledge of information and computer technology as I was compiling, editing, and submitting portions of the book to the publisher.

Lastly, I wish to thank my Saddle Lake Cree Nation people, (elders, former and current leaders, children, women, and youth), and the other Treaty Nations and Tribes of Canada, their elders, leaders, and peoples as I have had the honour and privilege to know and be associated with in the last thirty-five years.

CHAPTER 1

INTERNATIONAL DEFINITION OF A NATION—CONTRAST NORTHERN PLAINS CREE DEFINITION WITH THE STANDARD DEFINITION OF A NATION

MY UNDERSTANDING OF "nation" from my Cree perspective, through observation, reading, and listening to Cree leaders and elders of my area, is that there is no standard Cree definition of the term "nation" in the Cree language. There is no literal translation of "nation" in Cree. I asked one elder once what "nation" means or what a "nation" is. He replied that we, *iyiniwak* or *nehiyawak* on this island or land mass, *minstik*, now known as North America, define or designate ourselves by what we value and practice as *nehiyawak*. These values and practices were endowed to us by the Creator, *ekiymiykusiya*, and we rely on respect and the *Pipe*, sweet grass, fire, water, and rock. Also included is our indigenous Cree language and cultural practices, ways of worship, and relationships with people, the natural world, and the cosmos. Our creation stories and history were transferred from generation to generation through oral lessons, songs, drumming, ceremony, and other customs and norms that served to provide renewal, cohesion, and continuity of the tribe, clan, and family (both nuclear and extended), and also served as guides to engaging in relations of coexistence with other tribes, and later, with the first European and immigrants from other continents.

Cree tribes of the various regions of what is now Central and Western Canada, the Plains Cree, Swampy Cree, Wood or Bush Cree, traded, intermarried, skirmished with other tribes. The lands, rivers, lakes, and forests they occupied were shared according to season, though there were natural boundaries that served to indicate which tribe usually dwelled in certain land areas or harvested the natural resources (game, berries, medicines, fish, and other resources). *Siypiyk*, the North Saskatchewan River in my immediate area of Saddle Lake, was known to be the boundary between the Blackfeet of the south and the Cree of the northern plains and woods. The Cree did venture into what is now southern Alberta, into the United States, and as far south as Wyoming. The Cree may have ventured even further south and east of Central Canada and Central United States, as the language is related to the Delaware and other tribes. The Crees formed alliances with other tribes and made treaties of peace, friendship, or trade. Cree camps moved with the seasons, for traditional gathering, visiting burial sites, sites of worship (buffalo stones, medicines circles, the "Flying Rock"—*kapapamihat asini*), hunting, or fishing areas.

One interesting practice of another tribe in Eastern Canada was when a tribe or band (large group) was decimated by hunger, long winter, disease, or other calamity; they would venture into another tribe's traditional area to obtain women to bring back to their camps to replenish the numbers of the affected tribe or band. It may not be far-fetched to surmise that this was also the practice of my tribe, the Crees. In listening to elders of my area and in my readings, there was no mention of constant or ongoing vicious hostilities between tribes in Western Canada, although there were notable battles between the Crees and the Blackfeet with the last great skirmish in about 1870. What some of the warriors would do is take horses from another tribe as needed or, to show their bravery, would ride or get close to their "enemy" and touch them without harming them. This tells me that other tribes were considered friends and neighbours with whom natural boundaries overlapped, resources shared, and alliances formed.

Now, one definition of a nation, as in a nation-state, is a collection of people that has occupied or occupies a land base and has a history, a common language, laws, an army or naval force, a religion or religions according to regions, and a medium of exchange, currency or barter. Present-day Canada was formed with nation-states of Europe competing for lands and resources such as gold and other precious metals, fish, whale oil, spices, sugar, coffee, tea, textiles, furs, lumber, and later, oil and gas. Wars were fought on this continent by Great Britain, France, Spain, and later, the United States. There was Upper and Lower Canada and Maritime provinces which were all colonies of Great Britain. There's no Canada prior to 1867. It was still a colony up to the Statute of Westminster (UK, 1931). This act of the British Parliament implemented the imperial resolutions of 1929 and 1930 and declared the autonomy of Canada, Australia, New Zealand, and South Africa. Even today, some people question whether Canada is a nation as Quebec did not sign the final draft of the Constitution Act of 1982. Canada has no consistent history of one people having a common language. It has a system of English-derived common law and civil law (French civil law based on the Napoleonic code). Canada does not have one religion but has generally adopted the separation of church and state, and it has armed forces. Canada's immigration policies admit people of other ethnic origins, religions, languages, and customs from around the world, making Canada more of a modern nation in principle but in practice a country of diverse peoples, origins, and have linguistics and customs that vary from region to region. Within this current scenario, the Native peoples of Canada, specifically the Treaty peoples are mentioned in Sections 25 and 35, but are not accorded the full implementation or enforcement of the Treaties as understood by their elders and leaders, and as historical interpretations and Supreme Court of Canada (SCC) rulings would support. Instead, the federal government has been weak by not adhering to the SCC decisions, ignoring the true spirit and intent of Treaties, and failing to protect the constitutional rights of the Native or indigenous peoples of Canada.

CHAPTER 2

LAW, LEGISLATION, AND COURT DECISIONS - CONTROL AND IMPACT ON FIRST NATIONS

FEDERAL OR PROVINCIAL laws can be formalized, proposed, written, debated, amended, and given first, second, and third reading and, if agreed upon, ratified by Royal Assent before they are proclaimed as acts or statutes. I view this version of laws as an inadequate process. Without an effective oversight mechanism that will ensure the effective implementation of a law, then a law is a law only on paper. To control the Indian people of Canada, including the Cree of my area, the federal government of the past, wielding plenary power, legislation, and policy, was urged by the vested interests of the day (the mining companies, railroad magnates, and settlers from overseas) with the blessing of Great Britain. These powerful interests viewed the riches, the natural resources, and the land in Canada as profit generators and had no particular interest in the Native peoples or in their ways of life. These powerful and vested interests viewed the Native peoples as obstacles to the expansion, settlement, and development of the colonial West.

The Indian Act was the legislation that controlled the Indian peoples since 1876, the same year that Treaty No. 6 was signed at Fort Pitt, North Western Territory. This Act was used by the governments of the day, whether they were Liberal, Progressive Conservative, or now Conservative, to restrict the movement of Indian people, outlaw their ceremonies, curtail the hiring of lawyers to defend their rights and interests, and to control the produce of their harvests or sale of their furs or livestock. Since the Canada Act 1982 enactment, various Supreme Court of Canada (SCC) decisions have ruled in favour of the Natives' interests and Treaty rights highlighted with central terms such as "the duty to consult," "accommodation," "compensation," and the like. Or the SCC has encouraged the federal and provincial governments, and by extension, other parties such as companies or corporations, to negotiate fairly with Native interests and avoid costly and adversarial litigation. However, the federal government is known to not fully cooperate with the rulings of its own courts but instead to acquiesce or to let the private interests continue developing to the detriment of the rightful interests of the Native people.

The structural authority of British and Canadian law is premised and has been applied on a system of hierarchy. There is the Crown or Monarchy, the governor general of Canada, the prime minister (who is really the leader of a political party), the judges at the provincial and the federal levels, and the Supreme Court, and there are the ministers of the Crown with their ministries and administrative bureaucracies. This system of hierarchical power, authority, and jurisdiction took many decades to evolve and continues to evolve as it deals with modern challenges and realities such as the call for participatory democracy, accountability, new demands of technology (the internet with attendant disclosure and privacy concerns), population increases, demand for services, aging workforce, demand for more efficient use of resources, and increasing concern of the impact of fossil fuels.

The authoritarian structure of the British and Canadian systems of government controlled the Native peoples from the Native peoples' birth until death. Indian agents, acting on the orders of the various bureaucrats up to the level of the prime minister and minister of Indian affairs of the day, applied the various sections of the Indian Act or sometimes acted as if what they were doing was for the best interests of Native peoples. The Indian agents, farm instructors, and later socioeconomic development workers would register births, marriages, and deaths; issue seed grain, agricultural implements, fishing and trapping equipment, and livestock when available; and attempted to teach Native people how to make a living. The agents would also restrict the movement of people within and beyond the confines of the reserves and control the produce or surplus production of the Native people. The Native people were considered as wards of the government.

A particularly nefarious means of control by agents of the Crown was the false accusation of Beardy's and Okemasis First Nation members (and members of other First Nations) of engaging in the Northwest rebellion of 1885 with the forces of Louis Riel at Batoche (as recorded in the *Edmonton Journal*, July 29, 2011). Since 2001, the band has been in the process of recovering a $4 million claim from the federal government. The federal government had withheld the treaty annuity of $5.00 per band member for consecutive years 1885 to 1889. The federal government is disputing the claim. A continuing observation or conundrum is the federal government is both the trustee and the dispenser of monetary or other benefits and, for that reason, always appears to have the upper hand over dealings with the Native peoples. The federal government's control, oversight, and alleged trusteeship over First Nations continue today in one form or another. For example, it will threaten to withhold funds appropriated by Parliament should First Nation leaders refuse to sign funding agreements in a given fiscal year. Government workers will threaten, intimidate, and be recalcitrant while at the same time remain convinced that they are acting in the best interests of affected First Nations' peoples.

On the other hand, the Cree of my tribe practiced a system of equilibrium of relationships of the families, clans, various interrelated bands, and formed alliances of trade or friendship. Traditionally, there was a chief, an *okimaw* at times of calm and peace or a war chief and soldiers (warriors) took charge during times or circumstances requiring protection. Elders held the guiding hand to advise the council and the chief. People were skilled in hunting, protecting, healing, and maintaining order in the camps. Transgressors of tribal customs and laws could be banished to the edges of the camp or even away from the camp for an indefinite time. Though the individuality of the Native person (man, woman, and child) was respected and his/her role valued, individualism was secondary to the integrity, cohesion, continuity, and stability of the clans and the tribe. Relationships, roles, and responsibilities of men and women, children, extended family members, and elders were valued. The unfortunate, the disabled, the orphans, and the elders were given compassion, respect, and protection. Surplus food (game, fowl, fish, berries, wild edible plants) was shared or preserved and stored for future use. Medicines from plants were collected and preserved by medicine men and women. Anything beyond that was considered greed. An adequate supply of game, fish, fowl, or other natural resource was available almost everywhere. A surplus of food could not be easily carried from place to place. Therefore, preserved food (*pimiykan*, berries, *iywaiykana* or crushed meat mixed with fat and berries) was cached at certain locations of a clan's or tribe's territory.

Today, my people, the Native people, must take the tools of education, modern technology, and better access to land and resources to not only meet their minimum caloric needs but also to attain and maintain a better standard and quality of life. I have confidence that my people can use modern education tools while reaffirming their indigenous identity, language, and cultural knowledge.

On leadership styles, both non-Native and Native leaders must rely less on top-down leadership as the best way to run affairs. In an increasingly uncertain world, overall clear and forward vision and understanding by leaders or people in responsible positions will result in a measure of control over uncertainty in an increasingly complex world. There is no certainty in an uncertain world. There are only variations of uncertainty. Wise management, innovation, and ideas must be valued. Decisions may take longer because other players in a community or a nation must be included. Wise decision-making relies on consensus, networking, and sharing knowledge in different fields. No one person is revered because of position, birth, privilege, or the perception of entitlement. There is no "one-upmanship." No one person will be blamed if things go awry. Native people need to rearrange the system and be allowed to constructively work their own affairs through traditional methods, through tribal law and customs, and through trial and error if necessary.

Native treaty people have both inherent and Treaty rights. These rights are constitutionally guaranteed and supported by Supreme Court decisions. We Native people may make errors, but we will also offer constructive solutions to continuing challenges in meeting our needs as well as the needs of the wider society. Our people are getting educated. They have always contributed to the gross domestic product. They have assisted the fur traders, trappers, farmers, fishermen, miners, and ranchers; have been producers or middlemen in their own right; as well as have been allied with the British or the French against a prevailing common invader. My people are gaining knowledge, sharing divergent views, and adjusting to new realities while retaining their identity and cultural norms, values, and interests. My Cree Nation of Saddle Lake has produced doctors of medicine, doctors of philosophy, lawyers, bankers and financial specialists, teachers, professors, and an assortment of other professional and paraprofessional workers. In the field of public life and policy, there must be a balance between centralization and decentralization in Native and non-Native communities. Variation of opinion, new ideas, or a reworking of old but reliable ideas must be applied to meet changing situations in time and place. One can see that the government and business practices in Canada are characterized by a system of top-down leadership and are centralized, promote certainty, and allow minimum or no dissent to the political party in power or chief executive in control. The control the federal government over Native people since the eighteenth and nineteenth centuries continues today. This pervasive control manifests in the no recognition of specific Treaties or a misunderstanding of the spirit and intent of legally binding Treaties, unresolved land and resources sharing, and the misunderstanding of the Treaty benefits of health, education, and development as sourced from taxpayers or from the benevolence of the Crown.

CHAPTER 3

GOVERNMENT OF CANADA AND FIRST NATIONS—CONTRASTING VIEWS OF LAND, UNRESOLVED TREATIES AND THEIR ENFORCEMENT IN RELATION TO HEALTH, EDUCATION, AND OTHER DEVELOPMENT BENEFITS

THE ELDERS AND leaders of the Native peoples in my area say without hesitation that the land was not sold, as in fee simple, or in any other way seceded, given up, nor surrendered forever. They all say it was only to be shared with the settlers with the sanction of the Crown in Right of Great Britain at Treaty negotiation. To the Native people of my area, we are connected with this land, this island (*ministik*), from which we were formed. We cannot sell the land. Sale of land was an option permitted by the written text of Treaty No. 6 with our consent, or was it? There was no fully informed consent. My elders and leaders could not speak or write English at Treaty negotiations. They could not have understood the meaning of "cede, release, surrender, yield, or give up forever" as there was very little discussion as to what was actually being given up, though there is mention of boundaries of territory. The leaders and the people of the Northwest Territory were not informed that the Crown had previously granted a charter to the Hudson's Bay Company for certain interests in the land. After the Treaty, the reserves or *iskonikana* were lands to be kept exclusively by the Treaty Indian people. The Treaty Indian **people** were promised they could continue to live off the land and continue to practice their beliefs, customs, and laws. The leaders, the chiefs, by making their marks on the Treaty, did not give up the right to govern themselves as peoples.

    The written text of Treaty No. 6 is not entirely what was negotiated. If it was not a valid Treaty, then perhaps it was a pretext to take over the land for settlement and future extraction of natural resources. The honour of the Crown in upholding solemn agreements by her representatives is at stake. According to my elders and leaders the Treaty is valid as understood by them and what was told to them by their elders. My own grandmother would mention occasionally of the Treaty that was made at Fort Pitt and that certain benefits, including education and health benefits, and a $5.00 annuity are to be paid by the Queen through her representatives. As a child, I witnessed at Treaty time in Saddle Lake all the tribal members had to have an X-ray taken of their chests prior to the issuing of the $5.00 annuity payment. The people would gather at the community central grounds for a week to celebrate with ball games, horse races, hand games, card games, and to visit one another. Tribal members from other near and far reserves would also visit Saddle Lake.

The enforcement of the Treaty is unresolved. Perhaps there should be an international monitoring or oversight body to ensure that the Treaty is being observed and enforced by the Ministers of the Crown in Canada. Much work has been done by First Nations leaders from my Treaty area in Geneva and in New York working with the late Alfonso Miguel Martinez in the drafting and completion of the United Nations Study on Treaties and other Constructive Arrangements between States and Indigenous populations (UN ECOSOC June 1999) and the United Nations Declaration on the Rights of Indigenous Peoples. Also, First Nations leaders and elders were instrumental in the United Nations General Assembly's passage of the Declaration on the Rights of Indigenous Peoples in September 2007. Both the UN Treaty study and the Declaration of the Rights of Indigenous Peoples make strong recommendations for the recognition, validity, observance, and enforcement of Treaties, rights to land and resources, customs and laws, and other rights and interests of indigenous peoples. It is now up to Canada, as a signatory state to the Declaration of the Rights of Indigenous Peoples, to adopt and to build into its legislation, policies, practices, and actions to ensure that Native peoples in Canada are receiving standards of care and attention.

In relation to health, the Treaty people of my area retained their right to practice medicine according to their own understanding of holistic healing. They retain the right to their own medicine chest or "wiyw-wat." Medicine men and women used natural healing treatments, medicines, and ceremony to support and bring balance back to a sick person. To lessen the effects of new diseases from European contact, the medicine chest clause was set in Treaty No. 6 to ensure that medical treatment and medicines were available. Today, this is nothing less than access to full and comprehensive health benefits. At Treaty negotiations, the leaders understood that with the diminishment of the big game (buffalo, and other large game), the Crown must ensure that alternatives like education, symbolized by a school house built on the reserve, were available to their people and to their descendants in the future.

The leaders knew that education would provide their people the skills to survive and flourish. The Treaty promises that agricultural assistance (seed grain, implements, and cattle) and medicine benefits to protect from new diseases remain today but are delivered only as programs or services. Very early in the Federal-Indian relationship, two of the Treaty promises—education and health—were applied with concurrent policies and impact. Industrial education and residential school policy were selectively applied to both "do away with the Indian in the child" and to assimilate Indian people by placing their children in secluded industrial and residential schools. Industrial schools and residential schools were ostensibly set up to teach and train Indian children in European methods of learning and basic education. The schools were characterized more like Dickensian methods of control, while the affected children's bonds with their parents, extended families, and homes were severed or had and continue to have an impact on the surviving students, their children, intergeneration descendants, and communities. No one knows what the long-term effects of the Indian residential school experience will continue to have over every aspect in the lives of the surviving former students, their children, grandchildren, extended families, clans, communities, their leaders, elders, and their tribes. It has been stated elsewhere that there are more Native children in the provincial governments' child welfare systems than the estimated one hundred and fifty thousand children that resided and attended industrial, mission, and Indian residential schools.

CHAPTER 4:

INDIAN RESIDENTIAL SCHOOLS, POLICY, IMPACT, AND THE CHALLENGE OF RECONCILIATION

A BRIEF REVIEW of the colonial history of the British possessions in North America regarding the design of the residential schools concept and its development reveals that the residential school policy was one step in the assimilation of the Indian people into the numerically larger body politic that reflected European law, political orientation, and values. The assimilation process began with the passage of the Gradual Civilization Act in 1857. The Gradual Civilization Act, properly designated as, "An Act to Encourage the Gradual Civilization of Indian Tribes in this Province, and to Amend the Laws Relating to Indians," was legislated by the Province of Canada. This statute initiated the concept of enfranchisement, a process by which Native or Indian people lost their Indian status, and were transformed into British subjects possessing the right to vote, or so it was desired by the colonial authorities. The concepts of assimilation and civilization were the tactics the colonial authorities used to enact legislation that induced Native people to do away with their Indian status and to be included in the colonial society as ordinary citizens or subjects of the British Sovereign and thereby deemed to be "civilized." Under the Gradual Civilization Act, only Native men could enfranchise voluntarily, but they had to be over twenty-one years of age, be literate in English or French, be functionally educated, be free of debt, and be of good moral character. An enfranchised Native man's wife and children also lost their Indian status with no consideration for their desire otherwise.

For the period 1870 to 1910, Christian church clergy, workers, and federal government representatives collaborated to assimilate Aboriginal children into the mainstream society. In 1920, compulsory attendance for children seven to fifteen years of age was applied. Children were removed from their families and homes by clergy, Indian agents, and police. In 1948, there were seventy-two residential schools with 9,368 students. By 1979, 1,899 students attended twelve residential schools. In the 1980s, residential school former students began revealing abuses including sexual abuses they suffered at residential schools. In 1991, several individual lawsuits by Indian residential school survivors against the federal government are initiated. In 1996, the Royal Commission on Aboriginal Peoples (RCAP) Report was published. It recommended that a public hearing be convened to examine and report Indian residential school abuses. The Gordon Indian Residential School in Saskatchewan was the last federally operated residential school to close. The Assembly of First Nations (AFN) began negotiations with federal representatives to settle residential school abuses out of court. Mutual tentative talks also began with the AFN, church, federal government, and survivor representatives to develop guiding principles to resolve residential school claims.

In 1998, the federal government admitted wrongdoing, but not malfeasance, and published its regret to former students in the Statement of Reconciliation. The Aboriginal Healing Foundation, with a budget of $350 million, was established for counselling residential school survivors and funded community workshops and attempts at healing. A few residential school former students in my area mistakenly thought this fund was for individual financial compensation. I observed the beginnings of anger and anxiety expressed by former students at national and regional conferences and personally disclosed to me by, especially, elderly men as they were triggered by negative memories of residential school. Most of them said that no amount of financial compensation can pay for the loss of the spirituality, language, culture, family, and home life, and for the indignities they suffered at residential school. In 2000, law firms filed class actions or statements of claim on behalf of residential school former students. In 2003, a process called Alternative Dispute Resolution (ADR) was begun to settle some lawsuits out of court. This process affected possibly up to 250 former students in my area. Many of the claims were not settled, (or are still outstanding), or not dealt with to the satisfaction of the claimants or their heirs. Claimants who saw lawyers or form fillers (one form was a questionnaire) became confused with the growing number of forms, meetings, and workshops with lawyers and form fillers. In 2004, in response to the flaws in the ADR process, the AFN began to advocate for an equitable settlement for all Indian residential school (IRS) former students. The elements of a proposed settlement, as contained in the *Report on Canada's Dispute Resolution Plan to Compensate for Abuses in Indian Residential Schools,* called for a lump sum payment for a survivor for the years a former student attended or resided at a residential school, a truth commission, a healing fund, a commemoration fund, and an expanded equitable process for the compensation for serious physical, sexual, and psychological abuses suffered by former IRS students. In 2005, the parties to the proposed agreement signed an agreement in principle which included all the main recommendations of the AFN.

In 2006, all the parties signed the final agreement known as the Indian Residential School Settlement Agreement (IRSSA). In May of the same year, the Conservative Government Cabinet gave its approval to the IRSSA. An $8,000 advance payment was made available for eligible former students who were sixty-five years of age and over as of May 30, 2005. Courts in jurisdictions across Canada began hearings to discuss the merits of approving the agreement. Through a lack of a communication strategy by both the court(s) and the parties to the agreement, former students and communities were left wondering what was happening. Even I thought that the purpose of these court hearings was to obtain input from former IRS students. Instead, the hearings appeared to continue to fine tune the terms and conditions or to get clarity and certainty of the legal jargon contained in the articles of the 160 pages plus agreement. Some information about the phases or projected timeframe of the agreement was announced in the newspapers, some was sent to First Nations offices, and some was made available through the Internet. There was much second guessing and wonder at the survivor and community level. The IRSSA was implemented nationwide on September 19, 2007.

The financial compensation aspects of the IRSSA continue to be the focus of the former students as they rightfully claim what is legally due to them. Many of the former students are struggling to make ends meet and ensuring they have the basic needs of food, shelter, and clothing. Many are unemployed, underemployed, lacking skills, and are older. Other former students have various physical ailments or medical conditions such as hearing problems, failing eyesight, diabetes, chronic obstructive pulmonary disorders, and other conditions requiring treatment or medication. This is in addition to or co-occurrence with relationship issues involving self, family, and community, lack of trust, anomie, and having feelings of marginalization or being the focus of the settlement agreement, and especially, realizing that this perceived dysfunction could be a result of the residential school experience. Many of the former students have faced police, lawyers, judges, and have been incarcerated in provincial or federal jails for various offenses. They are now meeting lawyers, an adjudicator, and engaged in legal-like processes in the IAP abuse claim. Then there are former students who are deceased. There are a number of former students who claimed their years of residency at residential school but who have not been paid for those years. There is frustration there. There is also frustration in the IAP abuse claim process. Many former students are triggered by their retelling of their residential school abuse. They disclose to their lawyer, support worker, perhaps to a therapist or cultural person, and then again to an adjudicator at a hearing. They think they are not being believed. There is also the stigma of mental dysfunction and of not been associated with it or affected by it.

A critical observation is the residual effect of the lack of functional education in the basic reading, writing, and numeracy skills that should have formed the foundation for further education for the former IRS students. Without proper education, adequate resources, and qualified teachers with better expectations of their students, I believe many former IRS students were cheated of their education and by extension cheated out of a better quality of life for themselves, their families, their communities, and their tribes. In the early years of the industrial and residential schools, for the better portion of a school day, the students were obliged to perform hard physical labour tending cattle, vegetable fields, cutting logs, cleaning barns and yards, milking cows, mending clothes, washing dishes and pots, washing and polishing floors and stairways by hand almost always under strict supervision. Granted there were clergy, nuns, and lay staff that were kind-hearted and did not abuse students. One sad episode that I was recently reminded of, occurred in the IRS I resided at. At about the grade two level, a certain boy was exceptionally proficient in tracing or copying letters of the alphabet and probably numerals. He became so proficient in making an exact copy of a letter. But he could not understand what the letter symbolized or learn how letters of the alphabet could be arranged to mean something. As I recall, that boy remained in the residential school only about a year. It is an example of how the boy was cheated out of the future benefits of attending school.

As another phase of the IRSSA, the commemoration phase allows for community projects, activities, or events that honour, commemorate, and celebrate both the negative and positive outcomes of the residential school experience. In my area, our custom is to honour the deceased, or as we say, those that have gone ahead, *kahniykanutehcik,* and that their remains or burial places are honoured with ceremony. Other projects can be undertaken by communities such as compiling a history of the IRS, reconnecting with families, initiating projects involving recovery of language and culture, genealogy, family tree, and other positive projects. These recovery activities are crucial to the reaffirmation of the identity of the IRS survivors, their family, clan, and tribes, and to transmit this relationship rebuilding to their descendants.

There is no accurate translation of "reconciliation" in my plains Cree, "Y" dialect. "Reconciliation" can only be described with certain words in Cree. It would be translating or closely translating the phrase, "It is being fixed, something that was broken." One other term for "reconciliation," as suggested by someone else in a report I have recorded is *chakascikewin*, meaning "piling things on top of one another." But that is not quite the meaning of reconciliation. The difficulty of tackling the meaning of "reconciliation" is that, while it is mentioned in the IRSSA, there is no definition in the agreement for it. I believe reconciliation between Native and non-Native societies may take many decades to achieve as the IRS experience occurred over many decades. The IRS experience, legacy, and its effects are imbedded in attitudes and behaviours that will take many years to change. The survivors and their communities are not the only players that should be expected to reconcile. The broader society, its institutions of law, church, State, commerce, schools, universities, media, and individual Canadians must also take up the challenges of reconciliation and review, consider, and revise their perceptions of Native people in general, and of residential school former students, and their families in particular. It will not be easy. There will be denial, incredulity, embarrassment, as the silence regarding the residential school experience or experiment is broken and truths are revealed. The challenge for everyone is to consider the risks, benefits, and opportunities in this engagement of reconciliation and how to bring a measure of balance to relationships that were fractured, extremely difficult and will be difficult. The challenge today for both Native and non-Native people is to continue to coexist so that the future generations of all peoples in Canada will benefit together, equitably share land and resources, and live in harmony and peace.

CHAPTER 5

FUTURE TRENDS—DEALING WITH RUPTURED CANADA AND FIRST NATIONS RELATIONS, INCREASING FIRST NATION YOUTH POPULATION, DIMINISHING INDIGENOUS LANGUAGES AND CULTURE, ALIENATION, MARGINALIZATION, ANOMIE, DESPAIR, AND DEPRESSION IN FIRST NATIONS PEOPLES; RESPONSIBILITY OF THE GOVERNMENT OF CANADA, SECOND LEVEL GOVERNMENTS (PROVINCIAL AND MUNICIPAL), AND FIRST NATIONS GOVERNMENTS TO WORK IN TRUE PARTNERSHIP

CANADA AND FIRST Nations relations have, historically, been bound by a trustee or fiduciary type relationship. In this relationship, the trustee, the Government of Canada, is the developer of policy, control, and the financial dispenser of benefits, services, and sanctions that affect First Nations peoples' affairs from birth to death. From the first Indian Department created as a segment of British imperial authority in 1755, superintendents were responsible for dealing in relations with the Indian people and obtaining their alliance with Great Britain in the conflicts with France, and later, with the American forces.

In 1830, the Indian Department was located in Upper Canada and in the control of the lieutenant governor. In Lower Canada, the military secretary held the control. In 1840, Upper and Lower Canada became the Province of Canada, and the two offices of the Indian Department were placed under the symbolic authority of the governor-general, but the daily departmental control was exercised by the governor's secretary. In 1860, imperial authorities transferred British responsibility for Indian affairs to the Province of Canada. The Crown Lands Department became the first department for Indian affairs with a commissioner appointed as the chief superintendent. After 1867, Indian affairs were controlled by the federal government through the secretary of state for Canada. In 1873, the responsibilities of registrar general and superintendent general were transferred to the secretary of state for the provinces. Also in 1873, Indian affairs and the North were placed with the Minister of the Department of the Interior.

In 1936, the Department of Indian Affairs was made an arm of the Department of Mines and Resources. In 1950, the Indian Affairs Branch was put under the Department of Citizenship and Immigration. In 1966, Indian affairs were placed under the Department of Northern Affairs and Natural Resources. The Department of Indian and Northern Affairs was formed by Parliament in 1966 and headed by various ministers. Later, the department was renamed as Indian and Northern Affairs Canada, and was again amended foregoing developments, control, providing and withdrawing of financial benefits were all rationalized and applied with the plenary authority of the Government of Canada including successive cabinets, ministers, legislation such as the Indian Act, and departmental policies, regulations, and directives. There was no input from the Indian peoples affected. The government departments (Indian Affairs, now Aboriginal Affairs, and Health Canada) have various mechanisms that give the impression of approval and acceptance by First Nations. These mechanisms are referred to as consultation, co-management, and dialogues. But the departments, ministries, and the government in power have the final approval for any initiative, policy, regulation, guideline, and directive for the implementation of Indian Act provisions.

The various Native nations or peoples in Canada cannot be said to have relinquished to nations of other hemispheres their right to govern themselves according to their own histories, languages, culture, beliefs, customs, and laws. The Cree of my area have always professed a close link to the land, forests, rivers, lakes, mountains, other living creatures, and the cosmos, the stars, the moon, and the sun. They have also valued the kinship ties to parents, grandparents, extended family members, to ancestors, and to the well-being of future generations. If the Canadian government continues to exercise its plenary power to override the significance of the "honour of the Crown" and fails to acknowledge the true meaning of the Treaty relationship with the First Nations, it will be most difficult for the First Nations to get a fairer share of the control of their affairs, land, and the natural resources of Canada. If the courts, including the Supreme Court, continue to disregard the constitutional and Treaty rights of First Nations peoples by rulings based on "justifiable infringement," then the First Nations peoples, as indigenous peoples, will have to rely on the international support, mechanisms, and the public through urging the Government of Canada to implement the Treaty study of Miguel Alfonso Martinez and the Declaration of the Rights of Indigenous Peoples. The Government of Canada, the institutions of legal power and commerce, and the public will need to consider the risks and benefits or disadvantages and benefits of conditions or developments that will allow the public interest to override individual rights and to protect the collective, Constitutional, and Treaty rights of Native peoples. My humble opinion is that the collective rights of a nation or a people have greater merit than individual rights, while at the same time, the system must allow individual, Constitutional, and Treaty Rights to be observed, protected, and enforced.

The challenge of Canada, Canadian citizens, and Treaty First Nations peoples is to engage with one another and to carry the responsibility of ensuring their relationships are based on trust, honour, commitment, respect, and integrity. Individuals, families, communities, and regions of the country must work continuously on bringing some balance in their interrelationships. There must be an acknowledgement of past injustices to Native peoples and recognition of the risks and benefits of coexisting with a diversity of peoples with variety of beliefs, practices, customs, and norms. There must be acknowledgement of the contribution of First Nations people to the continued society. The dominance of a numerically greater people only underscores their responsibility and privilege to the continued existence and protection of numerically challenged constituent segments of the populace. The Treaty rights of the First Nations peoples must continue to be acknowledged and implemented. The rights to health, education, and development benefits must be provided and adequately funded; otherwise, Canada will continue to be confronted with higher social welfare rates, unemployment, minor and major legal infractions resulting in incarceration, and high rates of physical morbidity and mortality. This is the cost to everyone not only in terms of financial resources, but in the loss of potential knowledge and abilities and in the lateral human pain and suffering to individuals, families, and communities in Canada and in First Nations.

Elected representatives of the federal, provincial, and municipal systems must revise their legislation, statutes, and policies so that the legislation, statutes, and policies adhere to the recommendations of the UN Treaty Study (M. A. Martinez 1999) and so that the legislation, statutes, and policies also conform to the articles of the UN Declaration of the Rights of Indigenous Peoples. The first and second levels of government must ensure that the rights and interests of First Nations people continue to exist as recognized in Treaties. First Nations governments must be allowed to exercise their inherent powers of governance as sanctioned by their peoples. Various oversight controls such as consensus, gatherings promoting understanding, and ceremony can be reaffirmed. Or the idea of an ombudsperson can be explored.

At the federal level, legislators and the electorate should consider amending the Constitution to permit a bicameral federal structure to ensure that Canada's affairs include First Nations representation or that guarantee a system where First Nations representatives constitute or occupy a certain minimum percentage of seats in Parliament, such as with the Maori in New Zealand. Rather than being based on the original British arrangement where the Crown, nobility, clergy would occupy a chamber and the common people would occupy another chamber, a unique bicameral system would allow two associated but distinct chambers, where one would represent the Crown and the elected representatives of the Canadian electorate and the other chamber would be occupied by the representatives of the First Nations peoples. The first chamber would reflect the values, traditions, and institutions inherited from British parliamentary practices, while the First Nations chamber would reflect First Nations' inherent powers, authorities, and jurisdiction to govern their people and also would reflect the Treaty relationship with the Crown.

Leadership styles and practices of both Native and non-Native societies must be based more on reliance on the expertise of citizens from the various occupations of industry, commerce, government, professionals, paraprofessionals, Native elders, and Native peoples with traditional knowledge. Leadership styles and practices should not be based solely on hierarchy, cronyism, or level of authority. Consensus seeking, inclusion, consideration of the risks and benefits of development, and working together, *mamawokamatowin*, must be emphasized by leaders and followers.

There must be a clarification or review of land and natural resource ownership so that First Nations are guaranteed access to land and resources benefits. The federal government, court system, and Parliament must revisit the nature of the Treaty relationship regarding the land and resources sharing envisioned by the Native representatives during the Treaty negotiations. Native peoples should be reassured that their link to the land is protected and that their right to the produce and benefits from the land, lakes, rivers, forests, and minerals is guaranteed. The Native peoples must be allowed to practice their right to access and harvest game, fowl, fish, fruits, roots, and medicinal plants they value for sustenance, for ceremonies, and for linking their families and communities together. Treaty rights to development benefits, education, and health (prevention of disease, treatment, and postvention) must be recognized as Treaty rights by the federal and provincial governments. These

Treaty rights are crucial reinvestments for the future survival and attainment of a higher quality of life for First Nations peoples.

The Indian residential school experience, its legacy and impact, is a complex topic that is currently being reviewed and engaged by the federal government and its agencies, churches, lawyers, former students and their families, communities, and educational institutions. The various parties to the Indian Residential School Settlement Agreement and associated players such as academics, bureaucrats, and researchers are studying and assessing the impact of the residential school experience and its effects on former students, their families, and their communities. Documents related to the genesis of the industrial and residential school concept and implementation are being accessed, examined, and reviewed. It will take several generations to adequately weigh or determine the value of the benefits and disadvantages of the Indian residential school experiment. One forgotten group or segment of the First Nations, Métis, and Inuit survivors, as far as critical impact is concerned, is their children who are impacted through lack of parental love, closeness, and guidance. Intergeneration impact may also have resulted in more Native children in government care in the child welfare system than the estimated one hundred fifty thousand children who resided in Indian residential, mission, and industrial schools. The settlement compensations, the truth and reconciliation activities, and the attempts at healing are also lost to the deceased former residential school students.

There is an expectation or perception that the former Indian residential school students are being asked to forgive the government, the churches, and the staff who sanctioned, were complicit to, and worked in residential schools and activities. But the full impact of the Indian residential school experience is just beginning to be explored. The silence is being broken on this most unfortunate and flagrant era of education policy and practice. The relating of experiences of former students, staff, clergy, and through government, Church, and private documents are revealing the physical, sexual, and psychological/psychic harms that former students suffered at residential schools. The healing or full recovery of some students may not ever happen due to catastrophic harms to their mental, physical, and emotional integrity. But part of the recovery process, in terms of changes of attitudes, begin not just or only with residential school former students, but also with the institutions of government, churches, the legal system, media, education systems from kindergarten to post-secondary, and above all, by individual Canadians. There will be incredulity, blame, and denial as knowledge of the

Indian residential school experience and impact becomes known. But the knowledge gained will need to be examined with empathy, acknowledgment, understanding, and acceptance.

Everyone must be involved in dialogue, workshops, conferences, study of new research findings, urge and ensure that there are revisions or additions to this sad chapter of Canada's history. Recovery should entail recovery from traumas that may be unrelated to the Indian residential school experience. Lessons can be learned from this experience. These traumas, whether internalized by individuals or exhibited in fractured relationships of the various constituents of Canadian society including the unfinished Treaty acknowledgment and implementation, will require everyone to learn foresight, consider forgiveness, and continue dialogue. The challenge for Canada, as a State in the international arena, is to come clean; gain knowledge from unresolved issues such as Treaties; acknowledge the discrepancies, structural or functional imbalances in its domain; and support the hopes and initiatives of the Native peoples of Canada. Perhaps only then can Canada claim to be in the forefront of human rights and be the society where justice and egalitarianism are visible and truly valued.

REFERENCES

Column: *Beware of leaders who promise certainty. Forget top-down politics – the best way to run things is through trial and error,* Don Gardner, Edmonton Journal, May 23, 2011

Indian Residential School Settlement Agreement 2006, www.residentialschoolsettlement.ca

Ministers Responsible for Indian Affairs and Northern Development 1755 to 1999, www.inac.gc.ca/pubs/information/info38.html

National Library and Archives, www.collectionscanada.gc.ca

Pipeline to B.C. a magnet for controversy, Edmonton Journal, November 18, 2011, p. A13

Remembering the Children – an Aboriginal and Church Leaders' Tour to Prepare for Truth and Reconciliation 2008

APPENDIX A

HEALTH CARE AS A TREATY RIGHT POSITION PAPER READ AT A RALLY IN CALGARY, ALBERTA—SEPTEMBER 19, 1995

CHIEF ERIC J. LARGE

<u>GOOD AFTERNOON MY BROTHERS AND SISTERS:</u>

My mandate as Chief of the Saddle Lake First Nation includes, but is not limited to, the protection of Treaty and indigenous rights, the delivery of programs, and policy development. While my nation has pursued numerous initiatives in the area of health, the leadership believes the negotiating position on these issues has been comprised of the lack of a full understanding of the Treaty right to health and its potential scope. The weakness of this position has been further exacerbated by confusion, as to which federal bureaucracy, Health Canada, or the Department of Indian Affairs and Northern Development has ultimate responsibility for the delivery of these services.

Today, the federal government's absence in dealing with its responsibility for the health and well-being of First Nations has resulted in a rally to express our discontent. There is ample evidence that the federal government's interpretation of our right to health as a Treaty right has been diminished. Today, the barriers that prevent my First Nations peoples from experiencing vibrant health are the result of

A. the federal government's misinterpretation of First Nations peoples vision of health,
B. the federal government's low prioritization of processes that encourage the establishment of healthy First Nations communities, and
C. the fact that attaining commitment from government for affirmative action is next to impossible.

As a result of these failures of the federal Crown, my community has encountered and been involved in numerous situations that are unacceptable to us. Examples of these include the issues around Blue Cross, constant federal reviews of noninsured health benefits, no consultation, and no community-based training programs to deal with reforms. In addition, First Nations peoples have limited access to health care services. The portability of our health care right is challenged. Home-care services that meet our needs are not provided in our communities. Our requests to the federal government for rehabilitation services fall on deaf ears. It alarms me greatly; the list that I have just read is not a complete list of our grievances.

The Treaty right to health care is not being honored. The Saddle Lake First Nation endorses the need for the recognition of health as a Treaty right if our peoples are to survive.

We must stand together behind our Treaties and safeguard them. We need to look forward to our children's inheritance. Our ancestors did this on our behalf; we can do no less.

APPENDIX B

NEWS ADVISORY—SEPTEMBER 11, 1995

COUNCILOR ERIC J. LARGE

RE: DALTON HALFE-ARCAND—FATALITY INQUIRY

The Saddle Lake First Nation and Alexander First Nation have decided to observe the proceedings of the fatality inquiry first announced on March 3, 1995, into the death of thirty-four-month-old Dalton Halfe-Arcand who was a member of Saddle Lake First Nation. What was requested by the chiefs of Treaty 6, 7, and 8 of the provincial government was a public inquiry into the infant's death under the Public Inquiries Act. However, the decision made was the announcement of a fatality inquiry under the Fatality Inquiries Act of Alberta.

Saddle Lake First Nation and Alexander First Nation are not satisfied with the fatality inquiry as it will only officially establish in the public eye certain facts of the death, such as the identity of the deceased, date, time and place of death, conditions under which it occurred, and the medical cause and manner of death.

A fatality inquiry is narrower in scope than a full public inquiry, which may raise questions of why the death occurred at all. Nor will a fatality inquiry delve into the standard of health care delivered by the medical care system on behalf of First Nations peoples or whether health care cutbacks may contribute to a decline in the quality of health care for First Nations peoples.

APPENDIX C

NEWS ADVISORY IN REGARD TO DALTON HALFE-ARCAND—DECEMBER 6, 1995

COUNCILOR ERIC J. LARGE

I would like to thank the news media for coming here today to listen to us in respect to the families of the late Dalton Halfe-Arcand. Essentially, we want to bring to light what we feel are important issues surrounding this case—issues that were not brought to the attention of the community at large.

Before I begin addressing these issues, first, I would like to express to the families of both Crystal Arcand and Blair Halfe our most sincere hopes that they may be able to find the answers to the questions that they still have. Many of the questions that you have remain with us also. It is important that we continue to find the answers until we are reasonably assured that what happened to Dalton will not happen to another child.

On behalf of Saddle Lake First Nation, we are expressing our extreme disappointment regarding the outcome of the fatality inquiry into the death of young Dalton Halfe-Arcand. We believe that more can be said, and we certainly expected definitive recommendations from the inquiry.

Throughout the inquiry, we heard evidence and testimony from expert witnesses that indicated more could have been done for the care of young Dalton *prior* to his release from the Royal Alexandra Hospital. In the opinion of these experts and many others who did not testify at the inquiry, Dalton was still a *very* sick child prior to his transfer from the Royal Alexandra Hospital. One could only ask why he was transferred. *Why was he placed in a taxi cab?*

We grant that the immediate cause of death by the pulmonary thrombosis is fatal. However, we must point out, in light of the opinions expressed by the presiding judge, that we must differ. That is, if due care and attention had been provided to Dalton, he may very well be here with us today. In our opinion, if the care that Dalton required had been provided, it would have altered the tragic outcome or may have been averted altogether.

We know from the testimony from the inquiry that specific signs and symptoms displayed by Dalton prior to his release were consistent with those of a *very sick* child. We also know that not enough was done to determine whether these signs and symptoms were attributable to a specific cause. We also disagree with the attempt to refer to the testimony offered by various experts at the inquiry as immaterial and speculative. The purpose of an inquiry is to shed light into circumstances surrounding an individual's death. Expert witnesses at the inquiry have stated if certain procedures were initiated, then the death could have possibly been averted. Our question in response to this is "How come they were not done?"

On the day of transfer from Royal Alexandra Hospital to St. Theresa Hospital, the mother, Crystal, consistently repeated her objection to the use of a taxicab as the method of transportation. The testimony at the inquiry established that she had repeatedly requested for an alternate mode of transportation, via ambulance. Crystal had also offered to pay for the cost of the ambulance so that Dalton would be attended to. She was denied any choice. We can only state here that the needs of Dalton and his mother were overwhelmed by the insubstantial savings to the health care system. To add to this, the health care system did not take the time or put any effort in reconsidering circumstances in response to the mother's appeals.

The real tragedy of it all is that young Dalton had died in a taxicab, while in his mother's arms. How can one comprehend the feeling of the mother without thinking of one's own children or family? We emphatically state that "our children should not die in a taxicab while in the care of the hospital care system!" If this was Dalton's destiny, then it should have been under the best of care and with the best of efforts. Only our best and the best that hospital care can have to offer should be good enough.

You may ask, "Where do we go from here?" Our only purpose, as we had stated in earlier conferences, is to prevent similar or other circumstances that besotted young Dalton. We in Alberta are experiencing the effects of changes to the health care system. We know too well the numerous questions as to the effects of these changes. Specifically, in this case relating to circumstances of death, did any of these changes have any bearing on the quality of care given to young Dalton?

With that in mind, we again would call upon the leadership of Alberta to examine the care more fruitfully so that assurances can be provided to First Nations and the people of Alberta that we have a responsive health care system—one that puts lives before cost and one that puts the word "people" back into health care.

Thank you.

APPENDIX D

UNREPRESENTED NATIONS AND PEOPLES ORGANIZATION (UNPO) MONITOR WORKING GROUP ON INDIGENOUS POPULATIONS SEVENTEENTH SESSION, JULY 26–30, 1999 [PARTIAL EXCERPT FROM UNPO TRANSCRIPT]

CREDIT: UNPO

Disclaimer: This monitor is not an official transcript of the Working Group but represents substantially what was communicated during the meetings. UNPO apologizes for any inaccuracies. If you have corrections, comments, or suggestions, please contact the UNPO Secretariat in Room A 388.

Monday, July 26, 1999

Day 1, Afternoon session

1. Chair Mrs. E. Daes: Declared the meeting on IP open. She informed the participants of the results of the private meeting that in view of the large number of speakers wishing to present a statement during the meeting, all speakers' interventions are to be limited to five minutes only. The only exceptions are to be made for high-level representatives of governments who have come to provide comprehensive information about government policy. She encouraged all delegates to respect a five-minute limit in order to give the opportunity to other colleagues to deliver statements. She urged participants to consider the possibility of delivering joint statements. She further stated that consideration of item 4 was to take place during the course of the afternoon and on Tuesday. On Tuesday and Wednesday, items 5 and 6 on land (and health) would be discussed. Then there was to be a review of developments pertaining to human rights and fundamental freedoms of IP. She recalled that the discussion of these items would offer all delegations the chance to provide recent information in countries relating to IP, and not for complaints citing other mechanisms are

better suited for such statements. The floor was then passed to Gloria Stickwan/Atna Athabascan Tribe.

2. Gloria Stickwan/Atna Athabascan Tribe: Thanked Madam Chairperson for the opportunity to speak. She explained that she was an Atna Athabascan Indian from the Copper River region of Alaska and the subsistence coordinator for her area. She wished to discuss the issue of subsistence in the state of Alaska. She explained the geographical and harsh physical conditions of her region and noted that the population of the area was between four thousand and five thousand people, of which 20 percent were Alaska natives. She stressed the importance of subsistence activities in providing food for families and material for shelter and clothing. In particular, she mentioned the importance of fishing, hunting, gathering plants and berries activities, which had been carried out for thousands of years. Since the 1940s, the Atna people have changed their lifestyles and no longer travel between summer and winter camps as they did previously. They began to settle down and send their children to a Bureau of Indian Affairs School, administered by the U.S. federal government. This change in lifestyle has forced Atna people to take on low-paying and seasonal jobs and has resulted in them being unable to meet their subsistence needs. At the same time, their situation of poverty prevents them from being able to invest in off-road vehicles to facilitate hunting. She requested that subsistence be given a priority for fishing and hunting, where there is a shortage of resources.

3. Chair Mrs. E. Daes: Passed the floor to Jose Morales/Conejos de Organizaciones (CUTO), Tukum Umaw, Guatemala, who was not present. She clarified a point regarding the absence of speakers. The practice of the WG is that those who are absent—with the consent of the participants—will not be able to take the floor. This was decided owing to time restrictions. She thanked the participants for their understanding. She then gave the floor to the speaker Mr. Ahmed Ouma Omar Eihadji/Association ASSA (Sahel Solidarité et Action). He was not present. The next speaker was Neigulo Krome/Naga people's Movement for Human Rights (NPMHR)—also not present. The floor was then passed to Councilor Eric J. Large/Saddle Lake First Nation.

4. Eric Large/Saddle Lake First Nation: Read a letter related to child adoption in Canada. It stated that Canadian High Court had violated two major international instruments: the Convention on the Prevention and Punishment of the Crime of Genocide and the Convention on the Rights of the Child by awarding an indigenous child to adoptive grandparents as reported on February 18, 1999. The transfer of this child was in contravention to article 2 of the Convention on Genocide, ratified by Canada, as it denies the child the possibility of knowing his indigenous heritage and separates the child from his rights to indigenous lands and territories. The act of removing this child secondly violated the Convention on the Rights of the Child (art. 30), which states that linguistic, ethnic minorities and their children shall not be denied right to their heritage. He mentioned that the chief and council of Saddle Lake First Nation are considering taking action against Canada at the United Nations to have the conventions enforced and for Canada to be censured.

7. Chair Mrs. E. Daes: Gave the floor to the next speaker, Mr. George Wuethrich/Comite Sociale des Chagossiens. While he prepared, the secretariat made an intervention.

8: Secretary Mr. J. Burger: Requested that all those receiving grants from the voluntary fund—of which there is sixty-two—leave to collect their bursaries. The administrator was due to leave in ten minutes.

9: Chair Mrs. E. Daes: Gave the floor to Mr. George Wuethrich/Comite Sociale des Chagossiens.

10: Mr. George Wuethrich/Comite Sociale des Chagossiens: Insisted on the fact that the Comite Sociale des Chagossiens was the only legitimate representative body of the Chagossien people. He underlined that the Chagossien cause was greatly helped by the Mauritian president who made a speech at the UN tribunal in September 1998 for Anglo-American recognition of the fundamental rights of the Chagossiens. This brought a new element to the Chagossien struggle. He underlined that many families from Archipeli islands were displaced to Maurice Island thirty years ago by the British government to make way for an

American military base on one of the islands (Diego Garcia) and that, even now, many still wish to return to their own islands. He further stated the PM's conclusion was to respect the rights of the Chagossien people, including the right to return to their land. He encouraged constructive dialogue, which Mr. George Wuethrich confirmed as the preferred method of cooperation of the Chagossien people, bar one or two detractors. Mr. Wuethrich insisted on negotiations with the British and Mauritian authorities with a view to finding a solution.

11: Chair Mrs. E. Daes: Introduced the next speaker Mr. Bart Bernhard/ The Mena Maria Foundation Human Rights for the Moluccas.

12: Bart Bernhard/The Mena Muria Foundation Human Rights for the Moluccas: Talked of the recent riots in the Muluka and underlined the suffering of the people of the Moluccas. He explained how a difference of opinion between a bus driver and a passenger escalated into full-scale riots in which religious Muslims and Christians were killed. Mr. Bernhard indicated that the cause of the riots was due to other factors than religious tensions. He indicated that IP felt that tensions between IP transmigrates and migrants from central Java and South Sulawesi also played a fundamental part. He suggested that the population transfers had disturbed the way of life of the IP. He underlined that migrants were often favored over IP for jobs, education, and land ownership. The indigenous common law system and, in particular, the "pela-gandong customary law" system has been disturbed by the riots. Peaceful coexistence between all religious groups and indigenous and nonindigenous peoples has to be established, while respecting mutual trust and democratic reforms in harmony with the fundamental rights of IP.

13: Chair Mrs. E. Daes: Introduced the next speaker Senor Alejandro E. Cruz Lopez/delegate of the Consejo Indigena Popular de Oaxaca "Ricardo Flores Magon," Mexico.

14: Alejandro E. Cruz Lopez/delegate of the Consejo Indigena Popular de Oaxaca "Ricardo Flores Magon," Mexico: Expressed his concerns regarding the rights of IP and indicated that he wanted approval of the new legal instrument as soon as possible in order to contribute to improving the situation. He said that the people of Oaxaca had suffered invasion with terrible results and that now they were suffering internal colonization. He further stated that the indigenous people on Mexican territory in Oaxaca were in poverty and marginalized. The government had catalogued the area as one of great poverty with the lowest employment. Immigration and emigration had broken families. He stated that those who return come back with customs, which break up the communities. He commented that the local and national government had tried to destroy organizations, such as the "Ricardo Flores Magon" organization. He further states that 106 indigenous people had lost their children through beating and that survivors still suffer torture and beating. He called for individuals to be brought to book. Local government is not investigating crimes, and the second most important post in country is occupied by someone involved in the crimes. The Mexican government violates human rights, without the voice of human rights being heard and investigated under a system of the rule of law. On behalf of his organization, he asked the UN to look into this.

15: Chair Mrs. E. Daes: Gave the floor to Xiong Chuhu/Hmong International Human Rights Watch.

16: Xiong Chuhu/Hmong International Human Rights Watch: Stated that instances of genocide of the Hmong still continue in Laos in the jungles of the Phou Bian Mountain and the surrounding countries though the Vietnam War ended nearly twenty-five years ago. He highlighted that no observers or international monitors had been allowed into this area in the past twenty-five years. He further stated that in 1975, the newly formed Lao People's Democratic Party (LPDR) instituted a renaming process of the area and designated it a Saysomboun Special Zone. Displaced Hmong have been attacked with over forty thousand killed and another sixty thousand displaced into the jungles. Presently, over ten thousand are hiding in the mountains waiting for the killing to end. Since 1979, there have been a series of attacks on Hmong people, including in June 1990 and February 1998. Three military...

APPENDIX E

NEWS RELEASE RE: SIXTH SESSION WORKING GROUP ON INDIGENOUS POPULATIONS NOVEMBER 20–DECEMBER 1, 2000, GENEVA, SWITZERLAND

COUNCILOR ERIC J. LARGE

Councilor Eric J. Large recently attended the Sixth Session of the intersession working group established in March 3, 1995, under the Commission of Human Rights—Economic and Social Council of the United Nations at the *Palais des Nations* in Geneva, Switzerland. Councilor Large attended the November 20–December 01, 2000, session of the working group, which was mandated for the purpose of elaborating a Draft Declaration on the Rights of Indigenous Peoples. The forty-five-article draft declaration had previously been tabled by the Working Group on Indigenous Populations (WGIP) with the Sub-Commission of the Prevention of Discrimination and Protection of Minorities on August 23, 1993, with the goal of its adoption by the General Assembly of the United Nations. Up to now, only two of the articles had been previously adopted.

Large delivered a six-page presentation stating the position of Saddle Lake First Nation in relation to the draft declaration. The Saddle Lake First Nation presentation outlined its geographical location, its ongoing relationship to the land, occupancy and use, and its previous interventions with the WGIP.

The presentation also stated Saddle Lake First Nation's position in the exercise of its inherent right as an indigenous nation in Canada; the control of our people under the Indian Act; the taking of lands and resources contrary to Treaty No. 6 of 1876 and the coerced land surrenders; child apprehensions by provincial agencies; outlawing of traditional ceremonies; and continuing division of its sovereignty by governmental policies, legislation, and court decisions made without its consent while diminishing its right to its own procedures and processes, such as membership and leadership selection.

Councilor Large's speech supported the fundamental principles of the declaration to which Saddle Lake First Nation is committed, such as the inherent right of self-determination, referred to in thirteen articles, and inherent title to its land and resources, referred to in at least five of the articles. Self-determination and title to land and resources are recognized in the Royal Proclamation of 1763. This relationship was reaffirmed by the Crown of Great Britain and Ireland in the Treaty No. 6 of 1876 where the Cree Nation agreed to share land in consideration of the Crown's Treaty obligations to provide, without further conditions or restrictions and not limited to access to education, medical services, exemption from military conscription, assistance in times of pestilence and famine, extraterritorial rights, the retention of tribal customs and laws, and hunting, fishing, trapping, and gathering. Today, these rights, unlimited in scope, are recognized in section 25 and 35 of the Constitution Act of Canada 1982, including freedom from adverse discrimination as recognized in the UN Charter and human rights law. Articles 44 and 45 refer to the no extinguishment or diminishment of rights indigenous people may gain and that no state, group, or person has any implied or otherwise, right to engage in actions contrary to the UN Charter.

Councilor Large made two interventions in the debates. He elaborated on article 44, which states: "Nothing in this declaration may be construed as diminishing or extinguishing existing or future rights indigenous peoples may have or acquire." Large said that, in Canada, existing Aboriginal and Treaty rights are recognized and affirmed under Section 35. These rights pertain to First Nations who are indigenous peoples defined by distinct customs, traditions, ceremonies, languages, worship, governance, social norms, and who have a special relationship to the land and resources, which is basic to their being and forms their worldview. Second, he referred to articles 12, 13, and 14, which would state that indigenous peoples have the right to their cultural traditions and customs; the right to use and transmit their spiritual and religious traditions and ceremonies; the right to their religious and cultural sites; the right to ceremonial objects; the right to repatriate human remains; and that states ensure that sacred places be preserved, respected, and protected. Article 14 would declare that indigenous people have the right to use and transmit their histories, languages, philosophies, symbols, and to identify communities, places, and persons using their own names. Councilor Large declared, for example, the use of sacred objects forms a relationship to the Creator, to our people, to other people, and to the natural world.

Many of the state governments, including Canada, stalled the adoptions of articles 1, 2, 12, 13, 14, 44, and 45, by trying to limit the inherent aspirations of indigenous peoples by tabling certain words or clauses for future discussion.

These words or clauses include "peoples," "applicable instruments," "adverse discrimination," "in conformity with domestic laws," and other clauses. The fear that states have, related to the possibility that indigenous peoples would affect territorial integrity of a country in their efforts at self-determination and that control of land and natural resources would somehow diminish the power of the state.

The nation states were unwilling to concede the full enjoyment of all the human rights and freedoms to include indigenous people that these same nation states have endorsed in the past in such agreements as the Charter of the United Nations, the Universal Declaration of Human Rights, and the International Covenant on Political and Civil Rights, to name a few.

The Sixth Session ended after a lot of debate, discussion of positions, consideration of alternate language, stalling, meeting in caucus, and no consensus or adoption of further articles. The Working Group for the Draft Declaration, under the chairmanship of Luis-Enrique Chavez of Peru, will summarize the session, which will be adopted in a report format.

Attending the UN Intersession were 362 representatives from forty-one countries, two nonmember states, one UN research body, thirty-six nongovernmental organizations in ECOSOC status, twenty-six indigenous organizations approved by Commission on Human Rights, ten other organizations, and two other general representatives.

APPENDIX F

REPORT OF CONFERENCE HOSTED BY THE INDIGENOUS BAR ASSOCIATION – OTTAWA, ONTARIO OCTOBER 20–22, 2000

COUNCILOR ERIC J. LARGE

I attended a conference hosted by the Indigenous Bar Association. The theme was Globalization: Indigenous Law in the International Context and was held in Ottawa, October 20–22, 2000.

Day 1 included speakers from eastern and western Canada, New Zealand, and the USA. Workshops were then held in relation to governance and justice in Canada and international fora, First Nation lawmaking, and an update on Corbierre.

The afternoon agenda covered Aboriginal title and treaties through panel presentations. The first speaker spoke on a subject of great interest to Treaty No. 6. The UN special rapporteur of the UN Treaty Study Report was Miguel Alfonso Martinez, who is now a professor at Cuba's Higher Institute for International Relations, Cuba.

Martinez said the final UN Treaty Report was tabled in July 1999. He said he was proud and thankful to have had opportunity to listen to the elders in Canada, Aotearoa (New Zealand), Chile, and many other places. He attached great importance to the conclusions and recommendations. He urged us to have a follow-up what is there in the UN Study on Treaties. He said this follow-up may serve to start a new effort throughout the United Nations. He said, "We had to defend every niche we had to conquer." He recommended that this effort has to continue with new initiatives. Mr. Martinez said he sees certain negative trends developing within the United Nations and in the field of indigenous issues, such as the following:

a. The adoption of the Draft Declaration of the Rights of Indigenous Peoples. Adopted by the Working Group of Indigenous Populations (WGIP) in 1993, the WGIP had adopted only three of the forty odd articles of the declaration. Martinez said that this speaks clearly of the reticence of most national governments to the adoption of the document. The main problem, Martinez sees, resides in the recognition [or lack] of the right to self-determination of indigenous peoples. In 1945, at the United Nations, states recognized the right of peoples to self-determination and that the right is inherent to all countries and to all peoples. Indigenous peoples want to protect their inherent right to self-determination and their cultural wealth. A nation state's right to self-determination is not the only avenue of the expression to self-determination. Martinez referred to article 33 of the present draft declaration whereby indigenous peoples have the right to promote, develop, and maintain their institutional structures and their distinctive customs but within the parameters established by the UN body. To Martinez, that is discrimination.

b. The other worry Martinez has is the very probable demise of the WGIP. He said that the WGIP was established in 1982 to

(1) establish new standards of the rights of indigenous peoples, and
(2) review recent developments of indigenous peoples' issues and concerns.

The WGIP had been established with the support of Indigenous peoples.

c. The third initiative, on which Martinez has a very strong reservation, is the Permanent Forum for Indigenous Peoples, which was established this year by the UN. The problem, as he sees it, is in the composition of the forum, the nature of the mandate, and the weakness of its recommending role. He said that this is not the wisest way to advance the causes of indigenous peoples in the UN. There is no reason the WGIP and the Permanent Forum can coexist. But both cannot exist without adequate finances. Also how will the eight indigenous peoples' representatives on the forum be selected as full voting members? The forum's only mandate will be to act in a consultative capacity. The full power to act will be in the hands of the president of the Economic and Social Council (ECOSOC) of the UN.

Last, Martinez referred to the dark side of success of the WGIP. He said that many people are now claiming to be indigenous and that "indigenous" is a term of the colonizer. The result is that many allies of the indigenous movement are concerned that this will result in further confusion and turmoil. He concluded by stating that there are effects of globalization on indigenous peoples. Globalization is a fact. Martinez's problem is the present kind of globalization is of a neoliberal nature, for example, in North America, Europe, and Africa, which affects the most vulnerable groups in society of which indigenous peoples are included. He is afraid of globalization affecting indigenous people's access to finances and resources, and limiting their rights and interests.

The rest of the conference included issues of trade and natural resources, intellectual property, traditional knowledge and environment, and options and practical tips for bringing issues to the international fora for indigenous peoples. These issues were arranged into panel discussions, a plenary presentation/session, and workshops involving speakers from the legal and academic worlds from the national and international scene. The participants were indigenous lawyers, First Nation representatives, indigenous law students, and members of specific agencies.

APPENDIX G

REPORT ON THE INDIGENOUS BAR ASSOCIATION CONFERENCE—OCTOBER 19–20, 2001, VANCOUVER, BC—THEME OF BUILDING TREATIES AND RESTORING RELATIONSHIPS

COUNCILOR ERIC J. LARGE

The keynote address was made by Grand Chief Ed John, hereditary chief of Tl'azt'en Nation and graduate from University of British Columbia Law School in 1979. Grand Chief John dealt with the history of First Nation and government relations beginning with the prohibition against claims and the hiring of lawyers to pursue claims. This prohibition was lifted in the 1950s, which saw the renewed discussion of rights-based initiatives and the increase of Native lawyers and judges.

Grand Chief John said First Nation leaders have the continuing problems of indigenous people, the social and economic and political-relational problems. He said leaders have taken the tools of laws. In finding solutions leaders said, at one point, that we need more teachers and social workers, but don't recall saying we need more lawyers.

Grand Chief John said he was told that we have to take care of the young ones, old ones, and the less fortunate, and that this was his approach in his background. He said in British Columbia, the late 1960s saw the grants to Bands initiative taking place with the taking over of social services and the hiring of a secretary in his First Nation. Today, he said ninety to ninety-five people now work in providing a "civil service," allowing his nation to look at the very survival of his people. He said that young people now are the greatest risk of the loss of language and culture. He said his nation is putting together a strategy to address this reality through various ways provincially and adding efforts internationally, such as through the Inter-American Commission on Human Rights. Also tried were remedies through domestic courts, but the onus is for First Nations and indigenous people to prove that they have rights: Aboriginal title, fishing, and other rights, e.g., *Marshall* and *Sparrow* cases. Grand Chief John said some First Nations have passed their own legislation and are accountable to themselves and to no one else. All of these developments since the lifting of the prohibition against claims and the hiring of lawyers allow the First Nation people to take their rightful place in this country.

But Grand Chief John said there are still problems, e.g., the BC Treaty process where there are three parties. He said the BC government wants time out to have a referendum to get a mandate to pursue the treaty process, while the Wetsu'weten asked for a process of forwarding their views and history but were refused, and instead there are committee hearings held to advance the government's agenda.

The grand chief then posed the following questions. Where do we start in the struggle to address the challenges we face? What do we do to break these cycles? What do we do now to lay the foundation for future generations? What do we need? He said that in his First Nation, they do a lot of soul searching and said that one tool and expertise is lawyers in courts and advocacy, also teachers and professors. Another tool is the passing on of knowledge and in the foundations of our nations, and restoring relationships and building treaties through meeting with governments. Other obstacles confronting the treaty process are directives by the BC government in the areas of lumber supply and oil and gas industries, as these impact First Nations' rights and which require the consent of indigenous people.

Grand Chief John concluded by saying that all of these challenges of the last twenty to twenty-five years require the expertise of the lawyers present, knowledge, skill, and commitment. He further posed the following questions: Where do we go in the next fifty years? Where do we put our strategies to try to improve the conditions that challenge our people?

The first plenary session dealt with "Building Treaties" and was chaired by Miles Richardson, BC treaty commissioner. Richardson began by saying BC First Nations have been negotiating treaties for eight years and that the main issue is funding. Mr. Richardson advocates change on how treaties are negotiated and said no treaty has been negotiated in the BC treaty process though nineteen recommendations were made. He said that we need to move away from the big bang theory of negotiations where negotiations are dealt with for ten to fifteen years and nothing happens, while the government is saying we need a referendum to get a mandate. The treaty commission favors taking incremental steps and interim measures, accessing economic initiatives and partnerships, and to complete these and roll them into the negotiations later. Mr. Richardson added that there are huge issues, e.g., certainty, which can define the essence of the new relationship or, "is its use only for the benefit of the Government negotiations?"

The first panel speaker was Dave Joe, a lawyer of Southern Tutchone descent from the Yukon and chief negotiator for the Council of Yukon First Nations. His presentation was on land claims and self-government agreements. Mr. Joe compared two final agreements—the Nisga'a and the Champagne and Aishihik First Nations (CAFN) in which certainty, lands, harvesting, and self-government are the focus points. While conceding that the Charter of Rights and Freedoms applies in the Nisga'a Final Agreement (NFA), Mr. Joe said it was not his peoples' value system and would prefer a standalone document. He said the weakness of the Charter is that it applies to provinces and that Canada does not mention the Aishihik or the Nisga'a. A further desire was that the Aishihik and the Nisga'a employ their own common law and that they have the right to invoke the notwithstanding clause. The CAFNFA extinguishes all claims, titles, interests, and rights in all nonsettlement land and all other land and water; the mines and minerals within all settlement land; and would install fee simple settlement land. The NFA sets out the Nisga'a Section 35 as Aboriginal rights, including title in Canada, of the Nisga'a Nation and its people in Nisga'a lands, other lands and resources in Canada; the jurisdictions, authorities, and rights of the Nisga'a government; and other Nisga'a Section 35 rights.

The next speaker was Ed Wright, secretary treasurer of the Nisga'a Lisims government and Laxgibuu member of the Gitwilmaak'il for the House of Duuk'. Mr. Wright said that the Nisga'a Agreement was concluded in 1998 with about $50 million being expended by the Nisga'a. He further said that the NFA has been a challenge and is being challenged today.

Regarding certainty, Mr. Wright said that they have stated clearly that they did not surrender but that they put Aboriginal rights and land claims into a box and put them into a larger box. He said they also did a self-appraisal and looked at their culture and traditions and of how lands evolve. Other questions arose such as what kind of self-government model did they want? He said the Delgamuukw decision recognized the community of Aboriginal people in Canada. He said that in 1913, all of their leaders put all land and resources holdings in one pot. Later, in the issues they faced, Canada and the Province of British Columbia came united in areas such as taxation, whereby land taxes exemption is lost in eight years and income taxes in five years. In their negotiations process, Mr. Wright said they involved the four communities of their people who also live in urban areas and have representatives from all locations. The negotiations got their mandate from annual assemblies of which they had forty-two.

Regarding certainty, Mr. Wright's people had to communicate with the federal government whose version was modification and release of all Aboriginal rights to land but which process would be triggered only if the court found that any provision in their treaty couldn't withstand the legality. His people's version of certainty was modification and continuous modification. He said that courts have further crystallized what they had done in their treaty. But the government challenge, despite the Section 35 recognition of Aboriginal and treaty rights, is its argument that Aboriginal self-rule was extinguished in 1867 but which stance was dismissed by the courts more recently.

Mr. Wright said that they just did not make their own powers in the Nisga'a Agreement but ensured that those powers would be consistent with federal and provincial laws. Regarding lands and because fee simple is in the agreement, there has been a lot of confusion he said. For the Nisga'a, preexisting right is the original fee simple. They say they own all the mineral rights on their traditional lands and on reserve lands. For the present, the Nisga'a have their own government system with their own legislation house of thirty-nine members of which there is a president, chairperson, secretary/treasurer, and chairperson of the council of elders all of whom are elected. There are also village governments with elected representatives. To date, four laws have been enacted, for example, the Legislative Amendment Act. Mr. Wright concluded that the proposed Governance Legislation by Indian and Northern Affairs really is an Indian Act Amendment impacting elections, leadership selection, and accountability.

The next speaker was John B. Zoe, of Dogrib descent and chief negotiator, Dogrib Treaty 11 Council. Mr. Zoe spoke on regional claims. Their elders advised their people to restore relationship with their own people. He said that any treaty involves land, that their people have to look at their own land base, and they know their own history is written into the land itself. He said that they have a history of building, adding on and renewing relationships. Sacred sites were used where geographic changes occurred due to interaction between animals and people, for example, beaver and people resulted in the forming of tributaries of rivers and dams and the use of place names. All of this necessitated coexistence and called for the formation of relationships. Conflicts arose from excursions beyond tribal territories and the meeting of members of other tribal groups and later into trading activity with non-

Natives. Mr. Zoe said coexistence with the natural environment is a way of fending off extinction of tradition. Government followed to set a new chapter, and because government is interested in the subsurface resources to raise revenue, it called for a treaty attended to by representatives and elders of the Dogrib treaty area. Encroachment and settlement by other people emerged and called for the setting up of a territorial structure. The building of a treaty also called for the Dogrib to retain their culture and stem total assimilation. Their treaty building is an extension of the prior agreement of what the treaty means to the Dogrib for "as long as the sun shines and the rivers flow." Mr. Zoe concluded by saying that the current concept of certainty is only an interpretation by the government, but the Dogrib are saying they provide their own certainty as they were here before.

The next speaker was Shannon M. Cumming, a Métis lawyer from Fort Smith, Northwest Territories (NWT), who is in involved in the BC Treaty Commission which has produced a Report on Treaty Negotiations. She reported that there is a shift in focus to incremental treaties, interim agreements, and funding for agreements. The issue of extinguishment keeps surfacing, while there is lack of substance to the issue of self-government. She briefly mentioned the South Slave Métis Framework Agreement, which began in 1996, and deals with lands, resources, and self-government. She advised the audience, when incorporating traditional values, that it is important Aboriginal lawyers make provisions for this, as indigenous law is about relationships and building community consensus through workshops on constitutional law.

Ms. Cumming said it is also about information gathering from their own people on how they governed themselves traditionally. In their case, this involves making a treaty that makes sense to their people in the NWT. There is interim protection of lands, which may make for greater protection through actual identification of lands. On the issue of self-government, Ms. Cumming said that Section 35 is recognized by the government as the right of Aboriginal people to govern themselves internally. She concluded by saying that the NWT prefer the right of government to apply mechanisms that are based on public institutions and legislation. Last, those negotiations are important to keep community on side and with courts directing legal people to negotiate [rather than to litigate].

The next topic was interim measures, with the first speaker being Terri Lynn Williams Davidson who briefly dealt with the BC treaty process and treaty renewal in general.

Concerns and discussion raised from the audience were the following:

- Interim measures are taken to protect traditional land and the treaty process. An example of traditional lands is the five-mountain area in BC called Thunderbird. This and other areas are protected against harvesting of logs by large companies.

- Negotiating interim measures in the BCTP involves government-to-government negotiations that have a beginning and an end and require a government to have a clear authority to negotiate and to have a constituency.

- The purpose of the BCTP is to reconcile Aboriginal title with Crown title and to reconcile First Nations' version that they had preexisting and continuing title versus government's version of an assertion of Crown title deemed at discovery.

- Issues of permanent settlement of non-Native people and protection of sacred sites. The balancing of conflicting interests may require interim measures, which indicate a measure of trust.

- Interim measures are political agreements.

- While negotiations take place to protect land and resources, resource extraction takes place, e.g., logging continues in BC. This results in frustration of First Nation members. Issues need to be identified, such as the impact of forestry activity and parks development. Solutions need to be put forward.

- The issue of maintaining peace and human safety when tensions escalate needs to be addressed, as when road blocks are made by First Nation members and the reaction of, for example, the Department Fisheries and Oceans and the RCMP. How is this issue dealt with? Considerations are:

- Protection by the province of certain areas, such as parks.

- Permit system.

- Cost of litigation.

- Land use planning measures by certain tribes, First Nations, and government.

The luncheon speaker was Roberta Jamieson, who is of Mohawk descent of the Six Nations Grand River where she began articling. She said that she and fellow First Nation lawyers had great hopes in trying to make a difference in helping their people with their interests. The truth is, she related, very little progress is being made with the exception of the prime minister's recent promise to take steps to make dramatic improvements and Indian Affairs Minister Nault's governance initiative. With the PM's promise of improvements, a Committee of Cabinet Ministers has been appointed to implement a blueprint for a change agenda. Ms. Jamieson asserted that now is the time to act and to connect the promises to take practical steps for the blueprint for it to come through on its promise. The current relationship of government to First Nations requires a dramatic change. She said this is an opportunity to fill this policy vacuum and to build a new relationship that requires new institutions capable of looking back to redress grievances and rebuilding for First Nations. This requires

1. confidence of both First Nations and governments created by and responsible for both to maintain healthy fiduciary relationship;

2. a national body established by order-in-council, which would act as a mediator and independent court to review and mediate decisions and where First Nations have been done harm regarding land and resource issues. Aboriginal law, common law, and international Law would need to be considered.

3. an ombudsman to assist, monitor treaty implementation, and the achievement of Aboriginal self-government;

4. The creation of First Nations for their own attorney general;

5. The need for fresh thinking of the fiduciary relationship, to preserve the honor of the Crown, and to preserve First Nation land base and rights.

The specific recommendations that Ms. Jamieson made were:

1. Strategic action with the legal community by getting ready to take unresolved cases to court and by getting more First Nations people and Metis to take legal education.

2. Public education is essential to support change as the government responds to public pressure. Also advised is the creation of an indigenous law section in a law firm.

3. Astute use of the international arena in finding new ways of protecting our rights. The governments no longer want to take land but our intellectual rights, our medicines, and our DNA. Also advised are United Nations forums and affiliations, e.g., Permanent Forum for Indigenous Peoples.

Ms. Jamieson concluded with the recent terrorist attacks in the U.S., there will be greater demand for public funds to go into the war against terrorism. She said that legislation is being drafted to restrict protest and dissent as part of this war. The climate is ripe for the public to react to First Nations vocal concerns. She said that our people can use our skills as lawyers, leaders, negotiators, diplomats to remind the government to fulfill its fiduciary duties. It is also important that we dedicate our values and what we hold as important.

The afternoon plenary session on comprehensive claims policy was chaired by Roger Jones who is of Sagamok Anishinabek descent and is presently employed with the First Nations Governance Institute. Mr. Jones stated that the last revision of the claims policy was made in 1987 or 1988.

The first speaker on this topic was Elmer Derrick, who holds the title of Yoobx in Wilps Wiigyet in Gitsegukla and is on the Gitxsan Treaty negotiating team. Mr. Derrick said the Wilps is the only entity that can provide certainty. He said that the lands that belong to their house groups have a very long history. One of the options is to structure the treaty in the form of a trust where there is no mention of where the respective authorities lie. Derrick said the treaty would indicate that the trustee/beneficiaries of the trust would be the three levels of government. The trust would be an outcome-based strategy to advance the treaty process. One of the means toward a treaty is the building of an interim agreement in one resource area, e.g., fisheries where a revenue sharing arrangement with the Crown is negotiated, and to consider the situation where the province claiming exclusive jurisdiction of oil and gas resources is a continuing issue of contention.

The next panelist was Mark L. Stevenson, who made a presentation, titled "A Commentary on the BC Treaty Process and the Federal Comprehensive Claims Policy." He said that treaties are very brave processes and deal with very difficult issues. He remarked that the claims policy does not work. The last revision was in 1987. The policy makers could not understand what Aboriginal and treaty rights meant at that time. The major court decisions since 1982 had not been made. Mr. Stevenson covered the recognition of Aboriginal title and rights or lack of recognition by the Crown, extinguishment as a condition, overlaps (overlapping traditional territories), compensation, section 91(24), and a treaty tribunal.

David Nahwagebow then made a presentation, titled "An Analysis of the Comprehensive Claims Policy Review in Relation to the Changing Legal Landscape." In part 1, he presented a historical overview of the developments leading to the establishment of the CC Policy. In part 2, he reviewed Aboriginal rights and title and their impact on the CC Policy. In part 3, he offered suggestions to policy and process options. In part 1—Historical Overview, Mr. Nahwagebow related how the Royal Proclamation of 1763 is the earliest acknowledgment of Aboriginal rights and as such formalized the treaty process. He said the Royal Proclamation set out the Crown's policy of legitimizing colonial expansion into Aboriginal territories while setting the stage for future Crown/First Nations relations. The first important aspect of the Royal Proclamation recognized that First Nations hold title to their lands and set Crown policy in the acquisition of those lands. The Royal Proclamation provides that Aboriginal lands cannot be acquired by private individuals without first being surrendered to the Crown.

Chief Arthur Manuel, of the Neskonlith Band of the Shuswap Nation in the south interior of BC, said the government has two choices in dealing with trespass issues, protests, and blockades. One is to keep the current approach and apply the law. Two is back down and recognize Aboriginal rights. Chief Manuel said that the Shuswap Nation people don't want to extinguish their rights to land but to reconcile these by recognizing Aboriginal title.

I next attended a workshop on claims policy and fiduciary obligation. Discussion raised the viability of a claim body or tribunal and whether it would be truly independent. In regard to a fiduciary, the question of conflict of interest on behalf of the Crown was raised, as well as the question of the role of a province, if any, in relation to the Natural Resources Transfer Act (NRTA). Negotiating in good faith on the part of the government was raised and the concern that the government resorts to threat to stall or stop settlement. The option of a First Nations attorney general was proposed and who would serve as a watchdog, but the question arises of how is Her Majesty compelled to adhere to her duties and obligations to First Nations? Also discussed was the reconciliation of the Crown's and First Nation people's interest as a nation by the upholding of the fiduciary duty. An additional question was "How do you make the Trustee accountable?"

The dinner guest speaker was the Honorable Judge Steven Point, an indigenous person from the Mission, BC area. Judge Point began his speech by stating judges are not allowed to speak freely. The book of ethics that is read to them does not allow them to speak on politics or current political issues. They can't criticize other judges or their decisions. He said today's leadership is faced with a dichotomy in treaty developments and other issues. He questioned why we are spending so much money and not progressing. He said that in his younger days, when he was chief, people believed in our leaders and that people believed in the decision the chiefs made. He said that nowadays, leaders believe in individual sovereignty. What he observes in First Nation communities is the moral authority of our people operating separately of the councils. The people of moral authority are the people who organize feasts and other events. Structure is based on consensus building, and discussions involved many hours.

Judge Point continued by saying that in the old days, they behaved together, hunted together, and decided together. When leaders today face their people, they act differently. They are strong, gregarious, and able to speak to the media. But many leaders are also humble, quiet, and listen before deciding with consensus. He asked how are we going to deal with treaties, certainty, and Supreme Court decisions. He said when he goes home, 80 percent of the people are on welfare and that there are many deaths. People have to face fetal alcohol syndrome and a high alcoholism rate. But Judge Point said we are also making tremendous progress, building houses, graduating more students, and seeing more judges and law graduates. He said First Nation people still face Aboriginal issues, like Aboriginal title. He said he tells the newcomers that it's his homeland. But he wondered how he tells them that while the Supreme Court recognizes our rights, the government won't recognize our rights. He said that issues are complex; they are legal and political on one hand and socioeconomic on the other hand. Leaders are stuck in having to make decisions on these two worlds. They get stressed and sick.

Judge Point suggested an idea he borrowed—that ancestral reaction is a thought, that's how we bring into creation that which is not in creation. In facing the complex issues, he said we should be forming discussion circles to discuss fishing, hunting, and the difficulty of explaining fiduciary obligations to community members. He said we have to be strategic in the political arena, in the highways, and in the international arena. He said the torch is passed to this generation and that it is a challenge that we cannot avoid. He was convinced that it can be done and that we can and must achieve meaningful treaties. The community members cannot wait any longer while the young people are getting restless.

On the second day, the opening speaker was Miguel Alfonso Martinez who has held various positions in international bodies in the fields of international law, human rights law, and international humanitarian law specifically within the United Nations system.

Mr. Martinez began his talk by identifying himself as holding the chair of the United Nations Working Group on Indigenous Peoples' Rights. He stated that he always says to himself when he comes to an indigenous conference that he has the opportunity to learn more of indigenous people. He said he came here to learn and that he was very impressed from the quality and the debates of yesterday. He had participated in the workshops and found them to be thought provoking. He stated that last year, he completed the final report on Treaties, Agreements, and Other Constructive Arrangements between States and Indigenous Peoples (also referred to as the United Nations Treaty Study). He said he and his colleagues continue to fight at the UN General Assembly to have a full-fledged conference on land issues. He said if we have to deal with this land issue, we have to deal with equity.

Martinez said the one thing that struck him yesterday in Ms. Jamieson's speech was when she stressed the need for the title of this conference in "Restoring Relationships" as indigenous peoples have to restore relationships not only with Canada but other Nations. New jurisdiction is being built to restore structure. He said that, as a rule, if you want a new relationship, you cannot trust the present one because you have to apply nonindigenous paradigms. Legal norms, concepts, and principles from indigenous people have been alienated. He said if we do not deal with these issues, conflict resolution becomes challenging. He said that follow-up to his treaty study needs our help. A new study is needed that does not skim over indigenous matters. He said that he is determined to introduce an indigenous chapter.

Mr. Martinez then spoke of human rights and human responsibilities. He said that the views of indigenous people need to be heard. What do indigenous people feel that an individual learning about them must know? He said this was the challenge he brought to us and will request of other indigenous people all over the world. He stated the international community deserves to learn what the views of indigenous people are on human responsibility. He briefly summarized the state of affairs in connection with Indian or indigenous people and the United Nations specialized bodies of the Working Group on Indigenous Populations and for indigenous peoples, of the Working Group on Indigenous Peoples of which 2002 will be its twentieth year. Martinez continued by stating that we are in a very critical moment as indigenous peoples in the United Nations. He highlighted the following issues of concern:

1. The present sorry state of the Draft Declaration of the Rights of Indigenous Peoples, which has languished in the Working Group on the Draft Declaration in the last seven years. Indigenous people have to take the decisions, which are the options to advance their interests. The next session is in November–December 2001, where three or four articles will again be dealt with. Hopefully, he said, all this work of dealing with the forty-five articles will be completed by 2003–04, but that it will take longer due to the lack of political will of many governments. There has to be an internal recognition or participation of indigenous people in the drafting of the declaration. Without it, credibility will be lacking. The other option is for indigenous peoples to have their own declaration.

2. A number of key issues with the new body, the Permanent Forum for Indigenous People, are still unclear. This body is to substitute for the Working Group on Indigenous Populations when the draft declaration is adopted by the working group. There is also the issue of representation on the forum by indigenous people.

3. Continuation or survival of the Working Group on Indigenous Populations. This group was to meet regularly.

4. State of the Decade for Indigenous Peoples. There are no funds and very little activities transpiring due to the financial crisis of the UN.

5. The effect of the financial situation on staff. The United States is practically in arrears with its dues. No people are assigned to indigenous peoples issues.

The next presentation was a panel discussion chaired by Sharon McNeill on the topic of treaty interpretation and renewal.

The first speaker was Bernd Christmas, who spoke on the Micmac treaties and *the Marshall* case. Mr. Christmas gave a brief history of the Micmac, Maliseet, and Passamaquoddy Peace and Friendship Treaties of 1725–1794, which acknowledged nationhood that is strong and continues today. The land located in this area is today experiencing oil and gas development. Governmental regulatory boards are acknowledging these treaties. Aboriginal rights and Aboriginal title are central. Mr. Christmas said there is no phrase in the Micmac language for ceding or surrendering of rights. No evidence exists they did. He said the Royal Proclamation of 1763 recognizes the rights of Indian nations and right to land. To date, there has been an Aboriginal person charged in New Brunswick with logging. In *the Marshall* case, the chief justice dealt with the principles of treaty interpretation. Essentially, he ruled that treaties must be liberally construed in favor of Indians. Treaties were signed to mutually benefit each party. *Marshall I* and *Marshall II* (clarification of *Marshall I* decision of the Supreme Court) confirmed that the Micmac, Maliseet, and Passamaquoddy treaties are valid treaties. *The Marshall* ruling involves the honor and integrity of the Crown and impinges on securing the peace and friendship with the Micmac. Mr. Christmas concluded by saying that he believes that all indigenous peoples in the country believe in the rule of law, which strengthens democratic values.

The next speaker was Gerald Morin, QC and Provincial Court judge who spoke on the treaty renewal process, which he describes as being an exploratory process of two parts:

1. Finished business, which resulted in the tabling of the medicine chest clause and the education clause. These were going to be left to interpretation however. This part of finished business relies on the written word used by the Crown and elaborates on what has been said.

2. Unfinished business in which the Natural Resources Transfer Act really comes into focus of resources in respect to *the Marshall* decision. The Treaty 7 litigation process was initiated due to the impact of limitation of action legislation.

In the exploratory process, elders look at the treaty that has involved the honor of the Crown and the Creator. Judge Morin said that for the first time in history, it happened that the Supreme Court revisited a decision it made in *Marshall I*, of which revisitation Morin views as atrocious. These discussions involve building treaties and restoring relationships. He said that Cree elders teach four principles:

- Link to the land
- Relatedness (Wah-koh toh-win)
- Good Relation (Mi-yoh- wi-ce-toh-win)
- Wiy tas kiy win (living together on the land in harmony).

The next speaker was Hugh Breaker who spoke on the courts and treaty interpretation. He stated the proposition courts romanticized Indian people, in particular, the Supreme Court of Canada has fallen victim to the Hollywood version that sees Indian people a slayers of game and fishers. This version views Indian people in the same way as explorers saw Indian people when the explorers arrived hundreds of years ago. Breaker said when Indian people want gambling rights, today the court gets confused for, among other considerations, it involves financing and taxation. Fishing is deemed a resource and economic benefit and is accorded by law some modest ability toward an income. Mr. Breaker mentioned other cases that do not have the preconceived notion. Internal right of self-regulation is recognized as it does threaten the rest of Canada. He asked the question of where the court goes now with treaty interpretation and renewal. He briefly referred to three points at issue in rulings.

1. *The Marshall* decision where generous rules of interpretation of treaties should not be used in after the fact largess (limiting of the application of principles they are comfortable with).

2. *The Campbell* decision, which recognized distinct culture but still had restrictions, established that treaties defined rights given protection

by Section 35 and recognized the ability to negotiate and the internal right of self-government.

3. The management of treaty lands involves the right to manage lands by First Nations. First Nations never get beyond lip service or beyond how Aboriginal perspectives relate to the other principles of treaty interpretation.

Mr. Breaker claimed that Indian people have moved past hunting, fishing, and wearing feathers. He said that other issues remain, for example, what does consultation mean? What is the relationship of Section 88 of the Indian Act to Treaty, to Section 35 of the Constitution, to provincial jurisdiction in adjudication and to Treaty Rights? He concluded by saying that there is going to be a lot of excitement in the court in relation to treaty renewal that is going to be challenging for Indian people and the rest of Canada.

The next speaker was Jean Teillet, who spoke on the *R v. Powley* case and Métis rights. She said there is no Department of Métis Affairs, Minister of Métis Affairs, or Specific Claims of Métis. There is no recourse but litigation with the goal of establishing relationship. The hunt is on for justice, for some kind of relationship with the government. *The Powley* case involves Métis harvesting rights and raises the relationship between treaty and Aboriginal interest. The Métis is now in that negotiation statement. Ms. Teillet said that she never underestimated the depth of the dishonor of the Crown. Powley hunted moose without a license. Powley won this case, with the judge putting a stay for a year to February 23, 2002, to allow the parties to negotiate with "utmost dispatch." But the government has put restrictive regulations and quotas. With this decision, Ms. Teillet said it is the first time ever that a Court of Appeal has made a statement that Aboriginal people have certain rights that must be considered before a decision affecting them is made.

The next workshop I attended was on incorporating First Nation values. Respect, reciprocity, keeping future generations in mind, consensus decision making, and responsibility were discussed. Respect means respect for the earth and people. Language retention and access to resources were also raised. The use of existing First Nation institutions, which are traditional, was raised, such as the BC longhouse setting and practices. A question arose, "Do we incorporate First Nation values internal to our nations, or do we use them in interfacing with the federal and provincial government?" An additional question arose of taking politics into a sacred place. This deals with the problem of not involving elders in sacred places and of involving all the elders in decision making. The question also involves the issue of getting the consent of a clan. Also raised was the status of hereditary chiefs and their role in the distribution of the traditional resources of the land. Another issue was that the real interests of First Nations are not on the treaty table, for example, the right of way interest and of resources used for livelihood. First Nation people also value their areas for spiritual purposes and that they use tribal boundaries, not just reserves to retain cohesion of our First Nation's values. There was an expressed need to meet with Crown representatives to deal with First Nation traditional values. For example, at the time of settlement, conditions were set on the railway right of way.

The luncheon speaker was an indigenous lawyer named Tomas Alarcon from Peru. His speech was titled "Challenges for Lawyers of the Earth (of the Land)." These challenges include the following:

- Existing law does not guarantee a people territorial integrity (sovereignty), which allows them to live according to traditions.
- Indigenous people do not have the legal personality that allows them to assume their destiny.
- Though our forefathers have entered willful agreements; history has shown the weakness of this arrangement through unfulfilled treaties, vulnerable Constitutions, and insecure laws.
- Contemporary governments do not allow the right to take back our lands.
- Governments in power have destroyed prairies, wetlands, and forests backed by their laws.

Mr. Alarcon said Mother Earth pleads to us that we must continue caring for her and defending her to ensure that humanity has a future worthy of an honorable future. He said this can only be achieved through the recognition of our people in international law. Under the present system, governments do not want to return to our people their sovereignty over our lands and the extension of self-determination. Mr. Alarcon gave the example of governments claiming their self-perceived authority over the biological resources that our people have conserved and coexisted with. Throughout history, our people contributed to the responsible stewardship of the environment and therefore in the promotion of international peace. Mr. Alarcon said there is no longer any excuse to deny our people a legal personality in the international arena, which will allow taking the responsibility they have with other people internationally. And finally, our people cannot be denied their right to care for the earth as the earth takes care of them and as the earth deserves to be care for by us. In concluding, Mr. Alarcon advised the indigenous lawyers to bring issue in every forum a call for reform of existing law to recognize our peoples' right, creating a new juridical doctrine of law in law school, in international settings, and in the internal mechanisms of our nations.

The other luncheon speaker was Mike Barnes, a Maori from New Zealand, whose speech was titled "Trick or Treaty." He began by briefly described the Maoris' worldview where the natural order of the world revolved in cycles. The Maori word for this natural order is "Tihar ooti ooti" (a world revolving). Next, he gave a short history of the colonization process, imperialization, and annexation of their people and lands variously by the Dutch, Russians, and the French. In 1840, Queen Victoria negotiated the Treaty of Waitangi with the Maori, which was a license for the white people and others to settle the land. In 1965 and 1985, the government acknowledged greater Maori autonomy. In 1975, the Waitangi Tribunal was affirmed to handle future breach of the treaty by the Crown. But also in 1985, the government was recalcitrant in its duty by establishing a disenfranchising body and allowing the use of colonizer rules to be used in the court system.

Mr. Barnes asked whether the Master is myopic and how does the Master view the Maori? Also around this time, punitive legislation was passed. It recalled the style of artists of the nineteenth century that portrayed portraits of Crown representatives along with the Maori at their feet supposed to depict a protective relationship. This paternalization of another people was deemed a God-given right by the colonizers. Barnes said in 1840, 540 chiefs and the Crown subsequently declared these chiefs as representing one people. The Maori put faith in the power of due process but felt marginalized. In efforts to preserve sovereignty and identity, the Maori sought to protest. This resulted later in the New Zealand Treaty Claims Process through political action and pressure. Barnes said in 1975, Wellington (headquarter similar to Indian Affairs) was willing to address Maori concerns in addition to the recognition of the unfulfilled promises of the Waitangi Treaty and the realization of reconstruction and compensation. The end results benefits to the Maori were 20 percent of the total of the country's allocation; licenses returned to the Maori; employment; economic growth; education and scholarships; Maori language protection; funding of preschools, primary schools, and secondary schools; Maori radio airwaves guarantee; forests to be returned; Maori natural resources laws; and Maori correctional facilities. The resulting deficits were the limited authority that the treaty tribunal has, as it can only recommend to the government. In conclusion, Mr. Barnes said the remedies needed are the removal of the fiscal cap; national guidelines in designing appropriate levels of claims settlements that are full, fare, and final; and ensuring a more sustainable way of making treaty settlements.

The plenary session on "Visions for the Future" dealt with other models.

The first speaker was June McCue, professor at UBC and hereditary chief within the Ned'u'ten Nation and a band member of the Babine Nation. McCue began by asking: Beginning with our families, how can we create a vision for the future? How do we apply ideas of sharing, feeling, envisioning on dealing with land disputes? She said visions can be accessed through dreams and stories and have to be clear. She said, back home, they are relying on kitchen table talks and the potlatch to deal with land disputes some of which stem from way back and are intergenerational. She said she is taking the responsibility as her grandfather would have liked on how to restore order. She acknowledged the frustration of their young members toward the elders. She noted some members are trying to use the legal system regarding questions of Aboriginal title. The potlatch, which her family is going to use, she said, already has a system to resolve land disputes and to reconnect to their land and family. Then she told a story. If you get lost in the woods, you have to stay still. Be calm and retrace your steps back to your camp. You cannot allow the trees to tell you where to go. You cannot allow outside forces to tell you where to go.

The next speaker was Dalee Sambo Dorough, a PhD candidate at UBC School of Law, who is completing her doctoral thesis on indigenous peoples' rights in international law. She is of Alaskan Inuit descent. She said, in relation to government and indigenous peoples' settlements for example the Alaska Native Claims Settlement Act, there needs to be communication, education, and consent. She highlighted the following current obstacles to settlement of claims:

- imposition of state-chartered corporations and owning lands,
- call for extinguishment clauses which were very ambiguous and far reaching, and
- impacts on Aboriginal hunting, fishing, and gathering rights.

She said that they are going to have to find ways to bury extinguishment. She asked, "Where does this come from?" Ms. Dorough said extinguishment is only an assumed power with no basis for it. It applies only to one generation leading to assimilation. She described the following three current developments:

1. Signed in 2001, the Yukon River Intertribal Treaty involves forty-five tribes and First Nations. The purpose of this treaty is to protect and preserve the Yukon River watershed based upon the tribes' and First Nations' customs and practices.

2. Intertribal Pipeline Initiative. She briefly described the impact of the Trans-Alaska Pipeline.

3. Tribal Justice. Ms. Dorough said this area saw advances among indigenous communities across Alaska, for example, the Bethel-Yupik people's child welfare and their retention in the community, the development of a Yupik Code on Child Welfare, the development of a Yupik decision making institution, the development of an Appellate Court System involving the taking a community's case to another community to resolve disputes, and Yupik control of language.

The last speaker, Herb George, a Wetsu'weten hereditary chief, said visions are critical for us to understand. He asked whether a vision statement is going to be sold or forced on anyone. Vision has to come from the people. We need to remind ourselves periodically of our vision and to create a new memory in the minds of the children. George said this can be done through the telling of stories of success, accomplishment, and pride. Children need to be told that they can be the best of what they want to become. Also, they need to be talked to about nationhood, what they see for themselves and their children.

Chief George said that our people need to get over the pain of past unjust treatments and experiences. He said if we don't know what we want, then it becomes impossible to talk about vision. We get preoccupied by talking about law and policy. We need to assume that we don't need anyone to recognize us or to negotiate extinguishment or to ask for Aboriginal title. George said the Wetsu'weten, in their negotiations, don't use whereas clauses but assert their title or jurisdiction. They worried about their children and how they can benefit right now. He said that we have to start rebuilding our economies. He advised that we should be ridding ourselves of the concept of fiduciary obligations but to look after ourselves based on sovereignty. Chief George concluded by saying we need to start making agreements and to create change to benefit us.

The question-and-comment session included but was not limited to the following concerns:

Greg Dreaver, from Saskatchewan Treaty Six area, announced that we are a nation of rivers and a river of nations. He said that an Aboriginal House of Parliament will be open in December in the former Library of Parliament in Ottawa.

On the issue of disrespect of indigenous people recently in view of the September 11 events, discussion centered why we cannot shut up though censure has been imposed against U.S. [United States] policy by certain elements of the public, rather we need to build our own structures, systems, and values. There are serious implications of the antiterrorism legislation being introduced in Parliament. We need to tell our children what really happened in First Nation and government relations. We need to think beyond the current processes that are in play. We need to find a way to mobilize the grassroots people for that is the only power we have. The fiduciary exists because everything we had and depended on was taken away from us. Last, it was noted that there is no political support for those First Nations (or their members) that are being charged with alleged law breaking.

APPENDIX H

A BRIEF ANALYSIS OF BILL C-7 (2002) THE FIRST NATIONS GOVERNANCE ACT

COUNCILOR ERIC J. LARGE

This bill, introduced by the minister of Indian and Northern Affairs on June 14, 2002, in the House of Commons, is yet another legislated method of controlling and limiting the full potential of the indigenous nations and tribes in Canada. A list can be made of the existing laws and policies that control our lives from our cradle to our grave: the Indian Act, the Financial Administration Act, the Criminal Code of Canada, the Firearms Act, the Budget Deficit legislation, the Natural Resources Transfer Acts (1929–1931), to name a few. Then there are the numerous regulations and procedures that stem from the above legislation and statutes, which require large bureaucracies to administer their implementation.

There are about eight other bills that the minister is ready to reintroduce in February 2003. Some details are available regarding Bill C-6 the Specific Claims Legislation and Bill C-19 the First Nations Fiscal and Statistical Management Act. Information on the other pending bills is scarce, but the minister did threaten to unload his department's trust responsibility and thereby let go of liability by transferring control by First Nations of their oil and gas resources. All this is being fast tracked by the minister, ostensibly in the guise of a "results" driven agenda and to build upon a legacy in First Nations affairs in the last year of the departing prime minister.

The Crown in Right of Canada and its agent governments continue to disregard the nation-to-nation relationship between it and Nehiyawak which relationship was recognized in the Royal Proclamation of 1763 and in the treaties that were signed. The Royal Proclamation and the treaties recognized Nehiyawak as nations and tribes ensuring their existence with continual access to land, natural resources, wildlife, and plants. This relationship was to mutually benefit the nations and tribes and the British Crown for "as long as the sun shines, the grass grows and the rivers flow." In the signing of Treaty No. 6, the Creator, Kiseh Manitou, was invoked with Sacred *Pipes* of the signatory tribes and in the presence of Christian clergy. The treaty making involved legitimate negotiations; the honor of the Crown; informed consent; the continuation of the First Nations' customary practices; rights to hunting, fishing, trapping, and gathering; access to traditional areas; education; health; freedom from military conscription; assistance in times of famine and pestilence; tax exemption, etc.

Through Bill C-7, the minister is to "give" greater authority and power to band councils to govern their membership. However, the minister will still retain final authority. There is no mention of the chief's authority. There is no mention of Treaty No. 6 or the promises made to our treaty peoples. There is no recognition of our traditional forms of governance and decision making by consensus. In addition, the acceptance and passage of Bill C-7 will not result in increased funding to meet the needs of our growing populations and the demands for additional housing, infrastructure, health costs, economic development, and support systems for tribal governance. The process of consultation for the promotion of Bill C-7 was improper, and the potential impacts of Bill C-7 for treaty First Nations will be far reaching.

Thus, Bill C-7 is a long continuing effort by the Crown in Canada to limit its treaty and Constitutional obligations to treaty peoples and to limit its liability. From treaty signing in 1876, the succeeding governments of the day were very conscious of the costs going to treaty peoples and sought to continually control treaty peoples so they may comply rather than complain. Or the selective use of rations and the tools, implements, seed grain, livestock, and other benefits were cunningly used by the Indian agents against the treaty nations and tribes in the guise of testing their loyalty to the Crown. The Bill C-7 legislation is very prescriptive with about ninety-three articles on band governance; powers of band councils; general provisions covering registries of codes and laws; regulations and orders; nonapplication; transitional provisions, related amendments and coming into force; and related articles. The minister is preparing medicine that he intends to give us for all that ails us. Like a doctor, he thinks that by prescribing this medicine, he is acting in our best interests. But the question is how many First Nations will take this medicine? We will have to wait to see if it will make them well. Or will the treaty leaders, elders, and people do all they can to retain their tribal customary laws and treaty rights and oppose Bill C-7 by lobbying members of Parliament and senators, informing the media, holding band information meetings, and reaffirming their positions with clear statements?

APPENDIX I

REPORT ON THE AFN CONFEDERACY OF NATIONS MEETING—DECEMBER 10, 11, AND 12, 2002, THE CROWN PLAZA HOTEL, OTTAWA, ONTARIO

COUNCILOR ERIC J. LARGE

On December 10, the welcoming address was presented by the hosting nation spokesperson, Ron Bernard, of the Algonquin of Pikwakanagan, whose message was that strength and unity are the only way to bring justice to every Anishinabe person in this land.

Next, National Chief Mathew Coon Come made his general opening comments. He said he believes that one of the greatest gifts of the Creator is the gift of choosing one has to do, finding accommodation and respect for diversity. He acknowledged the anger directed at the vice chiefs and the national chief. He urged focus on the perpetrators, the cutbacks on post-secondary education and Medicare. He urged the seeking of adequate houses, the rights agenda, and to continue tell the government our issues. He said he just returned from Geneva, Switzerland where the Working Group on the Draft Declaration of Rights of Indigenous Peoples was meeting. Crucial issues raised in Geneva were self-determination, self-government, and treaties. Coon Come said that Canada is trying to take the lead in drafting the articles. He said he told the Working Group of the lack of respect Canada has on treaties. Referring to this confederacy meeting, he said that in the last meetings, we focused on the government's legislative agenda. He pleaded in this meeting for the confederacy to let him and the executive committee report on how they implemented the resolutions.

A motion was raised for a resolution to adopt the Rules of Procedure for AFN Assemblies. A discussion followed that dealt with the legality of the current rules of procedure.

Chief Roberta Jamieson, Six Nations of the Grand River, said she would like to move on the agenda with two adjustments: (1) to add youth council presentation and (2) to propose the times we are in. Chief Jamieson said not since the 1960s has time been so critical. She said legislation on Parliament

Hill is moving forward in direct opposition to our will and resolutions. She asked where this concern on our agenda is. Chief Jamieson recommended work toward a fiscal relationship, which respects our inherent rights, and that we need a coordinated plan of action to oppose the suite of proposed legislation. She expressed a need for a three-hour block of time for Day 2 to move on a strategic plan of action. The Seconder to Chief Jamieson's motion agreed there is unfinished business to be done and asked what is being done about the environment as the Kyoto Plan is being voted on today in the House of Commons.

The Co chair of the assembly rules that resolutions will be made after each issue. A call for a vote for Chief Jamieson's adjustments to the agenda was called with none opposed, none abstained, and carried unanimously.

The National Youth Council members were introduced, who explained the goals of their initiative. The council is structured into a portfolio system in areas such as governance and fiscal, social and human resources, infrastructure, treaties etc. There are two youth representatives from each of ten regions. The youth representatives were very concerned about social turmoil in First Nations, and one of them discussed a gun incident at one First Nation.

The next speaker was Charles Fox, AFN vice chief for Ontario, who asked, "How do we begin to advocate health as a treaty right principle?" He said the challenge of our leaders is to effect change of the mind-set of the ruling members of this country. He mentioned the Romanow Report released last week on health as a national issue. One of the recommendations is the tabling of Aboriginal health in the first chapter, which indicates its priority in the level of importance. Vice Chief Fox said the contents of the recommendations involve the following:

1. The creation of a pan-Aboriginal approach with First Nations, Métis, and Inuit. There is no mention of additional dollars. Also there is the difficulty of working with other Aboriginal segments and being asked to share resources.

2. The creation of partnership with all levels of governments (federal, provincial, and territorial) and with nongovernment bodies. The issue of decision making is one that has been denied us and remains a challenge.

Vice Chief Fox continued saying the AFN has been lobbying for a First Ministers Conference on Health (to be held in February 2003) and requesting for a seat for AFN to deal with the Romanow Report. He said $1.63 billion has been budgeted for First Nations and Inuit health for 2003–2004 with $1.42 billion in projected expenses. A $1.75 billion is budgeted for 2004–2005 with $1.42 billion projected for expenses. He said we need a proper funding base to deal with the growing gap in health services. He said First Nations' health has improved only marginally since 1979 when the National Health Policy was initiated. There has been no movement by the government to accommodate changes in closing the gap for off-Reserve First Nations people.

Vice Chief Fox said we have to ensure, through political action plans, to keep the government honest in its approach to First Nations concerns in health and also to create awareness that First Nations' health is no different from others in the improvement of health. Also, how we tackle this from the treaty position, Vice Chief Fox said, "Also we have to correct the image that we are unable to manage our affairs, that we are corrupt and that we are a burden on taxpayers. We must shame this government in the lack of health services as a priority." He mentioned that the Chiefs Committee on Health is dealing with health renewal through a tripartite relationship with First Nations, Medical Services Branch and Inuit to tackle the growing gap and how to influence Cabinet to recognize the funding short fall to health services. With regard to the pro forma agreement, First Nations are still dealing with outstanding items.

Vice Chief Fox said the Chiefs Committee is still trying to work with an overall strategy based on health as a treaty and Aboriginal right. With the issue of the NIHB Client Consent Form, there is a strategy developed to deal with it. Overall, the imposition of the consent form is morally wrong and legally challenging. The four or five pilot projects (out of an original fourteen projects) were trying to find a middle ground. The client consent form was introduced in September 2002. It is presently being introduced in BC, Yukon, Saskatchewan, Northwest Territories, and the Atlantic Region. It has not been distributed in Quebec, Ontario, Manitoba, and Alberta. It does not require signature until September 1, 2003. Vice Chief Fox referred to Dr. Charles Weijer, a bioethicist with Dalhousie University, who has said that the NHIB Client Consent Form is unethical. The vice chief said the strategy to lessen prescription misuse is education and prevention, enhanced traditional healing, and review of international approaches. Again there is the infringement of Aboriginal and treaty rights; human rights; and Charter

Rights of privacy as consent opens a patient to secondary and tertiary parties. Fox concluded by saying, "The government may as well open your information to public view." He called for political, technical, and media action.

A discussion followed in which the AFN was accused of being led down the garden path. It was revealed there is a Federal Social Development Framework and Policy being a consolidation that is occurring with no thought of meeting needs with additional dollars. It was said that the Romanow Report recommends that $15 billion is needed over three years with $3 billion be immediately injected to meet Canada's health needs. A question was raised as to how much of that will go to First Nations and that we must get Aboriginal health on the First Ministers Conference on Health in February with the emphasis of health as a treaty right. Vice Chief Fox responded by saying the Romanow Report does not call for new monies for First Nations and does not reference health as an Aboriginal and treaty right. Additional concern on the Client Consent Form said it is a breach of the Treaty Right to Health, in particular to our elders with the problem of illiteracy in being forced to sign the Consent Form.

At this point, Co chair Luc Laine announced a roll call of eighty-two voting delegates as present with a 60 percent of these needed to pass resolutions.

Vice Chief Perry Bellegarde, Saskatchewan, then made his report on "Education—Special Education and Post-Secondary/First Nations Veterans/Regional Initiatives." In reference to special education, he began by referencing health as a treaty right with the spirit and intent as being central. He said a National Policy Framework is being designed and that AFN hopes for new funds of $30 million for each of the first two years and $35 million for the third year. He urged First Nations to lobby Regional Directors General to ensure they use these monies for special education. Of post-secondary education, Vice Chief Bellegarde said there are ten thousand students on the waiting list. He said the AFN lobbying strategy is ongoing for the February 2003 budget. He said the AFN has made two presentations to the Policy Advisory Group (unelected First Nations people handpicked by Minister Nault). He said he hopes that this group will listen to the funding shortages in special and post-secondary education. He also pointed out how youth are impacted at the community level with duplication and overlap of services provided by HRDC Childcare, MSB Fetal Alcohol Syndrome, and INAC Special Education.

Vice Chief Bellegarde called for support for a resolution for the establishment of a National Award for Education Heroes of Our Times

Scholarship plus others in criminology, sports, political science, medicine, and law. In regard to veterans, the vice chief said information was sent to chiefs following the announcement of the government's offer of a thirty-nine-million-dollar payout, which includes an offer of up to twenty thousand dollars per living veteran, surviving spouse, or estate. Bellegarde briefly mentioned the status of regional initiatives of the Treaty Implementation Act, Macro Fund, Off-Reserve Jurisdiction, and Natural Resources Transfer Acts in the context of the *Queen v. Delgamuukw* decision, gaming, the suite of legislation, and the firearms legislation. He invited the delegates to the June 21, 2003, grand opening of the Saskatchewan Federated College in Regina. Lastly, Vice Chief Bellegarde urged the chiefs to push for changes in the justice system as there is over representation of our people, in effect, creating a job industry.

Resolution no. 1/2002 Heroes of Our Time—Seventh Scholarship was moved, seconded, and carried unanimously.

The next presentation was made by Ken Young, vice chief for Manitoba on the Aboriginal Human Resource Development Agreement (AHRDA)/Taxation/Residential Schools. He reported that the AHRDA is under the Economic Development Secretariat of the AFN and that its strategy is responsible to the Chiefs Committee on Economic Development. He said that the Federal AHRDA works with each of the five major Aboriginal organizations (AFN, Métis, Inuit, Council of Women, and Congress of Aboriginal People). Work is pursued for influence and renewal of the AHRDA through a series of meetings across the country involving First Nations and the government. A review of the AHRDA will deliver on the Treasury Board requirement for an evaluation of same.

Young said that the Chiefs Committee on Economic Development will be working with a communication strategy to bring updates on developments including a successor strategy. Other areas Young reported on are the 1994 Employment Income Guidelines, First Nations Taxation Advisory Group, AFN/Canada Customs and Revenue Agency Regional Commissioners Meeting, Municipal Taxation Exemptions, and the CCRA First Nations website. On residential schools, Young reported that eleven thousand claims have been filed. The government is dealing only with mental, physical, and sexual abuse cases though many of the claims involve language and cultural abuses. He said the Alternative Dispute Resolution is referred to where the government recognizes only physical or sexual abuse with no room for language, cultural, or psychological abuse redress. An individual files a claim, while this process will define a class and will encompass all aspects of claims. A settlement amount will be identified of the total $12.1 billion that is estimated for which the government is liable but for which the government has admitted liability for only $3 billion.

Ted Quewezance of Keeseecoose First Nation, Saskatchewan, then made a summary of the Residential School Unit Report. In reference to residential school abuse, he said the priority is to recognize that some of the perpetrators of abuse are still living. There is a need to deal with social issues as abuse is still occurring. He said more money to our communities is not the answer but that everyone has to deal with the residential school syndrome. He said ninety thousand students attended residential schools, while there are twelve thousand claims. He said intergenerational trauma is associated with attending residential schools. The Residential School Unit was mandated by AFN Resolution no. 41/2000 with the mandate to work with a national residential school network. There is a framework for managing claims filed in the courts. A national working group composed of survivors of residential schools was formed. Mr. Quewezance said that strong networking needs to exist and needs to happen to determine the number of elderly and deceased survivors. There is a need for a communication strategy, but there are no resources. He said Indian and Northern Affairs set up the Residential School Unit with $54.1 million with expenditures of $43.2 million. A $13 million was spent for out-of-court settlements; $282,000 for court awards; $9 million for salaries and wages; $15 million for operation; $72 million for capital and equipment; and $5 million for other costs. Mr. Quewezance continued,

"We must prioritize issues as:

1. Amend all agreements to include language and culture. The national chief met Minister Goodale [Ralph Goodale, Minister of Public Works and Government Services, Minister responsible for the Canadian Wheat Board, and Federal Interlocutor for Métis and Non-Status Indians] and Sheila Copps, Minister of Canadian Heritage.

2. Claims of elderly and sick must be settled immediately.

3. Basic level of compensation must start at seventy thousand dollars. The government must pay 100 percent of compensation and go after the churches later. The Anglican Church recently committed $25 million for the next five years.

4. The government needs to accept responsibility of the removal of children as a basis for claims."

He said lifetime reconciliation processes must be supported and compensation made to families who have lost their children. Last, Quewezance mentioned six AFN resolutions made between 1999 and 2001 supporting residential school grievances and their mechanisms of redress.

The next report was made by Georges Erasmus, chair of the Aboriginal Healing Foundation (AHF), who made a slide presentation of the present situation of the twelve thousand legal claims with expected settlements in the hundreds of thousands, which could even reach a million dollars. He said the eleven-year mandate of the AHF expires in 2009. Of the total funded projects, $2.4 million went to the Inuit, $1.3 million for women, and a little under $27 million for Alberta. There was a 78 percent approval rating. Direct healing activities accounted for 47 percent, prevention for 19 percent; honoring survivors for 5 percent; conferences for 10 percent; and education and training for 19 percent. As of February 2001, criteria were added to include survivor driven selections be supported by statistics, best practices, safety and environment, ensuring clients have rights, and whole family treatment. Mr. Erasmus concluded by announcing the Aboriginal Healing National Conference to be held for July 2004 in Edmonton, Alberta, to deal with best practices and other issues.

The next report, made by Mary Jane Jim, vice chief for Yukon Region, was a summary of the AFN Languages Initiative. She said there are fifty-three languages in Canada of which only three are slated to survive (Cree, Ojibway, and Inuktitut). She said this portfolio takes guidance from the Chiefs Committee on Languages and as directed by the Chiefs in Assembly. She said work continues with lobbying Parliament to achieve change in policy. She reported that the Aboriginal Languages Initiative is funded by Heritage Canada. It appears that this initiative is undergoing evaluation, and it is not certain if Canada will renew it. Lobbying for the initiative intensified in October 2002 with the goal of establishing a language foundation.

The next report, the Firearms Legislation, was made by Vice Chief Bill Erasmus, NWT. Erasmus said the AFN began a discussion with the Canadian Firearms Center (CFC) consistent with an approach that we have a treaty and Aboriginal rights. The CFC and the AFN agreed to a system that will be implemented in Manitoba, Alberta, Yukon, and the NWT, and then the rest of Canada. A delay in the January 1, 2003, deadline is being asked for with a template for a draft letter that each First Nation can sign.

Discussion followed, which raised concern that First Nations must do more, perhaps launch a lawsuit against the Crown for breaching our treaty right to hunt and feed our people. Three hunters have been refused ammunition. It was reported that the Federation of Saskatchewan Indian Nations [FSIN] court case is hearing that the Firearms Act and regulations is an infringement of Treaty and Constitutional Rights. It was requested that the AFN change strategy and ask First Nations to support FSIN's case. AFN was asked how long the mechanisms it's taking will be. Grand Chief Louis Jourdain, NW Ontario, reported that Treaty 3 believes that they are sovereign nations and that they've advanced this position based on ethical and spiritual principles. "Sovereignty has no beginning and no end." Another chief said that First Nations oppose the approach that AFN is taking by stating the majority of our people are opposed to this legislation and will not apply for a license nor register their firearms. Vice Chief Erasmus responded by concluding, "We're not talking about compliance. I've said that before. I want to make that absolutely clear. I've said that before at the beginning."

On Day 2, December 11, Co chair Luc Laine asked for development of a proactive strategy for the months to come on the legislation that is being developed by the government.

National Chief Mathew Coon Come requested for a united front on the legislative agenda. He said the minister is allocating another $1.3 million on communication on the legislation. He said we have a work plan from the May 2002 AFN Confederation meeting but have limited resources. He said yesterday there was a national lobby by Chiefs on Parliament Hill. The AFN has lobbied on Bills C-6, C-7, and C-19; health strategy; languages; residential schools; veterans' issues; and others. He said the AFN Staff and Parliamentary Liaison have a list of lobbyists for today and tomorrow.

The national chief said in the last few months, he and the AFN executive have met with: Minister Nault twice, the Reference Group of Ministers, and along with Métis. They have made a presentation with the Standing Committee on Finance. The next agenda items are education and housing. He said the AFN has had fifty-six meetings with government representatives, MPs, and have appeared before Standing Committees a number of times on Bill C-6. He said they will make a presentation to Standing Committee on Bill C-19 and that meetings and lobbying will continue. He said the House of Commons will adjourn today and resume sitting January 27, 2003.

National Chief Coon Come said he met with the auditor general yesterday to commit streamlining of her audit report on the minister of INAC. He said the major media has been notified of positions, and the AFN is engaged in speaking opportunities at local, national, and international levels. For example, at the United Nations in Geneva, Coon Come said he worked with Chief Victor Buffalo and Wilton Littlechild at the second last meeting on the Draft Declaration on the Rights of Indigenous Peoples, which will be approved this summer in New York. Central to these rights is self-determination and inherent rights. Coon Come asked, "In the three hours we have, what is the best way to strategize?" He cautioned on not to implement on anyone else's treaty and to respect that. Also not just criticize but to move forward and set out a critical path of what it is we want to do. He offered the advice of looking at strategy politically, the negotiations of it, at implementation and delivery mechanism. The national chief concluded with "How do we move forward on Treaty and Aboriginal Title?"

The AFN Staff and Parliamentary Liaison then made his report. He said he has been involved in the coordination of chiefs' lobbying efforts since September to ensure there is a consistent message. Strategy was developed to respond to Bill C-6 Independent Claims Act. Issues were raised in the Liberal Caucus and a presentation made to the Standing Committee on Aboriginal Affairs on the shortcomings of Bill C-6. He said some First Nations preferred the addition of amendments and, if these are not forthcoming, then seek to have the bill withdrawn. He reported that Bill C-6 is at the Report Stage and said it is doubtful if it will pass before Christmas. He said there were twenty-three different meetings with members of Parliament held in October and November. The Parliament Liaison and Chiefs will be lobbying senators this week (December 9–13). He said that Bill C-6 will not make it through the Senate easily.

Regarding Bill C-7 First Nations Governance Act, the Liaison said the Standing Committee on Aboriginal Affairs hopes to have five to six weeks of hearings across the country. He said the position of First Nations is that the bill be withdrawn. If a First Nation wishes to appear, it must indicate by January 24, 2003. Locations have not been set yet, although twelve cities have been targeted but have not been revealed. The reaction of the opposition parties has not been made to First Nations yet. The Liaison said second reading of Bill C-19 the First Nations Financial and Statistical Management Act is expected this week. The issues concerning First Nations on this proposed bill are consultations were improper and that it infringes on Aboriginal and treaty rights. It appears that the bill will be delayed until the House resumes sitting January 27, and beginning February 3, hearings will start with national groups beginning with the AFN.

Open discussion resumed with Chief Dan Wilson of the Okanagan Nation Alliance/Okanagan Indian Band who was concerned there is no action by AFN on the proposed Endangered Species Act.

As the third speaker, I, as proxy for Saddle Lake Cree Nation and on behalf of the Confederacy of Treaty Six First Nations (Alberta), read a position statement on the current fiscal legislation (Bill C-6, Bill C-7, and Bill C-19). The statement includes rejection by the Treaty Six Chiefs of the proposed legislation on the grounds of improper consultation, violation of treaty rights, devolution of the Crown's fiduciary trust responsibility, and nonrecognition of First Nations as a distinct order of government. The statement further states that Treaty Six Nations maintain that the law of the Creator, natural law, and tribal customary laws will prevail over federal and provincial laws on First Nation land and that Treaty 6 Nations will continue to practice their inherent right of self-determination and in the reaffirmation and implementation of our treaty relationship with the Crown. The statement also mentions that the Treaty 6 Chiefs agenda is not represented by the AFN as per MOU previously signed by both parties. Last, the position statement serves notice that the Confederacy of Treaty 6 First Nations is designing a "Red Paper" to address Minister Nault's suite of legislation and desires a meeting with Prime Minister Chretien to present our position.

The fourth speaker, Chief Roberta Jamieson, said we know what our alternative is. She urged unity, and there should be short-term and intensive, sustained strategy and also long-term principled strategy.

Grand Chief Louis Jourdain, Treaty 3, said the Canadian Constitution does not and should not apply to our people but that we have the inherent right to sovereignty. He said our leaders are concentrating too much on administrative and program issues. He concluded by saying, by press release, that he is firing the minister of Indian Affairs as of this morning.

Vice Chief Perry Bellegarde then gave an update and status of the legal challenge of the FNGA by David Ahenakew and the FSIN. The claim is based on breach of trust by the Crown. It has been filed. Politically he said they, from Saskatchewan, met Paul Martin to try to get commitment now. Bellegarde believes that First Nations need a process to commit the government to implement Section 35.

Another chief raised the question of where First Nations are going and whether we can rely on the AFN anymore while there is challenge of creating jobs at home.

Deputy Chief Robert Corbiere said First Nations are sailing at the whim of the minister and asked, "Where are we going?" He said they, at his First Nation, don't have enough to meet the needs of their people. They are short five hundred thousand dollars in post-secondary education and that housing is desperately needed as their backlog is five hundred houses. Corbiere said it's time we build our own government, local, regional, and central government, but asked how do we finance it? He concluded by saying, "The way we're deliberating here, we're all speculating. I don't know where it's going to end. But it's time to wake up. I call for a court injunction to stop these developments."

Chief Margaret Swan said the hope is in our young people and that we need to educate them. She said that it is time to implement the National Action Plan Committee that we formed almost a year ago. Chief Hare said the minister should be fired, and we need to meet in the West. The chief of the Chippewa of Niwash Unceded Territory announced he will contribute one thousand dollars. He recommended that the chiefs go to the Standing Committee. Chief Roberta Jamieson said the first steps should be to deal with the plan prepared by the Implementation Committee to respond to the suite of legislation. She recommended meeting again in February and in March as an AFN General Assembly. She called for direct action and assertion of rights.

National Chief Coon Come said, "We'll put forward at the next AFN Assembly options for the reorganization of the AFN. Vice Chief Satsan (Herb George) asked for respect of the First Nations Summit of BC as they support the suite of legislation. He said, "Among differences of position, we can be seen as accepting status quo. Our strategy has to be related to our lands and other areas such as treaties." He said that we have exclusive legal interest to our land. Justification of infringement must be obtained by the Crown when such infringement of your land and resources occurs.

Two speakers from the National Youth Council spoke about engaging and involving youth in this process of dealing with the government's proposed legislation as one of the speakers said, "In three years, there'll be an entirely new generation in leadership. What are you doing to educate so they may address these important issues?" The youth speakers supported the call for more funding for post-secondary education and called for action.

Elder Fred Kelly then told the Assembly that "Anishinabe" has two meanings. The first meaning refers to "male of no value." The second meaning is "one descended from the sky." He said that not until 1850 was "Indian" used. Prior to that, Crown representatives referred to indigenous peoples as nations, their meetings as "congresses," and that treaties were made as acts of sovereignty of nations. Elder Kelly said, "You need an action plan to forward your treaty and Aboriginal rights." Another elder gave a brief background of the 1969 White Paper. He advised, "It's time for united action and to fight for the future of our children. No one can fight alone, not even the AFN."

After lunch, the meeting resumed with a head count of fifty-five chiefs and proxies at 1:45 p.m. A presentation of the World Festival of Traditional Games and Sports was made by Pierre Luc Brodeur, chief executive officer of the "Games of the World" to be held in Montreal July 30–August 8, 2004. The world festival is sponsored, in part, by the founders of ParticipACTION and by the government of Canada, government of Quebec, and the city of Montreal. It is part cultural and part physical activity involving seventy nations. It is not a competition but will involve people and nations participating in sports and culture. There are demonstrations in their culture and in their nations. The participants' village will be located at McGill University.

The final report, "Indian Act Membership Sections," was made by Vice Chief Ken Young, Manitoba, and by Grand Chief Francis Flett, Manitoba Kiwatinowi Okimakanak. Young said that the membership involves long-standing issues that are legally driven. Grand Chief Flett said, politically, Bill C-31 resulted in the extinguishment of our rights as Native people and that this bill needs to be dealt with as other pieces of the currently proposed legislation won't matter. He said Indian Act membership affects First Nations' own interpretation of citizenship in our own community. Grand Chief Flett urged the chiefs to form a national committee to deal with Bill C-31 along with the need for finances. He said there is a need to talk about this in assembly in our own Government House setting. Last, he said that the government can't dictate to us what we're going to do.

Resolutions 2 to 11 were then moved, seconded, and carried. Resolution 2 involves Opposition to the U.S. Army Corps of Engineers Great Lakes Navigation System Review. Resolution 3 deals with Representation of Urban First Nations Peoples by the Assembly of First Nations. Resolution 4 calls for a course of action to address racism toward First Nations Students in Canadian Schools. Resolution 5 requests Support for a Prayer Room at National Assemblies. Resolution 6 establishes a War Chest and Freedom Fund. Resolution 7 establishes a committee to coordinate and develop strategies for the recognition of First Nations rights to determine membership and citizenship. Resolution 8 supports the Ratification of the Kyoto Protocol to the United Nations Convention on Climate Change. Resolution 9 outlines the Proactive Strategy on the Indian and Northern Affairs Canada (INAC) Suite of Legislation. This resolution instructs the AFN to vehemently oppose the suite of legislation, immediately establish and support a command and control center (CCC) to implement an action plan, enable the national chief to ensure that the executive and the (CCC) are guided by the action plan, and call for a Confederacy of Nations meeting before February 15, 2003, to evaluate the action plan.

The action plan lists in detail the objectives, target dates in December 2002 to July 2003, key elements of First Nations political action, lobbying and legislative briefings, internal communications, media relations, public education, direct action/assertion of right, First Nations solidarity, challenge of Canada's accountability, international campaign on solidarity, and litigation. Resolution 10 calls for support for the Henry Traverse Fishing Challenge Court Case. Resolution 11 sets out A First Nations Approach to Firearms. It directs the AFN to "negotiate the extension of the January 3, 2003, registration date"; "complete the First Nations Approach to Firearms process and report back to the next Confederacy"; and "that if the Assembly of First Nations is unable to renegotiate the deadline or the process, that a legal action be prepared and brought back to the next Confederacy meeting."

On December 12, I drafted a letter to Inky Mark, Member of Parliament for Dauphin—Swan River—Marquette, Manitoba, and hand-delivered it to him at his office in the Confederation Building on Wellington Street. In the letter, I raised concerns, questions, and the position of Saddle Lake Cree Nation to the proposed government legislation Bill C-6 Independent Claims Act; Bill C-7 First Nations Governance Act; and Bill C-19 First Nations Financial and Statistical Management Act. The questions involved: the independence of the appointed commissions, boards, and authorities under Bill C- 6 and Bill C-19 and whether First Nations would have to meet extinguishment criteria, i.e., being prohibited from making any future claims to land, resources, and other benefits. Other concerns in relation to Bill C-19 are, that by allowing First Nations to raising their own source revenues for infrastructure capital projects, the Federal Crown will absolve itself from meeting its Treaty Trust obligation to ensure the health, safety, and well-being of our people as well as allow for a gradual system of taxation of our people. In relation to the proposed First Nations Statistical Institute, I wrote that more statistics does not mean more money from the government, as its fiscal policy is subject to the raising of its own revenues in any budget period. I argued that all the monies the government is spending in this legislation and the delivery mechanisms that will be created would be better spent by the government in meeting the basic needs of First Nations. Concerns related to the proposed Bill C-7 involve infringement of the Inherent, Treaty, and Constitutional Rights of Saddle Lake Cree Nation.

NEW DUTIES FOR THE CROWN AND ABORIGINAL PEOPLES FORUM, APRIL 26–27, 2005, FAIRMONT CHATEAU LAURIER, OTTAWA, ONTARIO — A REPORT

COUNCILOR ERIC J. LARGE

I attended the above forum, which explored recent decisions of the Supreme Court of Canada, such as the *Haida Nation v. BC* and *Taku River Tlingit First Nation v. BC* 2004 cases. As outlined in the forum brochure, these cases advance toward a refocusing of responsibilities and rights by the Crown and Aboriginal peoples and stakeholders. Topics to be covered were Crown duties, Aboriginal duties and their practical implications, how momentum must be developed so that all parties involved resolve cross-cultural differences, how court mandated duties must be morphed into legislation and agreements, and how a practical national policy on fair Crown dealings with Aboriginal peoples must be developed.

Day 1, dealing with "Defining Crown and Aboriginal Duties" began with a welcome and introduction by the Co chair of the forum, Peter Hutchins, of the law firm Hutchins, Grant, and Associates of Montreal and Vancouver. Hutchins said this forum will try to promote discussion of duties of the Crown, honor of the Crown, and the validation of these two ideas as well as their implications, in particular, new duties for the Crown in relation to consultation and accommodation. The question of the application of the *Haida* decision of 1994 is "How does it apply in relation to the duty by the Crown to act honorably and also whether the fiduciary duty applies prior to 1994 or whether the application begins from 1994?"

The Co chair of the forum, Alfred Caron, QC, of Indian and Northern Affairs Canada, said the theme of the forum is how do we work together in relation to the implications of various legal decisions? He suggested what is needed is a mutually acceptable solution to the challenges courts have placed before us regarding Aboriginal peoples, government, and stakeholders. He said, "If government is doing its job, the honor of the Crown is not a standard that is impossible to reach." Mr. Caron concluded that exchange of ideas is options in an open and transparent manner in contrast to

...enter was Brian Slattery, professor at Osgoode Hall Law ...ersity, and Toronto. In his topic, "The Honor of the Crown," ...e Haida and Taku River cases show the Supreme Court .... an approach that views the fundamental law governing Aboriginal rights as more dynamic than static—mandating a process that involves the active participation of Aboriginal peoples and the Crown in the identification of Aboriginal rights." He said the Court sees Section 35(1) Constitution Act 1982 as supporting this "generative constitutional order." Professor Slattery said the current or standard paradigm is that the Crown asserts it acquired sovereignty over Aboriginal peoples and their lands, which resulted in the embedding of Aboriginal rights in the common law of Canada. He contends, as such, Aboriginal rights are recognized and enforceable in the courts of Canada. However, Aboriginal peoples have to prove these rights court case by court case in order to have them protected in law. Slattery views this paradigm that has several challenges, such as

- Crown sovereignty—For many Aboriginal people, the Crown's de facto assertion of territorial control of their land was not a legitimate act that was done without the consent of the Aboriginal peoples.

- Proof of Aboriginal rights—If the Crown challenges the existence of a number of Aboriginal rights claimed by an indigenous collective, that indigenous collective must bear the burden of proving the existence of their rights in court.

- The static character of Aboriginal rights—The paradigm posits that Aboriginal rights, in general, morphed through the Crown's assertion of sovereignty and continue their existence in their original character, until or unless they are disallowed by legislation or by voluntary surrender by indigenous people.

According to Professor Slattery, the new paradigm is "a shift away from the approach taken in previous Supreme Court decisions, which suggests that we are witnessing the emergence of a new constitutional paradigm governing Aboriginal rights." Slattery stated Section 35 is seen as ensconcing a generative constitutional order by which the Crown is obligated to deal with Aboriginal peoples for the recognition of Aboriginal rights in a contemporary and workable format, which deals with the transformed needs and conditions of Aboriginal peoples and the larger society. This new paradigm recognizes that Aboriginal peoples possessed preexisting Aboriginal sovereignty and territorial rights prior to the Crown's assertion of sovereignty over Aboriginal peoples. A special relationship resulted from this process called the honor of the Crown, which mandates the Crown to interact honorably with Aboriginal peoples. Slattery said the honor of the Crown has several notable duties. These are

- "the duty to negotiate with Aboriginal peoples;

- the duty to identify their Aboriginal rights; and

- the duty to consult with Aboriginal peoples where Crown-authorized activities affect the Aboriginal peoples' asserted rights and, where appropriate, to adjust the proposed activities so as to accommodate these rights."

The new paradigm tries to correct some of the main challenges of the standard paradigm stated earlier:

- Crown sovereignty—While the court, in *Haida* and *Taku River*, concedes the Crown originally asserted de facto sovereignty in the face of the preexisting sovereignty of indigenous peoples and their rights to territories; it suggests that the Crown's assertion was bereft of legitimacy.

- Proof of Aboriginal rights—With the new paradigm, if the Crown disputes the existence or range of Aboriginal rights claimed by an Aboriginal group, the group need not bear the burden of proof of the existence of the rights in court so they may protect them from being disallowed.

- The static character of Aboriginal rights—With the new paradigm, the court highlights that the Crown is obligated to attain, by negotiation and treaty, a fair settlement of Aboriginal claims. The court appears to give a generative function to Section 35, which effectively means that the Crown, with the help of the courts, is obliged to create a new legal domain that accommodates Aboriginal interests and rights through negotiation and treaty. Section 35 binds the Crown to recognize the rights at hand and to act in a fair and just manner and, as much as possible, with the consent of the affected Aboriginal parties.

Professor Slattery lists some possible challenges:

Crown sovereignty—The existence of any Aboriginal rights in Canadian common law can be assumed to have priority over the existence of Crown sovereignty *de jure* because, otherwise, how can these Aboriginal rights exist as a function of Canadian law? The *de jure* nature of Crown rule rests on the established practice of governmental rule.

The static character of Aboriginal rights—The new paradigm cannot surpass the old paradigm without inviting court action amid competing policy considerations, in which the rights and interests of Aboriginal peoples may be infringed on in favor of the "common good." This challenge may be lessened by the courts deeming "that the Aboriginal rights claimed by an indigenous group exist at a relatively abstract or generic level but that the specific nature and scope of these rights need to be established by negotiation and agreement between the parties—and only in default of such agreement (and as a last resort) by the courts themselves.

Questions and comments were the following:

Participant: "Are you suggesting that there be reconciliation of the general population with Aboriginal people?"

Professor Slattery: "Aboriginal rights are still embedded rights, are not satisfactory, but need to be recognized in a process that is animated by the honor of the Crown, negotiation and care as the protector of Aboriginal people and, in some sense, as protector for all people. I am talking about Aboriginal rights and not treaty rights. Treaties gave people limited land. Historical treaties did not consist of the written memorandum, which the government kept, but on the oral negotiation of the people involved. In *Marshall*, the Supreme Court reads a treaty has underlying fundamental principles, the Crown as protector of Aboriginal people, would ensure Aboriginal people have a right of self-sufficiency, and Aboriginal people would have a treaty that is recognized. Treaty rights are not separate from Aboriginal rights but must be read in light of those principles of recognition, protection, and accommodation."

Sharon Venne, a lawyer with Treaty no. 8 North West Territories (NWT) Council commented the Crown is not adhering to Supreme Court rulings, that the Crown is not upholding its honor in dealing with First Nations with regard to fair negotiating, consultation, and accommodation of their rights and interests. There was no satisfactory reply by the Co chairs or Professor Slattery.

A representative from the Department of Justice raised a question on the Alberta Government's recognition of Métis rights and their implication. Professor Slattery's response was not clear.

Another participant asked for Professor Slattery's analysis in relation to the residential school experience and whether this experience was a form of assimilation of Aboriginal students or was a part of their assimilation into the larger Canadian society. Professor Slattery's response was "Honor of the Crown is a normative principle. It cannot change. What has been done has {been done}. But the honor of the Crown deals with what the Crown ought to have done. One of the principles is negotiation. It requires the Crown to favor, encourage, and help to ensure the economic self-sufficiency and prosperity of Aboriginal people today."

Another question raised was "Does the honor of the Crown require the Crown to ensure the Aboriginal peoples understand the implication of Treaty?" Professor Slattery answered, "The honor of the Crown requires that there should be no sharp dealings, that the Crown be forthright in its dealings with Aboriginal people." In other words, the actual treaty is what was actually agreed to, not what the government thought it negotiated. The government didn't go far enough in explaining the treaty during the negotiation process. Slattery said, "Part of the answer to the court ruling requires proof for specific Aboriginal rights is that the Supreme Court is gradually moving to recognizing generic rights, that all Aboriginal rights have some rights in some form."

An eastern Cree delegate said that the honor of the Crown is problematic to the Cree, emphasizing, "As governments have said, we have rights leading to lawsuits. Honor means dealing in good faith."

Another question was "How do we get the Crown to act honorably?" Answer: *"Haida* is the trigger to tell how to move the Crown to act honorably. Here are some legal remedies in moving the Crown to act honorably."

The next presenter was M. Louise Mandell, QC, of the law firm Mandell Pinder of Vancouver. Her topic was "Defining the Crown's Duty to Act Honorably." Ms. Mandell summarized the question of how Aboriginal people got the land and the government got the land. To make their case heard, Mandell said the "Aboriginal people in BC said they will bring their own songs and stories to court to establish Aboriginal title existed. Government said Aboriginal rights were extinguished. Recognition of Aboriginal title was reinforced by court-imposed duty of consultation." She mentioned the contribution of the late George Manuel with political and legal strategy in the early struggle for proving Aboriginal title. She said *the Haida* case "is a story of institutional shifting. It is

- A way in which honor of the Crown is rooted, to treat Aboriginal people honorably, to protect them, and is founded prior to assertion of Crown sovereignty.

- The aspect of the decision {that is important} is the legal duty to consult prior to assertion and to protect the land against unsustainable management of which Aboriginal people are the beneficiaries. The Crown said there has to be reconciliation, which requires negotiation and the duty is the honor of the Crown."

The Company Duty—In *the Haida* case, the Supreme Court ruled that the Crown's duty to consult does not apply to Weyerhaeuser nor can the honor of the Crown be delegated.

Regarding institutional shape shifting, Mandell and Pinder suggest that Supreme Court decisions requires Aboriginal peoples to enforce the decisions by getting governments to listen and to remind them of the meaning of respect and the demonstration of good faith and honor. Mandell and Pinder identify some of the elements of the Supreme Court rulings, which have transformative options. These elements are

- Institutional changes to laws and policies
- Treaty negotiation processes
- Aboriginal lawmaking is on the table
- The honor of the Crown: a new model
- The honor of the Crown to define and enforce treaty rights. Mandel and Pinder imply that the Crown is engaged in preproof stand and at the conclusion of treaty. *The Haida* case rulings implicitly oblige First Nations with treaties to compel the Crown to set a negotiation method to implement treaty rights.
- The honor of the Crown in negotiating interim agreements
- Protecting the land: consultation at the strategic planning stage
- Protecting the land: a remedy

- Developing capacity within Aboriginal communities and nations
- Third-party tenures granted without consultation.

A question was asked by a First Nation delegate from BC on the Forestry Range Agreement on Vancouver Island in reference to *the Haida* case. The delegate said his First Nation was denied an agreement, which he said is against the principle of duty to consult and accommodate. His view was that regional and municipal governments have a responsibility to consult and accommodate First Nations. Ms. Mandel replied, "There is no present process to include regional and municipal governments or even corporations."

Chief Dave General of the Six Nations of Grand River asked Ms. Mandell to summarize her talk as she went fairly fast. Her summary consists of what she called the four pillars:

- "Land use planning—the result will be a negotiated organized plan that can achieve protection for areas such as protection areas

- Shared decisions around management—our objective may be to protect a particular river with a particular species of salmon

- Tenuring system—consultation takes place with Aboriginal and third parties. Benefits can be built in for Aboriginal people and their impact for them

- Resource revenue sharing—[ensuring] hunting and tree cutting."

The next presentation, "A Comparison of the Duty to Act Honorably with the Fiduciary Duty and the Duty to Negotiate Section 35 Rights in Good Faith," was delivered by Prof. Michael Coyle of the Faculty of Law, University of Western Ontario. Coyle's view is "The duty to consult applies even when claims are unproven." For him, *the Haida* decision is a departure from previous decisions with its assurance that Section 35 rights are in fact implemented in our lifetimes. He said, "Aboriginal and treaty rights must be given effect immediately and leaving for later, definition. *Haida Nation* and *Taku River* decisions mandate that governments and other participants must consult as a requirement. The Supreme Court of Canada case-by-case approach has meant, for the most part, we have no idea what are the Aboriginal and treaty rights because it is time consuming, for example, there are two thousand four hundred present cases. To date, negotiation processes don't exist whether through legislation or otherwise. Negotiation processes and backlog of cases is increasing. Through *Taku River* and *Haida Nation*, the Supreme Court has called for action in identifying Aboriginal and treaty rights."

Professor Coyle said the origins of the fiduciary duty and honor of the Crown indicate they are arisen from the relationship of Aboriginals and the Crown's peoples through Treaty. He said, "The Royal Proclamation of 1763 provided protection of Aboriginal rights and land. It recognized Indian nations as autonomous nations. In 1764, Sir William Johnson met with two thousand First Nations people at Niagara and reiterated the Royal Proclamation. This formalized each party's commitment and symbolized the British and First Nations for treaty making. Honor of the Crown, in *Haida* and *Taku River*, was primarily defined by the court and admonished that the Crown refrains from sharp dealing and to act honorably. Fiduciary duty was first identified *in Guerin* where the Crown's legislation authority has given in to an exercise where the Crown is in a trust like capacity in relation to a First Nation. The Supreme Court *in Sparrow* ruled there is a fiduciary relationship between the Crown and a First Nation. For Professor Coyle, the impact *of Haida Nation* decision is relatively small. The fiduciary duty applies where the Crown has a specific duty.

In practical terms, Professor Coyle said the impact *of Haida Nation* decision {in terms of honor of the Crown} is that the Crown has a duty to consult First Nations even in respect of unproven claims. A province will be required to consult where its decision will have an impact on First Nations' interest. Aboriginal groups are called upon to participate in the consultation. In *the Haida Nation* decision, in all dealing with Aboriginal people, the Crown must deal honorably. Treaty principles of fairness apply. The court judgment states that the Crown has a legal duty to define Section 35 Rights, for example, title or other areas of interest to Aboriginal people and to participate in effective processes of negotiation. Professor Coyle's view is that the Crown's alternative to not negotiating will not result in successful negotiating. He said negotiating requires timeliness and setting the timeframe to resolution. "An honest disagreement between the parties requires a mediation process. Prior to *the Haida Nation* [decision], there were few Section 35 rights settled. With *Haida Nation*, the court is saying, it is time to give effect to Section 35 Rights." Professor Coyle said, "The result is new guidelines and new incentives created by the court leading to an effective negotiation process."

The next speaker was Alan Pratt, barrister and solicitor. His topic was

"Frustrating Consultations: Getting Beyond 'Trust Us.'" He said the duty of the Crown, as represented by the federal and provincial governments, to consult First Nations in relation to their rights and interests was affirmed by Supreme Court decisions *of Sparrow* 1990; *Badger* 1996; and *Delgamuukw* 1997. Pratt outlined some of the main elements in *Haida v. BC* [2004]. These elements are:

- Good faith on both sides is needed
- Sharp dealing is not permitted
- "Aboriginal claimants . . . must not frustrate the Crown's reasonable good faith attempts."

Pratt asked, "What will it take for First Nations to believe federal and provincial governments in their protestations of good faith?" He stated whether "First Nations are justified in wondering whether the *Haida* case itself might be just another false promise" in addition to the promises made in the Royal Proclamation of 1763, in the treaties, and in the Constitution Act 1982. However, in his frustration, Pratt agreed with the RCAP's proposal for a new Royal Proclamation that will commit the Crown to identify all of the current Aboriginal and treaty rights and to honor them. He also called for the renewal of the promises made in the Royal Proclamation of 1763 and hopes that the SCC "will continue to clarify what code of honorable conduct is required of the Crown, flowing directly from the principles it has restated and clarified in the Haida Nation case."

The next topic, "Arriving at a Common Understanding of Crown and Aboriginal Duties," was delivered by Michael Mitchell, district chief of Kawehnoke, Mohawk Nation at Akwesasne. He said Akwesasne is located in the United States and Canada. In 1986, the trade in tobacco was legally challenged. The government was alarmed, as it wants control. Mitchell said, "Our people believe in an inherent treaty right to cross the border." The Akwesasne cross border case became a test case where the charge was the evasion of GST and customs duty. Akwesasne went ahead and crossed the border in a truck with groceries and clothes. Akwesasne won the case ten years later. Mitchell said, "We leaders have a responsibility to have our own justice system. We are developing a nation law in health. First Nations must articulate their responsibility in health. We also made a nation law on firearms. We developed on how to work with other governments and jurisdictions. We are developing a wildlife conservation law to regulate hunting, fishing, and trapping."

Renée Dupuis, chief commissioner, Indian Claims Commission, was the next speaker. She dealt with recent history where there is a paradigm shift. She highlighted the 1969 White Paper, which denied Aboriginal and treaty rights; the *Calder v. BC* [1973] ruling that prompted the federal government to begin bargaining Aboriginal title claims, and the political and legal lobbying by First Nations in the international arena. She said the Constitution Act 1982 recognized Aboriginal peoples (Indian, Inuit, and Métis); existing Aboriginal and treaty rights; and the participation of Aboriginal representatives in Constitutional conferences regarding Aboriginal matters. Ms. Dupuis mentioned, with the change in the Crown's duties since 1982, there are new duties and obligations for the Crown, which goes hand in hand with the recognition of new rights. She said these new duties are

- A restriction on the powers of legislatures and governments

- Obligations imposed by the courts in the absence of political discussions. A fiduciary relationship giving rise to a fiduciary duty was affirmed by *R v. Sparrow* [1990] and *R v. Guerin* [1984]. The Supreme Court has ruled "that the Crown is bound by its honor and that no "sharp dealing" can be tolerated, owing to the responsibility deriving from the Crown's fiduciary relationship

- Duties for both parties to disputes (governments and Aboriginal peoples)

- The judicial approach: the clash of conflicting interests

- The need for a broader perspective

- Diverging and converging interests. There is often competing interests between the federal and provincial governments and within First Nations

- The Indian Claims Commission: a bridge between two different perspectives.

Day 2 began with the topic "The Duty to Consult and Accommodate Aboriginal Peoples: Expanded Obligations of Federal and Provincial

Governments" that was presented by Dr. Tony Knox of the law firm McCarthy Tetrault LLP, Vancouver. Dr. Knox stated the *Haida Nation v. BC* and, *Weyerhaeuser* and *Taku River Tlingit v. BC* rulings of November 18, 2004, affirm that Aboriginal law is part of Canada's general law. The Supreme Court obliges the Crown's duty to consult Aboriginal interests and rights. This trigger to consult is founded on "real or constructive" knowledge. Dr. Knox also advised the consideration of administrative law principles and fairness; standard of correction; adequacy of consultation; standard of reasonableness; spectrum of consultation; accommodation; changes to current legislation, policy, and procedures; possible reopening of current agreements; notice to industry; limitation of fiduciary duty; difference between duty and fiduciary relationship; provincial Crown's fiduciary duty; and impacts on municipalities and Crown corporations.

A question from a Department of Justice representative to Dr. Knox was asked in relation to the implications of overlaps of Métis' and First Nations' interests and claims in relation to the recent SCC decisions. Dr. Knox replied that the concept of reasonableness be applied case by case and that the "honor of the Crown may require the Crown to back off." Another question was "How does the honor of the Crown impact Treaty 4 and Treaty 6 rights where the Crown has asserted [in the text version] that First Nations rights to the land were extinguished?" Dr. Knox replied, "Where the treaty rights were infringed, the honor of the Crown is involved."

The next topic was "Aboriginal Peoples—Making Use of the Balancing Interests Framework." The first speaker was Gordon B. Peters of the Centre for Indigenous Sovereignty. Peters is a former chief and had brought a lawsuit against the Crown a few years ago for breach of duty and breach of treaty promises. The lawsuit was based on indigenous customary law. In today's address, Gordon implied that the steps being taken in relation to the term "fiduciary" have come from the court decisions and that this requires communication and interpretation. He said, "First Nations are not subjects of Canada, we have treaties. In Ontario, most treaties are pre-Confederation Treaties. We see treaties in the context of international instruments." He said this has been affirmed by the international treaty study by Alfonso Martinez.

Peters continued, "How do we reconcile our differences and seek opportunities to engage together? The Penner Report [1983] gave indication on how some processes may work, for example, reconciliation. The RCAP Report outlined a framework process of lawmaking on working together.

Today, we are still working with government with the same mentality as pre-1982. This requires education with federal government itself. Our capacity entails continued growth. In the 1980s, [the term] "bands" was used, then "First Nations" and "community." [This] "Requires collective action to forward our interests in resources and in our territories that are part of Treaties."

Peters raised the question, "How do we ensure we don't suffer consequences? For example, unilateral determination by government, court cases, criteria, and the definition of "situs." The solution is, let's agree how we're going to work together, to balance one element off to another and determine certainty. We need to look at what these standards are to be and what their application will be. Once accommodation is found, I think some of the recommendations of the RCAP Report will have been found. There is fear of taxpayers of settlement of First Nations claims [in terms] of costs. First Nations need to build capacity. It would be very good if we had some kind of institute to advance some of these issues to benefit our people. We have a relationship with Canada, and unless we have this, we will be hard pressed to realize there are two peoples and how we can coexist. We need to sort out these issues and move faster than we have had in the past with other processes."

The next speaker was Michael Mitchell of the Mohawk Council of Akwesasne. Referring to the cross-border case, he said there is a new interpretation of the 1987 remission order. In that case, the Mohawks argued that the community goods (groceries and clothing) were going to the community for its use. Despite the "Honor of the Crown," there was First Nation prejudice by law enforcement. Mitchell said, "First Nations for the last twenty-seven years have been ready to look at new models. It requires lawyers to examine one or two case studies, but we don't have any in Canada."

In relation to jurisdiction and authority, Mitchell asked, "How do we assume First Nations leaders come into the picture? Indian Act elections pit people against each other. It is a non-Native process that is alienating. First Nations have to rise above that. For one hundred fifty to two hundred years, we have been dominated by church and government and have become dependent. What are our roots of government? What are the weaknesses of today? [They are] denial and shrinking of land. Federal reports have come to the same conclusions with no action. How do we achieve harmony? Canadians are afraid of self-government. They don't know what it means. We need to use media, APTN, and go to university with our message. First Nations need to reexamine themselves and their strengths. It also starts with the legal professions. Don't assume we can run as we can barely crawl. We need institutions, a combination of legal, social, and economic strategy for what is possible for First Nations. We need to call on education institutions of this country and have our own projects similar to the Harvard project here in Canada. We need to recognize people, such as Harold Cardinal, who have gone through many years of trying to resolve First Nations and Canada's relationships. First Nations are in the mix in the tough world. [There must be] appeals to the legal profession and heads of government. What could we bring to Canada on First Nations issues? First Nations have tried claims in specific areas, e.g., environment, and have been rejected. Take these new duties to the Crown. A healthy Canada means building along with First Nations and having serious dialogue. Our treaties are like ... constitutions. There is importance to language and traditions. We need more content in this conference and build on it."

A question to Mr. Peters and Mr. Mitchell was "What are the major principles of First Nations and Canada working together?" Peters replied, "We need to work with First peoples, recognize treaties, and [make] reconciliation and reparations. We need to look at the current fiscal relations." Mitchell replied, "Over the past fifty years, the federal government has produced very costly studies and the Royal Commission. What models and solutions can come from there? The scary part for non-Native Canadians is the unknown."

The next presentation, "Implications of *the* Haida *and Taku River* Decisions for Industry," was made by Sandra Gogal, a partner in the McInnes Cooper law firm of St. John's, Newfoundland. Ms. Gogal's view was that, in the written record, there is uncertainty of what is "appropriate consultation with Aboriginal peoples; where does the duty lies, when is it triggered, what degree of consultation is adequate...?" She said the source of the duty to consult is that the "Honor of the Crown requires the Crown to always act honorably when dealing with Aboriginal peoples with a view to achieving reconciliation...in consultation...in treaty negotiations and treaty interpretations."

Quoting from *the Haida* case, Ms. Gogal further stated, "The duty to consult arises when the Crown has knowledge, real or constructive, of the potential existence of the Aboriginal right or title and contemplates conduct that might adversely affect it." She advised that caution be exercised by the Crown and private industry regarding the scope of consultation and that industry conduct its own analysis at the same time as the Crown. Gogal noted that the Supreme Court now obliges the Crown, as part of the duty to consult, to set administrative law principles or procedural and substantive elements for weighing Aboriginal interests and "further imposed standards of judicial review as safeguards in the process." The weighing of Aboriginal interests obliges the cooperation of the Crown, the developer/proponent, and the affected Aboriginal collectives.

Gogal emphasized that "ultimately third parties will be directly impacted if the consultation process is not fair or reasonable. Accommodation and Impact and Benefit Agreements will still be part of good corporate Aboriginal relations and will still address . . . part of the Crown's duty to consult and accommodate." She concluded with, "However . . . it is the Crown, who is ultimately responsible, developers should ensure the Crown is advised of the substance of the negotiations and is satisfied with the . . . consultation and . . . sign off on the agreement."

The next presentation was "How do the Duties in Canadian Law Compare with Duties in Other Jurisdictions?" This was delivered by Bradford Morse, professor of Law, faculty of Law, of University of Ottawa. Morse noted that the Supreme Court of Canada, in *Delgamuukw*, looked "to the Australian High Court in its decision *in Mabo* (no. 2) for aid in establishing that the content of Aboriginal title that is recognized by the common law emanates from. . . the substantive law of the Aboriginal community or nation concerned."

Morse also noted that, in *Haida Nation*, the Supreme Court borrowed from a policy paper made by the government of New Zealand in 1998 on the need for consultation filled by the Crown. Morse notes that the duty to consult in New Zealand arises from

- the Treaty of Waitangi,
- administrative regimes within the Crown, and
- the statutory regime of the Resource Management Act.

Morse said the Treaty of Waitangi made New Zealand a colony of the United Kingdom. The treaty, ratified in 1975, provided for the adherence of the principles of the treaty. The Waitangi Tribunal was created to listen and make recommendations for fair settlement of Maori claims against Crown breaches of the treaty's principles and omissions from 1840. Maori claims include land, access to food resources, burial grounds, and sacred sites. Courts still have the final say in giving force to the tribunal's recommendations. Morse said, in 2000, the government of New Zealand committed the following six guiding treaty principles:

- "good faith;
- restoration of the relationship between the indigenous groups and the government;
- providing just redress;
- creating fairness and consistency between claims;
- creating transparency; and
- having the government involved directly in all negotiations."

Professor Morse noted that the Supreme Court of Canada, in *the Haida* case, referred to New Zealand's seven conditions of ensuring the Crown's administrative duty to consult. These conditions are

- "gathering information to test policy proposals;
- putting forward proposals that are not yet finalized;
- seeking Maori opinion on those proposals;
- informing Maori of all relevant information upon which those proposals are based;
- not promoting but listening with an open mind to what Maori have to say;
- being prepared to alter the original proposal; and
- providing feedback both during the consultation process and after the decision-making process."

Professor Morse mentioned that the government of Australia has adopted the National Native Title Tribunal, which seeks to mediate native title claims. He said the tribunal is legally mandated to ensure that parties negotiate in good faith and to clarify the effects good faith will have on native title rights and interests. Professor Morse noted that in the United States, Aboriginal law is made around the notion that Indian tribes are deemed "domestic dependent nations" denoting a trust responsibility based on a government to government relationship. He notes that different meanings for the consultation duty are assigned by different authorities, such as the various branches and agencies of the federal government, presidential executive memoranda, orders, directives, policies, and court rulings. Professor Morse related the South American experience regarding the current situation in Brazil, Argentina, and Bolivia. He thinks that this experience seems to be motivated by global law developments via the ILO Convention 169 and the continuing work of the Draft Declaration on the Rights of Indigenous Peoples by the Organization of American States.

The next presenter was John Paul Murdoch, replacing Grand Chief Ted Moses of the Grand Council of Crees who was unable to be present. Mr. Murdoch said that the James Bay-Northern Quebec Agreement and the New Relationship is a follow-up to the James Bay Agreement. He gave a brief history of discussions on forestry but noted there was very little communication nor consultations. He said the Cree were deadlocked with Hydro Quebec and the government of Canada. The new relationship in forestry is an ongoing process. The Adapted Forestry Regime, for example, leads to a forestry company required to sit down with a trapper before the company goes ahead. In wildlife management, the Quebec Government delegated its authority to a body that makes regulations. In land management, leases are made to accommodate the Crees' interests.

Murdoch said this process began with the premier and grand chief meeting and each appointing a representative leading to an agreement and a standing liaison committee. A Quebec government representative was appointed as well as a Hydro Quebec representative. Murdoch said the Haida [court] decision calls for a process of meaningful consultation and accommodation. He said, "There is no obligation for third parties to consult. I believe they have a greater interest to consult rather than the government. There has to be something between the developer and the First Nation." Murdoch was concerned with the language "maximum" versus "minimum" work that is to be done. He further said, "This is the least government can do to reflect the honor of the Crown. This implies the setting of a minimum standard of duty to consult."

Mr. Murdoch was asked, "Do you have any difficulties getting consensual agreement within your community?" He replied, "It wasn't clear what process or route we'd take. Everyone decides his or her own question and put it into a referendum. Media was used to provide information."

The final presentation was a faculty roundtable of the previous speakers and open discussion by the forum participants. The topic was "Developing a National Policy on Crown and Aboriginal Duties." Fred Caron, the Co chair said, "What have we learned? There is a lot of common ground, speaking the same language. [There is need] for some sort of national policy framework to come together and advancing toward a national document. [There is need to consider] certain elements depending on the project in question and the timeframe. [There is need] for a concise statement of principles that should guide negotiations as in *Haida Nation* and *Taku River*. This requires some capacity. The government has initiated national policy sectoral discussions with national Aboriginal organizations. [There is need] for a baseline legal position and timeframe to allow us to move forward."

Peter Hutchins, the Co chair, asked, "How can principles *in Haida* and *Taku* be applied in modern-day agreements? We need a little more discreet discussion in the formation of a national policy document. It is good to recognize rights of Aboriginal peoples, but what are the remedies? *In Haida* and *Taku*, the words of the Supreme Court were given form [in contrast] to the waiting that occurred after *the Delgamuukw* decision. Can the Crown continue to insist that there are no remedies to injustices done to Aboriginal peoples that occurred one hundred, twenty years, or even today? Courts are there and will continue to assist. It is only what we put to them to advance issues. [What is the solution] for a federal government that does not have a national policy on consultation? I think individual nations need to form their policy approaches."

Questions and comments were the following:

- What institutional shifts would be needed if a national policy were to be designed?

- What criteria would be applied for the appointment of an accountable person or entity for policy design?

- Who takes the lead in monitoring consultation and agreements to ensure accountability? Would it be the National Energy Board to issue development permits and issue licenses or some other department or body?

- "I think a national policy to capture the principles *of Haida* and *Taku River* decisions should be minimizing senior level government support; bring policy statement to a forum, gathering or summit and invite the prime minister and leaders, and come up with some sort of statement with the leaders."

- An Alberta government employee said, "We had a hell of a time getting First Nations to come to the table to talk policy formation due to adherence to treaty rights while others would discuss."

- A Saskatchewan delegate from the Office of the Treaty Commissioner said, "I think there is need for a neutral body to deal with the issue of treaty rights and the importance of quality of life. [This neutral body] or facilitator-mediator is the way we'll work in the future."

- Mr. Hutchins suggested the idea that we all {Canadians and First Peoples} have a treaty and that we all benefit from the treaty.

- Michael Mitchell asked, "What would self-government be like? [One way would be to do it with] no federal interference but to have different partners. [There is] need to educate one another.

- Hutchins concluded by stating, "Why doesn't the Crown just let First Nations do their things rather than just talk and talk about it?"

Challenges that need work and clarification by Treaty First Nations leaders and peoples:

How do treaty leaders, elders, and their peoples compel the Crown to honor the promises and obligations the Crown made in the Treaties 1 to 11 such as that the land was not surrendered but was to be shared with the settler government down to the depth of a plow and that the subsurface natural resources and water resources were also not given up? How can the Treaty First Nations compel the Crown to take reconciliatory and recompensatory action for its failure to honor its treaty obligations in all areas, such as health, economic self-sufficiency, education, hunting, trapping, fishing and gathering, nontaxation, retention of tribal governance and law, and all other treaty rights?

At the above forum, Mr. Alfred Caron of Indian and Northern Affairs Canada advanced the notion of development of a national policy has had on Crown and Aboriginal duties. He asked, "What have we learned? [and that there be] some sort of National Policy framework... advancing toward a National document." He also recommended a "concise statement of principles that should guide negotiations as in *the Haida* and *Taku River* [SCC decisions]."

In relation to Mr. Caron's proposed idea, Treaty First Nations leaders should address the following questions:

- What have the Crown representatives (federal and provincial governments) learned? Can we trust these representatives, such as

Indian and Northern Affairs again, to forward our treaty rights and interests and design a National Policy document?

- How can post-1982 SCC rulings that recognize the preexisting rights of First Peoples to sovereignty and land be used to compel the Crown to honor the numbered Treaties of 1 to 11?

- Will Indian and Northern Affairs, in the design of a National Policy, only seek to further limit the Crown's legal and treaty commitments to Treaty First Peoples in relation to their lands, natural resources, revenue sharing, tribal and traditional governing systems, and all of the other Treaty rights confirmed in Treaties 1 to 11?

APPENDIX K

KEYNOTE ADDRESS NATIONAL CREE GATHERING 2005 AT SADDLE LAKE CREE NATION

AN UPDATE ON FIRST NATIONS AND CROWN/GOVERNMENT RELATIONS BY COUNCILOR ERIC J. LARGE

Wiyahtikwapew niya eysikasuyan. Ekusiy ekiysiwiyhit nokum. Nikan kihtatumiskatinawow okimawak, kahkicaymkawiyak kitayayak, onikaniywak and iskwewak, ekwa utaskewiyinewak ota oci ministiko kihtaskinak. Miyote oci kititinawow, tawow ota oma Niciskwapuwinih, Niykotwosik Tipamatowinaskiyk. Ewiyakayasiymoyan cikama kotakak iyiniwak upiykswewna puku nistotamok. Ma ka pukwowiyak osampikwu nisitotam akayasiymowin.

My English name is Eric John Large. My last name is derived from my paternal great-grandfather. On my father's side, I am descended from Chief Blue Quill who adhered to Treaty No. 6, and on my mother's side, I am descended from Chief Tustukswes who signed Treaty No. 6 at Fort Pitt in 1876. Honorable chiefs, respected elders, council and head men and women, and citizens of various nations and tribes of our home and native land Canada, I extend to you all a sincere welcome to Ohniciskwapewini, Saddle Lake, and Treaty 6 Territory. I will speak English as others may not understand Cree, as they understand only their native language. But almost everyone understands English.

I was a bit confused when I accepted, last May, to deliver this keynote address. Flattered and honored to address the Cree Nation, my first thought was that I should just summarize current First Nations and government relations, legislation, and policies, and First Nations' reactions to developments in these areas. My second thought was that a summary of current developments would be only part of the big picture. I also realized that there were and are more eloquent speakers than I, such as the late Eugene Steinhauer of Saddle Lake, Harold Cardinal of Sucker Creek, and Sol Sanderson of Chakastepesin. These Newoyawak, Cree, and others of like caliber, with their commitment in advocating our rights and interests, are true statesmen of our nation.

With their oratorical skills and belief in the advancement of our peoples, they raised above the normal leadership ranks. I honor and thank them for speaking on behalf of all our peoples of the various indigenous tribes and nations of Canada. Several key aspects of our national character need our thoughtful review and discussion. These aspects are our indigenous identity, tribal customs, our treaty status, unresolved Crown obligations, and current developments as viewed by us who are profoundly attached to the land and natural environment. I will talk about these aspects from historical points, current developments, and their future implications or impacts on the continued viability of our rights and interests.

- First Nations Nationhood and Responsibility
- Treaty Relationship of the Crown and Treaty First Peoples
- Current Crown Obligations, Policies, Programs, and Services, and Implications on Treaty First Peoples' Rights and Interests

FIRST NATIONS NATIONHOOD AND RESPONSIBILITY

I will begin this subtopic by commenting on some bases of indigenous self-identification and then contrasting the Western world's concepts of nationhood and First Nations' efforts to maintain intact our identity, our survival, and sustainability. The designation "First Nations" is sometimes used, along with "Natives," "Indigenous Nations," and now "Aboriginals," in reference to a collective or an aggregate of indigenous peoples of the Western hemisphere to signify their origin, or ancestral link, to the Western hemisphere. It seems that scholars, students, and critics of the Western world could not describe the indigenous peoples of the Americas at the "discovery" of 1492, so they had to rationalize the origin and existence of the indigenous peoples. One way they did this was to have, or to transpose, the closest rationale through a creation story or through the theory of migration. So they theorized that the ancestors of the present-day indigenous peoples, who are us, migrated here from somewhere. However, the original peoples of the various tribes and nations have always identified themselves according to their language, traditions, cultural practices, and worldviews. Through the study of ancient tools, artifacts, and animal remains, archeologists and paleontologists have theorized that the original peoples of North and South America are descended from big game hunters who arrived here ten thousand to thirteen thousand years ago through a land bridge between Siberia to

Alaska and gradually proliferated throughout the Americas. However, this theory is still only a theory. It has not been conclusively proven. There is even a theory that our ancestors of North America came to North America through the edge of an ice-bound Atlantic ocean seventeen thousand years ago from Europe not Asia. This theory is based on an amateur archeologist's study of DNA from ancient bones found near Ottawa as well as similarities in Paleolithic tools.[1]

American tribes and nations have their own stories of their origin and history. We, the Plains Cree, have our own story of creation and our place in the universe as Newoyawak, or as we more commonly pronounce it, Nehiyawak, which refers to four aspect or four directional beings. I am still searching for the origin of the word "Cree." One version I saw in the Custer County 1881 Court House Museum in South Dakota, two years ago, is that "Cree" is a short form of a French word, "kristaneaux," which referred to the indigenous peoples the French traders and explorers dealt with. Kristaneaux was supposed to describe the indigenous peoples as people who shouted or screamed loud. "Cris," in French, means screaming. It sounds like the Cree were screamers or people who shouted. It could also mean that the Cree were hard bargainers, good negotiators, or simply they had to speak loud so they could be heard better from a distance.

As Cree or Newoyawak, we are linked with the supernatural order, the natural world, to one another and to the other creatures of the earth. We are also part of the cycle of life. The four aspects or directions of Newoyawak are the dimensions of spirit, mind, emotion, and body. This four-aspect character is central to Newoyow belief and is used in ceremonies and in the formation of alliances and treaty making with other nations. More specifically, we, the Plains Cree of Saddle Lake, Paskwow Nicikswapiw Newoyawak, identify ourselves with a belief in a Creator, in our cultural customs and laws as a distinct tribe of the Cree nation. As part of a nation in North America, we deem our existence is affirmed as a tribe by the Royal Proclamation of 1763. This brings me to discuss First Nations nationhood. First, there is the domestic European notion of nationhood, which says that a nation must have a language, a monetary currency, a people, an army, laws, land, and government. Then we have a Cree version of nationhood that is based on our belief in Kise Mantu, the oldest, wisest, humblest Divinity, and on the *pipestone*, sweet grass, sage, water, fire, and air, as well as in the protocols associated with invoking Kiseh Mantu. The Cree also had a governing system composed of an Okeymaw, the main headman, sub headmen that had specific skills, elder men and women, warriors or dog soldiers, and tribal peoples. Each of these ranks had its roles and responsibilities that preserved and sustained the people. So while the Cree give Kise Mantu the highest rank in their spiritual and natural world, the European nations, such as Great Britain, have their heads of state that may be hereditary royalty and also are the heads of their national church or state-recognized religion.

Today, the federal Crown still maintains its assertion of sovereignty over our land, resources, and every aspect of our citizenship and our lives. The Crown can no longer continue to impose its concepts of domination and impose policies that gradually strip away our inherent responsibilities as leaders and citizens. Leaders, elders, and citizens of our Cree nation and associated nations must continue to revisit our customs and laws, speak our languages, and insist on identifying ourselves according to our beliefs and worldview. We must reaffirm our coexistence with one another and other living things in the universe. We need to continue insisting that we, indeed, are a unique people which the Crown and its own citizens must recognize and respect.

The Crown and other world states must succumb to this uniqueness that permits diversity that is in accordance with the variation that recurs in the natural world. The Crown and its agencies must allow Cree peoples and associated indigenous peoples to fully develop by supporting, wherever possible, initiatives that will let our people grow according to our inherent rights, responsibilities, and our customary laws. In summary, Newoyawak, the Cree must declare and assert the Cree way of life or Newoyaw pimatsiwin where all our citizens are included, the men, women, elders, and children who live the natural laws of sharing, caring, honesty, and determination.

TREATY RELATIONSHIP OF THE CROWN AND TREATY FIRST PEOPLES

I will speak in general terms on the subject of treaty, as I am still learning and cannot make conclusions. According to the *Merriam-Webster Dictionary*, the definition of a treaty is "an agreement made by negotiation or diplomacy especially by two or more states or governments."[2] In the case of Treaty No. 6, the treaty that was negotiated at Forts Carleton and Pitt in August and September 1876, protocols were performed by the chiefs as advised by elders and assisted by oskapewsak or worthy young men. The protocols were performed to signify the meeting of the two states, the negotiations, and the conclusion of the treaty. One state was represented by Governor Alexander Morris in right of Great Britain and Northern Ireland and the other state was represented by the chiefs and headmen in their own right on behalf of their nations and tribal peoples. The third party to Treaty No. 6 is the Great Spirit who was invoked by the elders in the presence of Christian ministers. Treaty No. 6 binds three parties and their respective beneficiaries in a treaty, which provides for mutual benefit, sharing of land to the depth of a plow, peaceful coexistence, annuities and promises to the indigenous peoples, such as the medicine chest, a schoolhouse, agricultural implements, seed grain, and livestock.

Other rights for our people established, prior to treaty and assumed to continue are freedom from military conscription, continued access to traditional lands for hunting, fishing, trapping, and gathering. Other rights reserved by the chiefs and their peoples are tribal customary laws, governing structure, leadership selection, child upbringing, subsurface resources, water rights, territorial ceremonial grounds, burial sites, timber berths, hay meadows, and access to the land of the long knives, the United States. However, the written treaty text that Governor Morris wanted the chiefs and headmen to sign appears to be a template of the previous five-numbered treaties in which the chiefs agree to "secede and surrender forever their right to the land."

Our elders have said the land and resources were never given up. They cannot be given up as we are a part of them in the scheme of creation. We can only share them. Governor Morris was urged by the Treaty 6 chiefs for additional rights not mentioned in the template. He said he was only authorized by his superiors to offer the terms and benefits in the template; he could not promise additional demands. However, the chiefs persisted to the point where Governor Morris said he would take their demands to his superiors. The chiefs insisted these were promises. My argument is that the chiefs and their peoples are still waiting for Governor Morris's reply. Is this why the government says that the provision of medical benefits and education benefits is a matter of policy and not provided as treaty rights as negotiated by our chiefs?

The recent (November 2004) Supreme Court decisions, *Haida v. BC* and *Taku River Tlingit First Nation v. BC*, compelled the federal and provincial governments, and to some extent, resource companies, to recognize and accommodate our rights and interests. These rights and interests must be taken into account in negotiations resulting in fair settlements, claims, and treaties.

The ethical principle of the honor of Crown is to be paramount in Crown/First Nation dealings. There must be no instance of "sharp dealing" on the Crown's behalf. There must also be adequate consultation, accommodation, and compensation. The difficulty here is that the legal system appears to take the position that they cannot compel the Crown to right the wrongs of past treaties but that they can only state what the *Crown ought* to have done at the treaty negotiation to uphold its honor.

Why does it have to take the Supreme Court to ensure the Crown deal honestly and fairly with the First Peoples who are still a party to a treaty? What if the Crown, its agencies, or resource companies still refuse to take our rights and interests into account? Do we go into more costly and time-consuming legal actions? The other problem I have is that most of the legal actions involving treaty rights appear to be criminal cases against us. Can anyone see what this implies? We should be taking the federal Crown to some kind of court for enforcement of our Treaty rights or for redress for the Crown's infringement of our treaty rights or for its failure to fulfill its treaty obligations. On July 12, 2005, I raised this question at a treaty conference in Calgary. In reply, the speaker to whom I directed the question suggested that treaty cases raised by First Nation people against the Crown be filed as civil cases. Lord Denning had suggested to Treaty 6 chiefs in 1993 that we take our Treaty rights, their observance, and enforcement to the International Court of Justice at The Hague.

CURRENT CROWN OBLIGATIONS, POLICIES, PROGRAMS, AND SERVICES, AND IMPLICATIONS ON TREATY FIRST PEOPLES RIGHTS AND INTERESTS

As I previously mentioned, the federal Crown and the provincial Crown are avoiding admission of any obligation that is treaty based. Two examples are the treaty rights to education and to health benefits. The Crown's view is that these two benefits are provided as matters of policy and are not provided as treaty benefits. They are provided at the Crown's pleasure as benefits to indigent or improvident citizens of Canada. Unless they are faced with legal action or international embarrassment, the federal and provincial Crowns avoid, when they can, the provisions and practices set down in the Royal Proclamation of 1763, Treaty No. 6 of 1876, the sections in the Natural Resources Transfer Acts of 1930 and 1931 that purportedly were made to protect our interests, the principles of informed consent, the honor of the

Crown, consultation, accommodation, fair compensation, and settlement. Meanwhile, the governments continue to rely on legislation, policies, and regulations that have Crown plenary or discretionary power to override our rights and interests. Since 1982, our Treaty rights and interests have been gradually affirmed by the Supreme Court of Canada on a case-by-case basis to a point where the Canadian state and the orders of government are legally compelled to recognize and accommodate our Treaty rights and interests.

There are unresolved areas that challenge us and require careful thought and response. One of these challenging areas is the potential impacts of Bill C-31, which became legislation in 1985. The unwritten intent of Bill C-31 is that the Indian status of treaty peoples will be phased out by a certain time, within one hundred years or less. Full status is gradually being phased out. Even children born after 1985 of full-status parents now have a different class of status in the Indian registry. I suppose the extreme action the government can take is to begin classifying us through our DNA. This may bring into question our rights and for our descendants to continuing Treaty benefits. On the surface, it appears that the government never rests in its goal of full assimilation and integration of First peoples into the Canadian society. Historically, where the government failed to get rid of its Indian problem, if I can use Chief Rose Lameman's words, "through bullets, Bible, booze, and bingo" (gambling addiction), it is now willing to legislate us out of existence so that it will no longer have to pay for Treaty rights. Leaders need to keep raising this issue to the attention of the federal government and in the international arena. At its annual General Assembly last month, the Assembly of First Nations announced its intent to host a national conference on the impacts of Bill C-31. With all the legislation, policies, and regulations of the federal and provincial governments, sometimes I think that we are still puppets whose heads and limbs are manipulated up and down ostensibly for our best interests. I recall the puppet Indian that is illustrated on the cover of Harold Cardinal's first book, *The Unjust Society*.

Another unresolved but related area is the issue of major funding for First Nations governments programs and services. Presently, chiefs and councils sign annual comprehensive funding arrangements or five-year flexible funding agreements with Indian and Northern Affairs Canada, Health Canada, and Human Resources and Skills Development Canada. The templates for these agreements are prepared by the government several months prior to the next fiscal year and given to the First Nations. Basically, the format is the same as well as the terms and conditions, guidelines, and the financial resources. According to the government of Canada, these are not treaty-funding agreements but are policy-based agreements with the relatively recent requirements of financial accountability and prescribed with terms, such as disclosure, transparency, and redress. The governments have stringent reporting that must be submitted. Among the aforementioned three major government departments, there are about one hundred sixty reports due them throughout a fiscal year. Here in Saddle Lake, chiefs and councils have insisted and continue to insist that these funding arrangements are linked to treaty obligations that need to be fulfilled even if they are partial fulfillments by the Crown. We have insisted that reference to the Royal Proclamation, Treaty No. 6, and its international aspect, Crown liability, comprehensive services, and full funding according to population need to be part of the agreement. We were only allowed to add these as clauses to the preambles in two of the agreements.

But ideally, the original Treaty understandings including resource sharing and fiscal arrangements need to be revisited by us Treaty nations with the Crown representatives. We need to scope out a treaty-based fiscal arrangement in all of the areas for which we require funding as commitments by the Crown. The treaty-based funding agreements would be a consequence of the inherent powers of governing ourselves we retained at the time of treaty making. I advise that Cree and other national and tribal leaders to address this unresolved but very, very important challenge that faces us and that will impact our descendants.

The final remarks I would like to make concern not only the Cree or Nehiyawak but also citizenships of other indigenous nations and tribes. I advise that we need to rediscover, revisit ourselves, our identity, our place in creation, and our roles and responsibilities as peoples. We can do this rediscovery every day and not just in annual gatherings or in certain days of the year, such as "Aboriginal Day" or other day to honor such and such theme. We need to act and practice our traditions, our languages, and our relationships of mutual respect with our immediate and extended families, our camps, tribes, nations, and in our relationship with the Creator. To sustain ourselves now and into the future, we, Cree and associated indigenous peoples, need to

- Reestablish traditional landmarks of community linkage, such as kinship, marriage, and adoption. Construct family trees and honor our loved ones who have made paths before us by visiting their resting places. Consider carefully the arguable "discovery" of 1492, when our ancestors entered a period of darkness and from which fallout disrupted our place in the universe. We were decimated and lost, as though we were lost in a forest at night. But we have the landmarks of traditions, such as kinship, relationships, and adoptions to guide us home until the daylight of reassurance and understanding comes.

- Reaffirm traditional international, intertribal friendship, and trade alliances. We need to make treaties, if necessary, to share overlapping territories and allow access to resources.

- Reaffirm our traditional ways of worship, storytelling, songs, ceremonies, recreation, dances, and especially our beautiful languages.

- Reaffirm and declare our rights to self-identification, self-determination, and inherent self-rule. Declare that we have a right to life as we inherited it from our ancestors and from the Creator. Ensure we do no harm to other beings and the natural world around us so that our future generations can continue to benefit.

I would like to thank you for your kind attention. I would also like to thank all the elders and indigenous peoples, who are too numerous to mention, who have guided me and continuing to assist me to discover myself and our Nehiyaw heritage. Hy Hy!

REFERENCES AND ACKNOWLEDGMENTS

1. Boswell, Randy. "Bridge over Ancient Waters," *Edmonton Journal*, Saturday, February 1, 2003, page Al.

2. *Merriam-Webster Incorporated* 1997.

3. I would like to acknowledge and thank all of the following individuals in my growth as Nehiyaw and for their support of the recognition of our treaty rights:

   Aulotte, Philomena (deceased)—elder and my maternal auntie, Unipahuos Cree (Frog Lake), Treaty No. 6
   Buffalo, Adolphus (deceased)—elder, Samson Cree, Treaty No. 6
   Buffalo, Marilyn—Senior Policy Advisor, Samson Cree, Treaty No. 6
   Bull, Jonathan—Councilor and former Chief, Louis Bull Cree, Treaty No. 6
   Bull, Sam (deceased)—former consulting lawyer, former chief, Whitefish (Goodfish) Lake Cree, Treaty No. 6
   Cardinal, Howard D.—elder, former Councilor, Saddle Lake Cree, Treaty No. 6
   Cardinal, George—traditional man, Whitefish Lake Cree, Treaty No. 6
   Cardinal, Harold—lawyer, statesman, former chief, Sucker Creek Cree, Treaty No.8; former President of the Indian Association of Alberta
   Cardinal, Noah—elder, former Councilor, Saddle Lake Cree, Treaty No. 6
   Cardinal, Norah—treaty supporter, Saddle Lake Cree, Treaty No. 6
   Cardinal, Raymond (deceased)—elder, Saddle Lake Cree, Treaty No. 6
   Cardinal, Ray G.—Cree language director, Saddle Lake Cree, Treaty No. 6
   Cardinal, Tom—elder, Saddle Lake Cree, Treaty No. 6, former President of Indian Association of Alberta
   Cardinal, Joe P. (deceased)—World War II veteran, elder, former Chief, Saddle Lake Cree, Treaty No. 6
   Chonkolay, Harry (deceased)—elder and lifetime Chief, Assumption Dene Tha, Treaty No. 8
   Crowchild, Gordon—elder, former chief, T'suu Tina Dene, Treaty No. 7

Crowchild, Regena—treaty advocate, Councilor, T'suu Tina Dene, Treaty No. 7, former President of the Indian Association of Alberta

Crier, Albert—treaty advocate, Saddle Lake Cree, Treaty No. 6

Currie, William (deceased)—Hobbema, Cree, Treaty No. 6

Delver, Louie—Councilor, Saddle Lake First Nation, Treaty No. 6

Denning, Lord Alfred Thompson (deceased)—British House of Lords, London

Ermineskin, John—elder, former Chief, Ermineskin Cree, Treaty No. 6

Freeman, Clifford—former chief and Councilor, Driftpile Cree, Treaty No. 8

Gladue, Helen—treaty advocate, executive member, Advisory Council of Treaty 6 Women, Beaver Lake Cree, Treaty No. 6; former executive member of the Indian Association of Alberta

Gladue, Joe—Korean War veteran, elder, Beaver Lake Cree, Treaty No. 6

Houle, Adrian—linguist, Saddle Lake Cree, Treaty No. 6

Houle, Eugene—former Chief and Councilor, Saddle Lake Cree, Treaty No. 6

Houle, Joe—World War II veteran, elder, Saddle Lake Cree, Treaty No. 6; former board member, Indian Association of Alberta

Hurde, Carroll—professor of international law, Wyoming, USA

Jackson, Andrew—elder, Saddle Lake First Nation, Treaty No. 6

Kakeesim, Margaret (deceased)—my maternal auntie, elder, Saddle Lake Cree, Treaty No. 6

Large, Joseph L. (deceased)—my father, former Councilor, Saddle Lake Cree, Treaty No. 6

Lameman, Rose—Chief, Papasschas Cree, Treaty No. 6

Lapatak, Roderick—elder, oskapews, Saddle Lake Cree, Treaty No. 6

Lapatak, Winston—Councilor, Saddle Lake Cree, Treaty No. 6

Large, Louisa—my paternal grandmother, Saddle Lake Cree, Treaty No. 6

Larocque, Lawrence—elder, Louis Bull Cree, Treaty No. 6

Lee, Gordon—elder, former Chief, Ermineskin Cree, Treaty No. 6

Littlebear, Leroy—lawyer, Blood Blackfoot, Treaty No. 7

Littlechild, Wilton—lawyer, Ermineskin Cree, Treaty No. 6

Littlechief, Roy—former Chief, Siksika Blackfoot, Treaty No. 7

McGilvery, Louis (deceased)—former Councilor, Saddle Lake Cree, Treaty No. 6

McGilvery, Sam (deceased)—traditional singer, drummer, storyteller, Saddle Lake Cree, Treaty No. 6

McLean, Dan (deceased)—elder, Sturgeon Lake Cree, Treaty No. 8

Memnook, Edith (deceased)—my paternal extended grandmother, elder, Whitefish Lake Cree, Treaty No. 6

Memnook, Paul (deceased)—my paternal extended grandfather, elder, Whitefish Lake Cree, Treaty No. 6

Morin, Peter—elder, Enoch Cree, Treaty No. 6

Morin, Veronica—elder, Chair of Advisory Council of Treaty 6 Women, Enoch Cree, Treaty No. 6

Moses, Finlay—former Councilor, Saddle Lake Cree, Treaty No. 6

Quinn, Carl—former Chief and Councilor, Saddle Lake Cree, Treaty No. 6

Quinn, Emile (deceased)—elder, Saddle Lake Cree, Treaty No. 6

Quinn, Morris (deceased)—elder, Saddle Lake Cree, Treaty No. 6

Pasquayak, Prosper—elder, Saddle Lake Cree, Treaty No. 6

Piepenburg, Roy—treaty supporter and self-described "World Citizen"

Saddleback, Jerry—traditional man, teacher, Samson Cree, Treaty No. 6

Samson, John (deceased)—elder, former Chief, Samson Cree, Treaty No. 6, former senator of the Indian Association of Alberta

Sanderson, Sol—statesman, Chief, Chakastepesin Cree, Treaty No. 6

Smallboy, Marie—treaty advocate, Ermineskin Cree, Treaty No. 6

Smallegs, Edwin—Councilor, Piikani, Treaty No. 7

Stanley, J. B. (deceased)—my maternal uncle, elder, Keeper of Treaty 6 *Pipe Stem*, Frog Lake Cree, Treaty No. 6

Steinhauer, Eugene—elder, statesman, former Chief, Saddle Lake Cree, Treaty No. 6; former president of the Indian Association of Alberta

Steinhauer, Joseph—treaty advocate, Saddle Lake Cree, Treaty No. 6

Steinhauer, Stewart—treaty advocate, Saddle Lake Cree, Treaty No. 6

Tobacco, Lawrence—elder, Treaty No. 6

Tootoosis, Eric—treaty advocate, Poundmaker Cree, Treaty No. 6

Two Rivers, Billy—former Chief, elder, Six Nations of Kahnawake Mohawk, Two Row Wampum Treaty

Whiskeyjack, Alex— former Councilor, elder, Saddle Lake Cree, Treaty No. 6

Yellowhorn, Albert (deceased)—elder, Piikani, Treaty No. 7

APPENDIX L

7TH WORLD INDIGENOUS PEOPLES CONFERENCE ON EDUCATION (WIPCE), NOVEMBER 27–DECEMBER 1, 2005

A REPORT BY COUNCILOR ERIC J. LARGE

I attended the above conference held at the Te Wananga o Aotearoa, Hamilton, New Zealand. As stated in the conference material, the overall theme of this conference was "Te Toi Roa—Indigenous Excellence." This theme called for indigenous peoples to celebrate their stories and beliefs in their principles, values, histories, and their uniqueness as indigenous people. Indigenous beliefs are said to reinforce the experiences and knowledge of indigenous peoples and serve to guide them in their effort for excellence in education. Three conference themes guided all presentations at the conference. The first theme, Leadership, is described in the conference package as, "This theme calls for presenters to share stories about leadership, where it has come from, where it is going, how it is being effected, and what leadership is needed by indigenous peoples for the 21st century." The second theme, Research and Development, is stated as, "This theme invites presenters to showcase approaches to and examples of research and development that will lead to significant advances for the development of indigenous peoples." The third theme, Horizons of Knowledge, is described as, "This theme honours the role of indigenous thinkers and educators in perpetuating and innovating to produce knowledge and insights for future generations."

On Sunday, November 27, the official welcome, *powhiri*, consisted of traditional Maori songs, addresses, a mass welcome chant, and a ceremonial challenge by warrior men and women on the shore and in war canoes on the Wakaito River. The Māori Queen was present and acknowledged the delegates. The ceremonies concluded with lunch served to about three thousand indigenous delegates. The Minister of Māori Affairs welcomed the delegates from Canada and other countries. The Minister said education and language are important to the Māori, especially to the tribes, the *ewi* (the people). He said, "It is important that we meet with you people. It's good to see you in your costumes, feathers. It represents something."

Dr. Luis Gomez Gutierrez, Minister of Education, Cuba, was one of the keynote speakers at the opening ceremonies after the lunch. He spoke in Spanish. The translator said Dr. Gutierrez has a doctorate in chemical engineering and has wide experience in education. The Minister acknowledged Her Majesty, the Māori Queen, and brought greetings of the Cuban government to the Māori government. He also acknowledged the delegates and said, "You are so friendly with nature." He said colonization wiped out the indigenous people, who unfortunately were wiped out completely in his area, and he admitted, "So I'm a descendant of the colonizer." He said he had reviewed the immigration of Africans, a history of colonizers, of sugar plantations where Africans worked in extreme heat which other indigenous peoples could not withstand. He said the colonizers "kidnapped Africans to Cuba, Caribbean, South and North America to do the hard work in extreme heat."

Dr. Gutierrez continued, "Cuban independence was a struggle in an already mixed population without any trace of the original indigenous population whatsoever. I'm impressed that you, as indigenous people, have been able to preserve something that is going to defend their culture in view of today where everyone is expected to be the same, to be of the same homogenous culture. We enrich a diverse world where everyone will be able to accept the way we are; to have every one respected. Why do we have this relationship? Every two years, we have a professional pedagogy. We have a modest experience in education, in particular, in adult education. You cannot educate the child the same as an adult. An adult experiences what is known to the known. Whereas the child learns something new as he or she has no previous experience. With adult education, there is a new approach that is from the known to the unknown. Adults have to develop different games, knowing how to count or combining letters with what is not known. We use the TV that is in worldwide use. Unfortunately, it is controlled by huge commercial interests. It controls what we eat, wear, say, and do. Pedagogues learn to use TV as a means of teaching. Our people get used to learning very fast through TV. For example, an illiterate person, in six weeks, can learn to read and write, and write a paragraph and expand his education. So we partnered with the Māori, and used English instead of Spanish. The experience of illiteracy in Cuba is it was eliminated in 1961. Before that, with no VCR, DVD, poor people couldn't have schools. They remained ignorant. That's why we had to have a revolution to teach people and for teachers to have jobs. Cuba became the first country in Latin America to be free from illiteracy. Cuba recently, in collaboration with Venezuela, became the second country in Latin America to be free from illiteracy.

After 1961, the first objective was to have the whole population reach sixth grade and later the ninth grade. The second objective was university study that is totally free. We have trained all necessary teachers. We have teachers with one teacher per fifty-five inhabitants. Why the education obsession? Education and culture will develop that country. A person that does not read and write cannot be free, cannot make choices, options, nor participate. Illiteracy has many risks. What could be the future for one hundred twenty million children not attending school? How can we prepare for the future? We, human beings, among the animals, have the capacity to destroy the human species. You that are the indigenous people understand the environment and its care. It is only in the last twenty years this environmental awareness has surfaced in the modern world. Destruction of the environment and energetic resources are predicted to be gone in two decades. We need to have a culture that understands the risks to struggle to produce food while nine hundred million people worldwide are starving. The struggle to control diseases from escalating into epidemics is there.

Our president, Fidel Castro, values the importance of education. He says only education can save humanity. We require from educated people who are conscious of complex problems we are facing. In Cuba, we have all public schools ensuring poor people a quality education. Each factory is also a school where theory and practice is learned. All Cuba is a university. A culture of economy, history, and culture to enable each Cuban will contribute to his society and where each Cuban can be equal and achieve social justice. In Latin America, we have high inequality. There are owners of ships and planes but where people are hungry, forty-two million illiterate, one hundred twenty million semiliterate, and 60 percent live in extreme poverty. We are developing an economy where people are literate. There is a lot of propaganda against Cuba, but with this education, we have people who are egalitarian, with more than twenty-five thousand doctors trained in our revolution who work in Africa and Asia.

When Hurricane Katrina struck New Orleans, the government of Cuba offered to send one thousand doctors and supplies, but the government of the United States refused the offer. We have doctors in Venezuela and in some African countries trying to eliminate the menace of AIDS. The menace of AIDS is a reality. The disease can obliterate humanity. It is possible for countries to develop together in health and education to benefit the people.

The world population increases, with eighty million in the third world, in the poor countries. Poverty will increase unless steps are taken to combat illiteracy. I will return to report to UNESCO to say 'I shared with your experience and of the continuation of your traditions.'"

Moana Jackson of Aotearoa, a law graduate of the University of Victoria, was the other keynote speaker. She said, "We share much in common, but we also have diversity. Aotearoa is the island, the power, and the enlightenment. There are two things that bind us as indigenous people. One, we have been colonized by people who came from somewhere else. Two, we have a common view of relationship with each other and the world. There is a small island on the east coast of this country of New Zealand. This island, Kahunu, or "Bitter Waters" as known by our people, is where they established a school of higher learning, adopted or "followed the thought" of elders, and used a basket that was bottomless as the pursuit of knowledge is bottomless. There is a certain power and privilege in seeking and finding the answer through "following the thought." This school of higher learning was destroyed by colonizers and replaced by other means of understanding the world. This other means of understanding used law, the law they had in the nineteenth and twentieth centuries, law as derived from what they called the Enlightenment. In this conference, I hope we can revel in and enjoy (1) in the power of knowledge and (2) in the knowledge of power we exercise among ourselves and the land in which we were born."

On Monday, November 28, the conference began at the WIPCE village at the University of Wakaito. Russell Harrison, master of ceremonies, said there are three thousand delegates expected to attend from eighteen countries, such as New Zealand Māori, Canada, Mainland USA, Hawaii, Alaska, Sammiland (Norway), Australia, Africa, Taiwan, Pakistan, Samoa, and others. The opening address was given by Bentham Ohia, Chair of WIPCE. He said, "We wanted to create a truly indigenous environment here with a wooden village typesetting with carvings and other things. Today, there will be one hundred and forty presentations."

The first keynote speaker was LaDonna Harris, a Comanche from New Mexico. She said, "We're here to celebrate our Indigeneity. This organization is symbolic of the things we'd like to be doing, for example, accreditation and next steps. Now, in this time of globalization, there is no sense of direction or leadership, but there is demand by Indigenous people for their culture and political autonomy. What should we be doing? We have to create our own institutions that reflect our values, how to live with one another, to find our voices, and to move to globalization that [considers] economic and resource development. You have to set your own values for your selves. I'm proud of who I am. I am proud that I am a Comanche. I don't feel victimized by colonization. Ask, how do I get out of this? Create new information, for example, the American Indian Ambassador Program. How do we value and trust our relatives? What is our responsibility to our values and to the universe that can make it a better world? It's time to speak up and say what our worldview is. You have the institutions and the values that will make that a realization. I challenge you to make this world a better place through your own Indigeneity. Questions to globalization, we need to grab globalization to reflect our values, taking care of our relatives, and prevent it from becoming a second form of colonialism. You have to love yourself, your tribe, and your people. If you go against your own values, you're more than likely not to accomplish what you want. If you stay at it long enough, you can see change. We don't learn history of ourselves. We have to do that. We are a government in our own right. Use our energy to be creative. That is what WIPCE is trying to do. Think out of the box. Be radical. Think positive. We have been conditioned to be negative. Go home and treat your relatives and be responsible for relationships. Because we are communal people, we understand how to share. How do we share and how to live? Talk and try to live them every day."

The first workshop I attended was on "Indigenous 'Self-Leadership' for Resilience, Guardianship, and Self-Determination: Case Study," which was delivered by Lesley Bradley-Vine, a doctoral candidate with the University of Western Sidney. Her message is, rather than criticize leaders, we have to support them and create a balance, also to move, as in the Greek concept, toward the wholesome. The presenter gave a short history of the Māori creation. First, there was nothing, and then there was sound. Then Māori appeared. There was a long migration and the heeding of all to that familiar plan, sailing on the ocean with *the waka* (canoe) with gentleness and grace to the sacred place. She said, "Māori have developed a highly sophisticated system, pathways, and indicators to sustainable development."

The next workshop I attended was called "Whakaaro Rangarita— Think like a Leader," which was delivered by a daughter Kym Hamilton and her father Atarau Hamilton. Ms. Hamilton said, "Government policy development has nothing to do with good common sense." She then described her family lineage from her ancestors from Aotearoa and from Scotland. She continued, "What is the challenge of self-determination?" She spoke of the importance of redressing the balance of power and the seeking of the knowledge of power. She asked, "What is going on between the Crown and Māori?" She said education now is non-Māori. She suggested it needs to be determined how much authority Māori assume and of making sustainability a difference. She said Māori managers and politicians need to go and take a process of decolonization. She said, "There are ways to exercise leadership, be it education, formal education, and recreation. All possess the vitality to exercise our ancestors' values? Economic development is secondary to our values."

The next workshop I attended, "Bridging Ancestral Values and Modern Challenges: International Perspectives on Serving Our Indigenous Communities," was presented by Mawae Morton. He said there is need for leadership like people in education, in resources, and the creation of peer groups. He asked, "What's the point of thinking about the future?" He talked of land claims and speaking our languages. He said, "The point is survival, physically and, more important, cultural survival. The creation of wealth for its own sake can sometimes be the problem. There are 585,900 Māori in New Zealand in the last census. How Māori are these people? One-third of Māori children are being educated in Māori. The last census of the Māori language showed that 42 percent of adult Māori speak Māori beyond simple words. One-half of the Māori speak Māori fairly well. In 2004, thirty-four thousand Māori adults learned in educational institutions. Three to one of the adults chose the Māori box in the census. Twelve to one of the Māori youth chose the Māori seats. By 2040, 40 percent of the workforce will be Māori. If we are looking for shifts, there is a shift from a Polynesian majority in this country of New Zealand. There will be tremendous challenges in education and leadership. There will be no single majority ethnic group in this country. We are going to need leadership who can crisscross between tradition and the modern world. This requires mature leadership who knows how to compromise and knows how to wield political power to ensure survival."

The second keynote speaker was Professor Konai Helu-Thaman, of Fiji, whose address was "Indigenous Education and Indigenous Knowledge Systems for the Peoples of Oceania—a Personal Reflection." He spoke of the importance of indigenous specific knowledge education. He said, "Today, the biggest challenge for people in Oceania is the sustainability of Pacific peoples and the need to center education in the face of globalization. The task for all educators in Oceania is there. We are focused in education for teachers." He classified the Western view as a closed predicament. This Western view speaks of minorities, sees indigenous knowledge as useful and practical, and that early gatherers of knowledge were of nonindigenous origin. On the other hand, the traditional view is an open predicament. This view is subjective, gut feeling, and always sure of the proof. Its time framework is in terms of thousands of years. He said, "Pacific people speak in terms of majorities in their regions. Indigenous knowledge systems are seen as important for the collective development and survival of Pacific peoples." He said the following points need consideration:

- Need to better contextualize university education
- The struggle for cognitive democracy in university education
- Mainstreaming of Pacific cultures in our program
- Recognition of cultures and languages developed over millennia
- Indigenous people are active partners in resources
- Inclusion in the curriculum of formal education by considering different perspectives of knowledge system
- Better collaboration and partnerships between indigenous and nonindigenous peoples, which will lead to better understanding.

Professor Helu-Thaman said he uses poetry and writing. He said, "It is ironic literacy makes illiteracy, possibly just as wealth makes poverty possible. We are trying to ensure that more indigenous students get an education so they may express their culture and knowledge systems, champion human rights and sustainable economic development. Teachers are the only people licensed to change people. It means colonial attitudes are no longer tolerated. We must be able to express our cultures and deconstruct and reconstruct knowledge-generated processes. We need to continue to acknowledge our indigenous knowledge systems in order to recenter ourselves."

At 3:30 p.m., a leadership panel convened. There were six panelists with representation from the U.S. (Comanche), India, Samoa, Australia, New Zealand (Māori), Norway (Sammiland), and the Māori Party. Discussion was on key leadership issues confronting our people. Comments were the following:

- Parliament cannot make you a Māori leader but only your people.
- Leadership takes many forms such as political leadership.
- Winning support for your party and support for your people
- Māori have had leadership for thousands of years.
- What makes a good leader? Is a leader born or is a leader made?

- A born leader and made leader is both in many ways. There're many traits that make a leader.
- The challenge will be to unite Māori. Leaders are working with their people.
- A good leader has a clear mind, knows where he/she is going. A leader is a good talker and a good walker of his/her talks.
- A leader is a doer, a visionary, and is able to work other people's vision. A leader works with all levels of people.
- A leader's work is to stabilize situations and to bring out issues so people understand each other and come to a consensus.
- Leadership is about vision, strength, with ability to listen.
- Leadership is being prepared, never retreating from injustice, not to give in but to demand same rights, for example, in education and being able to make decisions.
- Leaders can be artists and crafts people.
- Leaders have core cultural values and are not from a Western standpoint.
- Leaders are able to identify, reconfirm.
- To be a leader, you have to love your people, to really care, walk your talk, and be courageous.

KEY ISSUES INDIGENOUS EDUCATION WILL BE FACING IN TWENTY YEARS IDENTIFIED:

- There will be a paradigm of celebration rather than a paradigm of defense.
- Ability of teachers to pick out from existing systems and consider those that are relevant to this society, for example, blend values of Samoa in the face of globalization and maintain core values and principles of your own system
- Assimilationist movement, there is a false sense of hope. We are on a journey. Take our educated people and link with elders who can teach. Land use studies where elders go out and point out traditional usage areas.
- Beginning to get into language immersion programs
- That we don't over romanticize these values but use them to confirm our values

- To teach cognitive democracy. To be philosophical and poetic as indigenous peoples have something of real value
- Ensure we stay progressive and proactive
- Be able to set agenda. Getting the majority of people to see there are other values and rights. Of having our own educational curriculum, e.g., Sammi curriculum in Sammiland in Norway
- Getting more responsibility to get our own curriculum and make agreement between Norwegian Parliament and the Sammi Parliament
- Create positive images for indigenous people
- How to get indigenous people more visible in the larger society
- How to staff the Department of Paku Affairs
- Globalization is being countered by a Māori uprising, the expression of ourselves, doing research on Maori basis. Create ourselves out of the community
- Put Māori right out there today and in two hundred years.

The panelists' message to youth is "It is a simple process as knowing who you are. There is cultural contamination and other influences of the dominant culture. Never, never surrender to injustices nor retreat from intolerance but walk the walk as adults, which sends messages to our young. Every indigenous culture has high suicides. Young people said they knew who they were, their identity, but didn't know their culture and heritage, of what makes them Māori or indigenous. Be proud of who they are, in their heritage, culture, and in their identity, in their space, i.e., their minds and in their hearts. Find ways of enculturation, for example, youth becoming adults, being able to embody that Indigeneity that values that we talk about actually take place in their life. Encourage youth to participate in ceremonies, for example, honoring ceremonies legitimizing the direction they are going. Be proud of themselves at this time of history. Investment of your particular culture in the future as part and parcel of the whole society of which you are a part of and in which you will become an elder, enriching the world through diversity, for example, music and its link with nature. Leadership change should be a part of the school curriculum.

We need leaders. Create a better New Zealand, a better profile of ourselves. Create something they can identify with. Create positive things for our children. The enemy is 'one size fits all.' We must do it in our way of diversity. Poverty is another enemy. Consider what a basic living standard is. Why can't we live in exclusive and choice locations as others? [There must] be economic sharing of resources and benefits, training of leadership, and support for education, and being able to understand the advantages and disadvantages of the Western and indigenous systems of education. Participate and learn leadership. Take time to bring up the next generation of leadership. Don't imitate Western type of leadership. We're talking about leaders from politics, also teachers and others from the community. Be proactive and move forward. Educate our funders who tend to tell you what the seven key ingredients of a successful leader are. We need to develop our own leaders in politics and in education.

Think about how we are all related, to contextualize issues emerging in our country. As more-senior generations, we have to understand to contextualize what we are talking about when speaking of leadership. We must ask, How do we make our communities better, happier, and healthier? How do we create better human relationship? This is more challenging. The real answers to our journey lie within ourselves, to give hope to our communities, to the world, decolonize ourselves, and not be party to games that divide us. We've got to champion being Māori. Don't let the government keep dividing us. Let's be united as you are doing here."

On Tuesday, November 29, I visited a primary school in the city of Hamilton called Te Kura Kaupapa Māori o Te Ara Rima. According to an official handbook, this school "is a total immersion public school catering for children aged from 5 to 12 years of age." It is located in a low socioeconomic status area and was redesignated as a total immersion status in 1992. When we arrived at the school yard and entrance, there was a *Te powhiri*—official welcome by Kaupapa students and staff. There was a lengthy welcome ceremony with remarks by our hosts in Māori. We were offered lunch after which we assembled at an activity site. Activities included making shapes and waving objects such as rope, short and long sticks, and harikiki ferns used for making clothing and baskets. I then went to classroom Ruma 9 where a senior student taught a lesson to us visitors on creating patterns drawn on the board, which we replicated on paper. Words with symbols used were *koru, koruru, patiki* (flounder fish), *niho taniwha* (tooth of a monster), and *mangopare* (hammerhead shark). I observed that the students referred to Māori art with photos or artwork and the use of material objects such as grass and fern leaves. They study other cultures such as Polynesian. At Ruma 9 (classroom 9), a senior student introduced us to the Māori language. The student called these expressions "basics of Aotearoa." *Kia ora* is "hello." *Tena Koe* (pronounced "kway") is "how are you?" *Tena Korua* means "How are you?" (Hello to two people). *Tena tatou Katoa* is "How are you all?" *E pehea ana Koe?* is "How are you?" The answer is *E pa ana ho*, or "I am fine." *Ae* is "yes." *Kao* is "no." *Ko wai to Ingoa?* is "What is your name?" The answer is *Ko Eric toku ingoa*, which is "My name is Eric." *No whea Koe?* is "Where are you from?" The answer is *No Canada ahua*, which means "I am from Canada." End-of-visit activities were ceremonial physical movements using sticks, strings with balls, and hands free.

The three o'clock paper presentation was given by Dr. Eulyda Toledo-Benalli who has a PhD with distinction in Cross Cultural Studies. Dr. Toledo-Benalli's topic was the Boarding School Healing Project of the United States. She recalled the personal hurt she felt at a mission boarding school when she had her hair cut. She was also physically hurt by students or a matron. She said she cried a lot with other girls due to loneliness. There was no visiting and playing with one another. She said she was a second-generation boarding school survivor. The Healing Project involves research started in intervention involving eight former students. It is a pilot of a systematic study of physical, mental, and sexual abuse of residential schools. Dr. Toledo-Benalli said, "The focus is on healing ourselves and shared understanding that will evoke healing. The very act of seeking healing is intervention." She said this is a simply explained project that has a gentle approach with e-mailing of consent forms and the use of a trained counselor. What are being claimed are legitimacy and the seeking of past injustices. She said a human rights office has offered to facilitate this process. As an ongoing process, the Navajo Nation Education ensured standards are set as well as the use of experience and storytelling. Questions asked of survivors with responses on the following:

- Broad experiences at boarding school in terms of time frames (grand tour questions)

- Positive experiences, for example, making friends, playing in a band, singing in a choir

- Negative experiences, such as punishment, forced to obey, peer tattlers, lack of nurturing, intense loneliness, inability to share emotion, fearfulness, denial, lack of self-esteem, sense of betrayal when older students had to clean younger siblings, feeling of hate when talking of the past, dislocation of the Dene Nation when the U.S. Army employed General Kit Carson.

Dr. Toledo-Benalli then gave a short history of the Native experience in the U.S. In 1871, Congress recognized Indians as wards of the government. In 1879, the Carlyle Industrial School in Pennsylvania became the first industrial school building. Its goals were

- Civilizing the "savage" Indian; teaching of reading, writing, and arithmetic
- Teaching Indians how to work
- Christian training.

Over a forty-five-year span, data showed gradual enculturation of the Dene. Dr. Toledo-Benalli said revitalization of our culture and language is crucial. She said efforts toward this goal are being made by two tribal colleges, which are accredited as institutions of higher learning and that are supported by Dene philosophy. She said we have not restored healing of the residential school experience for "we continue alcoholism, rampant sexual abuse, domestic violence. We must restore healing to the physical, mental, and spirituality through medicine people and mental health workers.

No amount of reparation can lead to healing the cultural loss experienced as a result of the boarding school experience. The "bad man clause" of the 1868 Treaty of the Navajo Tribe and the United States, states no white man shall abuse Indians. The Dene population is reaching three hundred thousand but still has not addressed the residential school experience. Caring to remember is part of the healing process. Heal and transform this process. [There is need to] reframing to define the problem and collectively solving the problem in our communities. We have not even touched the surface of this healing because it is painful. The journey is to reclaim, intervene, and retrain through the use of traditional healers and reaffirm language."

I next attended a workshop called "Inca and Maya Heritage Update and Contemporary Education System—Peru and Guatemala," which was presented by Dr. Walter Fleming, a Kickapoo Indian, and Dr. Wayne J. Stein of the North American Studies Program at Montana State University, Bozeman, Montana. Dr. Fleming said this project is a part of the program at Fort Belknap College and is a five-week faculty and curriculum development seminar in Peru and Guatemala. Through a field trip in which photographs were taken, the project studied ethnicity, identity, and Indian education. It observed social realities, history, and culture in Lima, Peru, a "country in search of a Nation." Peru has a population of seven million five hundred thousand and has two major tribes, three geographic areas, and is 55 percent coast, 30 percent mountains, and 15 percent jungle (selu). The human population is 14 percent white, 49 percent Mestizo, and 36 percent Indian. Dr. Fleming posed a question, "Indian or Indian?" and said that "indio" retains a strong negative connotation and stereotypes, "*Campesinos*" or simple farmers and "peasants." He said Juan Velasco Alvardo (1968–1975) was involved in an agrarian reformist movement. He gave a short history of Lima, which he said was founded by a king from Europe in 1537 through Francisco Pizarro. He said the Inca *(Inka)* time line shows there was an Inca dynasty in the twelfth century and in the period 1450–1530. The pre-Inca cultures existed, one of which is the Mochica (100 BC–AD 500). He concluded by saying that Guatemala is properly pronounced as *"Guate-Maya"*).

The plenary keynote speaker was John Bennett Herrington (Commander, U.S. Navy, retired); NASA astronaut and member of the Chickasaw Nation of Oklahoma. His speech was "Living Your Dreams." He used a PowerPoint presentation with highlights from his career, such as the launch of his shuttle and flying in the space shuttle *Endeavor* and working with the International Space Station in 2002. He said the pronunciation of his tribe Chickasaw is *"Chi caw sa."* He recalled his early years in the 1960s with "What did it take for me to become an astronaut? I had a dream when I was eight years old that I was going to go to the moon. I recall when I was in a cardboard box at a playground. Going to space was a dream I had, but I did not think I could fulfill. It's about a journey, my journey from small town Oklahoma. My grandma was a full-blood Chickasaw. My parents told me I had to go to college. They preferred I go to school as they didn't have a chance to attend. They didn't tell what I should do. I wasn't motivated. I didn't put time and effort in school. It wasn't that I wasn't intelligent. My average achievement at high school continued at university where I was eventually asked to leave because of poor results. I went to work. It was the support of a boss at work who saw my potential that sent me back to university."

Herrington said the two key guides in his life direction were motivation and mentors. He said, "You have to be motivated. You cannot succeed without motivation, but you need mentors to stay motivated." He said he changed his college major from forestry to engineering and graduated in applied math. He joined the navy in 1983. He said, "People along the way gave me their opinion. I have flied airplanes about twenty years, still do. I liked making decisions, mitigated the risks, and studied hard. I have walked in space three times with NASA at the Kennedy Space Centre. It takes a whole team effort. Everybody has a purpose to serve." Herrington said being an astronaut is "probably the most satisfying job I've ever done in my life." He said he is grateful for the support of strong role models for helping to live his dreams of succeeding in reaching for the stars. He concluded, "It has a phenomenal impact on how you see your place in the world. You see places you grew up in, but you can't see any of the people who live there. It gives you a real sense of your insignificance in the great scheme of things."

On Wednesday, November 30, I attended a workshop called "Protecting Indigenous Knowledge in a Globalized World" presented by Debra Harry, a Northern Paiute from Pyramid Lake, Nevada. According to the *WIPCE Official Handbook* (page 339), she studied human genetic research and its implications for indigenous peoples. "She earned a master's degree in community economic development from New Hampshire College, and is currently a doctoral candidate at the University of Auckland, School of Education. She serves as the Executive Director of the Indigenous Peoples Council on Biocolonialism (IPCB)." Ms. Harry gave an overview of her talk stating there are "international discussions taking place, which may result in international standards for the protection of knowledge and intellectual property rights." She asked, "What is traditional knowledge?" She said the United Nations refers to it as "cultural heritage of indigenous peoples" and includes all moveable and immoveable cultural property. She gave a few examples of topics in current international discussions, such as

- The Convention of Biological Diversity, which has an international regime for Access and Benefit Sharing (ABS) regarding traditional resources and genetic resources
- World Intellectual Property Organization (WIPO), which has an international regime for the protection of traditional knowledge, genetic resources, and folklore
- Other UN fora, such as FAO, UNESCO, and WHO.

In a discussion of "Production versus protection," Ms. Harry said that intellectual property rights law says "protection" is the "creation of a legal right (patent, copyright, and trademark) to exclude others from using or reproducing." Indigenous protection is safeguarding traditional knowledge and resources that are inalienable. She stated that production versus protection has consistent themes of

- "Intellectual knowledge is a resource to be commodified
- Holders of intellectual knowledge should be compensated when such knowledge is commercialized
- A legal system to recognize rights and distribute benefits from the commercial use should be created
- A balance must be struck between promoting scientific innovation and rights of Indigenous peoples."

Ms. Harry outlined the following defensive measures:

- "Disclosure of origin of genetic resources and/or traditional knowledge
- Databases for prior art searches prevent bad patents. A shopping list of Indian traditional knowledge digital library, Biozula Database (Venezuelan National Academy of Science, American Association for the Advancement of Science TEKPAD)
- Indigenous response to databases. Indigenous technology is dynamic, not static and cannot simply be documented and fixed
- Database right. Create industrial property protection that ensures exclusivity to the use of the contents
- Public domain knowledge. Liability regime characterized by "use now, pay later." Allows use but requires users to compensate producers/providers. Have collective management institutions
- Inducements for participation. Prior informed consent is required but should be more than that and include indigenous peoples in decision making
- Benefit Sharing Agreements having mutually agreed terms."

Ms. Harry warned of real dangers, such as

- "Recasting indigenous knowledge in indigenous peoples' terminology
- Indigenous people can only protect property in a commercial and Western legal context
- Compartmentalizes and alienates indigenous knowledge
- Clash of worldviews. Indigenous peoples' rights versus monopoly rights. Indigenous systems hold resources collectively to benefit for future generations."

Ms. Harry concluded by offering the following strategies for protection:

- "Assert right of self-determination
- Ensure protection is collective in nature
- Develop a *sui* generic system that truly recognizes and protects customary laws
- Indigenous knowledge is truly protected through cultural practices. It must be lived."

The next workshop I attended was "Tribal Knowledge, Consciousness, and the Challenge to Education." This was presented by Murdena Marshall, a Mi'kmaw, from Cape Breton Island, Nova Scotia. She is described in the *WIPCE Official Handbook* as an elder and leader of her nation, "holds a Masters of Education from Harvard University and, is an Associate Professor at the University College of Cape Breton."

She said, "Tribal knowledge has spirit and lives in specific places, in stories, and in oral traditions. It is known through watching and listening. Tribal knowledge is dynamic and is experienced through song, ceremony, hunting, fishing, and gathering of medicines. It interacts with daily life. It is present in our dreams, ceremonies, and in all of creation. What is traditional knowledge? There is lots of interest in this concept from the outside of traditional culture. Research with elders from several communities provided understandings. Two-eyed seeing (First Nations sights) versus non-Native ecological understanding. Western science emphasizes physical characteristics and cultural significance. First Nations traditional knowledge is a result of cultural upbringing. It recognizes natural objects by designating them as he/she and respects an object as any human being, for example, it is okay to talk to trees. Use and thank a tree for products that serve you. Mother earth is life giving. Long ago, moss could be used to keep babies dry and comfortable as a diaper. This is part of tribal consciousness and also reflects scientific understanding.

"Elders try to pass on tribal consciousness to ensure the living preservation of our worldview. Loss of language among the young makes it difficult to live the traditional knowledge because the understanding is embedded in the language. The words of the elders have always reinforced our belief that one time all creation was one. All living things have DNA. Traditional knowledge is a reflection of your own tribal consciousness. One's possession of tradition or traditional knowledge becomes a mirror image of your spirituality. We need to bring the spirit back to science. We are both spiritual and physical beings. In merging spiritual guidance with knowledge, parenting is considered preparation of character. The mother will ensure the welfare of a child, both spiritual and physical, is a priority. Elders from the community monitor birth, which ensures connectiveness. Language has spirit. Language allows us to respect. Wounding of our connectiveness is separation of physical and spiritual being. All people must learn 'two-eye seeing,' so that knowledge of the physical is not separated from the wisdom of the spiritual."

The second keynote speaker was Dr. Manley Begay Jr., whose address was "Our Duties and Responsibilities as Indigenous Peoples." Dr. Begay has a doctorate in Education. As described in the *Keynote Speakers and Bios* (page 2), Dr. Begay "is both director of the Native Nations Institute for Leadership, Management, and Policy in the Udall Center for Studies in Public Policy and senior lecturer/associate social scientist in the American Indian Studies Program at the University of Arizona."

He said, "Greetings to the Native world. We must never forget to continue to greet the earth, thunderers, sun, moon, stars, White Shell Woman, the holy people, and the Creator. Things you do become your character. Keep our minds on thanksgiving and greet the world. Remember the people. We have been given the duty and responsibility to the people and all living things in balance and harmony. It is our responsibility to be wise, having mental smoothness, steadiness, thinking highest thoughts of oneself and one's community. It's about maturity and having a long experience. We have seven senses: sight, sound, smell, taste, voice, touch, and memory. Learn to remember stories of creation and life. Dene views spirituality, health, beauty, and life are inseparable. Heat, light, sunlight, rays, and zigzag elements interact with other material elements to form life at the beginning.

It is our duty and responsibility to maintain balance with each other and other living beings. All parts of the universe are alive and interdependent. The ideal purpose of education is to attain, know, and seek truth, completeness of life as sustaining power, so we can have unity and balance. Our duty and responsibility is to maintain the balance. Elders say the holy people are the ones who placed us here. Our physical bodies are made from corn, and parts of our bodies are precious stones. Earth mother supports our feet. Mother longs for us. Earth mother is us, and we are her. Earth was used to make our flesh. Mountains are our leaders, our thinkers, and our way of life, and serve as the foundation. Thank the waters for quenching our thirst and giving us strength. Make an offering to the river, so it can rain and so that fish will be in the water and who can clean and purify the water and provide food for us, and so our minds are one. Plants were instructed to sustain life forms as food, grains, and fruit. Give them thanks, and now our minds are one. To medicine herbs, peyote, sweet grass, sage, give thanks. The animals teach us, the deer, kangaroo, sheep, seal, ducks, elk, buffalo, [and] moose. Thank them for giving the food. Trees and their families provide shelter, fruit, and other things, cedar, aspen. With one mind, thank them, and now our minds are one. A bird with beautiful songs, the eagle is the leader.

The four directions is the foundation for thinking and intelligence. The four winds, give thanks to these powers that purify the air. Change of seasons gives us strength. This means all living things are related. Thunderers, our grandfathers, thunder beings bring us the rain. The sun brings light of a new day. It is the source of life and for the gaining of strength. Grandmother moon is the leader of all women and governs tides. The stars are like jewelry and help the moon to light the darkness, provide direction for the night, and give us time and seasons. Enlightened teachers teach us balance and serenity. Our uncles, aunties, medicine people, when these teachers leave us, we must prepare. To the holy people and the Creator, give them thanks, and now our minds are one."

The next workshop I attended was "Teaching methods/Techniques Based on American Indian Traditional Knowledge and Cultural Values" and was presented by Dr. Linda Oxendine, Rosemary Christiansen. It was stated that circle teaching in a student group was prioritized. Integrative learning was used in a group process, while personal integrity was ensured. The importance of oral tradition and traditional listening is an art and a learned skill. Also respect, reciprocity, and relationship are very important.

The next workshop I attended, "One Earth, One Universe: Professional Development on Native and Western Science Perspective," was presented by Isabel Hawkins and Rose Van Thater-Braan. These presenters described "One Earth, One Universe" as a professional development project and as an effort of work to bring Western science and Native science and to bring harmony. It is about building the capacity of fifty NASA scientists from around the U.S. and educators to hold divergent views as equals. It is also about providing a learning environment that honors both views respectfully and where all voices can be heard. Another expectation of the project is to "make the Native paradigm and Native science visible to Western trained professionals."

The presenters said the process consists of workshops of self-motivated participants. There is an application process, an immersive experience of

4.5 days in a workshop setting with access to nature and talking aides, small group discussions, presentations and opportunities for reflection and introspection. Learning that comes out of relationship is explored and finding that knowledge emerges from maintaining relationship. The process includes the open possibility of holding divergent views and preparing to suspend Western thought. The use of all of the senses is encouraged as well as the recognition and reaching consensus that says "I know and there is collective harmony that allows that life to continue."

The presenters said they had two workshops since February 2005 on "Relationships and Responsibility" and "Ethics and Native Science." They said the next steps for the learning community are to provide a language experience to share experiences and collaborative projects. They said, "We animate, prepare for quietness, and use an outdoor setting that will provide impetus for the transmission of knowledge through many, many ways that engenders respect and trust, suspends belief."

The inspirational speaker at the keynote tent was Dr. Papaarangi Reid of Aotearoa, New Zealand. Dr. Reid is a specialist in medicine and is head of Medicine at the University of Waikato. Her topic was "Decolonization and Trouble, Is Trouble Such a Bad Thing?" She began, "I'm in so much trouble in so many fronts. Trouble 1 regards Kaupapa Māori Research, which is quantitative in scope. On one hand, the purpose of the research was to be liberating and decolonizing. It used quantitative analysis to make qualitative analysis but became problematic. Defining, confining was an issue affected by a funding formula."

Dr. Reid stated quantitative analysis includes the right to be counted and considers classification of ethnicity, the right not to be minoritized, having equal explanatory power, an indigenous standard population, and the right not to be victim-blamed. She said she got to thinking about methods as tools and also innovation. She said Trouble 2 is Māori women as superwomen. She said that through midwife conversation, it was stated, "Though women expect equal treatment, it must be asked, 'Are we getting enough medical services in health care at childbirth?' It's about owning our colonial influences and the indigenous right to all." Dr. Reid said Trouble 3 is sex, sexuality, and gender roles. This is known through conversations about *karanga*, the treason of talking sexism, let alone looking at Christianity. She asked, "What about homophobia? Why do women wear dresses? Is our culture living?" Dr. Reid's Trouble 4 is culture and identity. She asked, "Who is a real Native (thinks right)? We have to ensure our history is a friend. We have to go beyond recreating our past. It is a process of both remembering and creating, being and becoming. Loving indigenous is not the same as hating colonizers. Challenges are

- Insist on our right to complexity
- Insist on our right to diversity
- Stop policing differences, embrace issue of differences as a right and as safe journey to decolonization
- Be critical friends, be able to give and take criticism
- Be in tune with the principles of our ancestors. Recognize it is a changing world but not change our principles as guiding points, but practices have changed, for example, laws where custom burials have been replaced by outside burial practices
- There is serious revolutionary work to be done. We have to have serious work when we engage with people and talk to more people about the journey of decolonization
- Creating a safe space for decolonization, not putting off topics such as sexism
- Love Indigeneity. Trouble is a compliment!"

On December 1, the first keynote speaker was Professor Akpovire Oduaran, PhD, head of Adult Education, University of Botswana, Gaborone, Botswana. His topic was "Excellence in Education and the Challenge of the HIV/AIDS Epidemic in Sub-Saharan Africa." He said HIV/AIDS is a problem plaguing the continent of Africa. He said December 1 is World AIDS Day and that "lots of people in the world have been wiped out by HIV/AIDS. There are thousands of indigenous nations in Africa, and many are on the verge of being wiped out by the scourge of AIDS. Africa is rich in minerals. It has 635.2 million people. Development is stalled by so many problems like HIV/AIDS, which poses a challenge to human capital investment. The epidemic has a negative impact on excellence in education, impacting the environment for learning and quality. Why? The context of the sub-Saharan HIV/AIDS epidemic shows Botswana [is infected] 33.8 percent; Zimbabwe 33.73 percent; Swaziland 33.44 percent; and Lesotho 31 percent. In 2003, between 25 million and 28.2 million people were living with HIV/AIDS in the sub-Saharan Africa alone. This is against the figure of 1.3 million recorded for Latin America and 300,000–500,000 for the Caribbean.

The education sector has not been spared by the negative impact of

HIV/AIDS. HIV/AIDS have affected individuals, communities, and nations negatively. It has increased teacher mortality. Good analysis is hindered by lack of reliable data. In 1999, one in seven teachers in Malawi is likely to die. Why teachers? HIV/AIDS in sub-Sahara African universities is a disquieting picture. There is ignorance surrounding the presence of the disease and supported by secrecy and silence. There are impacts and clinical effect and pursuit of academic excellence. There are no statistics, but we know of the prevalence of full-blown AIDS through its manifestations, such as progressive brain damage. Universities' response is that some have initiated sexual harassment policies, preventive care, and support services. Barriers or constraints are lack of government support and lack of resources. Universities want to confront the problem by educating the community, highlighting the incidence of HIV/AIDS in education systems and by preventing the loss of foundations of excellence in education at all cost."

The closing address, "The Way Forward," was delivered by Prof. Linda Smith, an international consultant on indigenous education in Australia and the author of a book titled *Decolonizing Methodology*. Professor Smith asked, "Through feedback of participants, what have we missed out in education? The conference filled our need. We're here because other people helped us. For everyone here, there's a people who no longer exists, who will lose language, or who will be killed and deemed they have no basic human rights to live. Think of those who are not here, those whose languages and songs will not be heard unless we take up the challenges through education, of growing individual spirit and intellect and a society.

As educators, feel good about what you achieved. Thank the ones that are not here, but go home and take up challenges. Indigenous education, as a result of this conference, should be able to say what it is. So what is it? Where have you been? You know what it is. Look to tomorrow. Think about leadership. Every one of you is a leader. Leadership is important to indigenous peoples. It is difficult. Expectations are high. What are we doing in education to support leaders of the community? Leadership requires a certain quality of leadership. Visions are only good if they take you somewhere. A vision is only good if it lives. A community has to share. It changes every day as more people are added to it. Education is about possibilities. We're past the victim mode. We're in a mode of confidence. Review what is, for example, Māori education? Education is amazing diversity and of critical capacity."

APPENDIX M

2006 WORLD INDIGENOUS HIGHER EDUCATION CONSORTIUM [WINHEC] CONFERENCE, FOND DU LAC TRIBAL COMMUNITY COLLEGE [FDLTCC], CLOQUET, MINNESOTA, USA, AUGUST 7, 8, AND 9, 2006—A REPORT

COUNCILOR ERIC J. LARGE

I attended the above WINHEC conference to get an update of developments related to world indigenous higher education. WINHEC began with the signing of the Declaration on Indigenous Peoples Higher Education on August 5, 2002, in Kananaskis, Alberta, during the Sixth World Indigenous Peoples Conference on Education [WIPCE] August 4–10, 2002. Founding member nations of WINHEC were indigenous peoples from Australia, Hawaii, Alaska, the American Indian Higher Education Consortium of the United States, Canada, the Wananga [higher learning institutions] of Aotearoa [New Zealand], and Saamiland [North Norway]. As stated in its brochure, WINHEC's vision is "We gather as Indigenous Peoples of our respective nations recognizing and reaffirming the educational rights of Indigenous Peoples. We share a vision of Indigenous Peoples of the world united in the collective synergy of self determination through control of higher education. There is commitment to building partnerships that restore and retain Indigenous spirituality, cultures and languages, homelands, social systems, economic systems and self-determination." WINHEC has a stated seven-point mission and goals through higher education, which provide direction to WINHEC as the international forum and support for indigenous peoples.

On Monday, August 7, an international welcome was conducted at the Fond du Lac Community College Amphitheatre. Shirley Defoe, director for International Programs and WINHEC 2006 coordinator, related the origin, vision, mission and goals, and the founding member nations of WINHEC. Representatives present in the 2006 WINHEC conference were representatives representing twenty-five Indian reservations in the United States, Maori of Aotearoa (New Zealand), representatives of Higher Education Network Australia, Saamiland, Norway, Taiwan, Hawaii, and Canada. Defoe said, "Respect for differences has made us better human beings." Among other Fond du Lac Tribal Community Colleges officials, Dr. Don Day, president of FDLTCC, welcomed the delegates. Delegates from WINHEC nations were asked to introduce themselves.

The representative from the American Indian Higher Education Consortium said, "It's long overdue that we have this kind of organization. The movement is still alive and growing and hope that more colleges in the U.S. will [become involved]."

Dr. Lionel R. Bordeaux, Lakota, president, Sinte Gleska University, Rosebud Sioux Reservation, and Co chairperson of WINHEC, began his introduction with his personal background, education up to his studies toward a PhD, and work experience with the Bureau of Indian Affairs (BIA). He said while with the BIA, he was "called home by an elder to help retain and regain culture and to be president of a college as I spoke Lakota. I resigned from the BIA position and withdrew from the University of Minnesota. I went to a ceremony and was told the *pipe* would carry us through difficulties. I was in a circle of elders and guided by a young woman. The elders told their dreams and difficulties. I listened to their encyclopedic knowledge." Dr. Bordeaux said he was inspired that he wanted a new order, which he said was "one, to work for cultural preservation, identity as tribal people; two, as present education was irrelevant, to own accreditation through tribal law and customs. I wanted a wedding between economic development and education starting with Head Start. Three, change the tribal government system, put BIA aside, and put the treaty forward. Four, need to change every colleges and universities and them to be part of the system. We must take tribal education to the four directions. Take education, at least hope. Hope is not a strategy but is a beginning. Every year, there is always some barrier but that it makes us strong. We've come a long way, and we have a long way to go. We're strong because we have spirituality."

The Vice Chair of WINHEC introduced Robert P. Four Star, instructor of Native Studies—Assiniboine Studies, Fort Peck Community College, Wolf Point, Montana, who sang a ceremonial song. Mr. Four Star said this song signified "a retreat" and was traditionally sung by warriors to bolster themselves and staked themselves to the ground when in battle standing to the end.

The Māori delegation of about five people from New Zealand was acknowledged. Trevor Moeke, a Maori spokesperson, "thanked the ones who have gone before who developed WINHEC and WIPCE and that we are stepping to the plate for culture and languages throughout the world. Though we have computer technology, we can never replace the humankind and relationship of our people. I bring greetings from our queen. WINHEC is young. I look forward to the day when we do like teenagers and become rambunctious and celebrate."

The Australian delegation of four from central north Queensland was introduced by one of their members. The member said he "has heard of WINHEC and their struggles, which gives us hope and that we learn of the effects of colonization."

There were about twenty delegates from Canada with myself and one other from Alberta. I gave a brief geographical description of Saddle Lake and that Saddle Lake was a member of Blue Quills First Nations College, which offered courses from the Universities of Edmonton, Calgary, and Lethbridge in Social Work and Education.

There were three delegates, two women and one infant, from Saamiland, North Norway. The spokesperson, Mai Britt Utsi, Rector of Saami University College, Guovdageaidnu, Norge gave a brief background of Saamiland and the Saami University College. She said there were about fifty thousand Saami people with nine languages.

There were two delegates from Taiwan but who were attending college and university in the U.S.

The one Hawaii delegate said, "Indigenous people take control of our own indigenous education, including accreditation and standards and truly appropriate criteria for curricula."

In the afternoon, Turoa Royal, executive Co chair of WINHEC, declared the WINHEC officially open and gave an eleven-page written report to the delegates. Minutes, reports, and matters arising from minutes of the WINHEC Conference from Hamilton, Aotearoa, 2005 were circulated and adopted. Mr. Royal invited comments on his report. I got up to provide a brief update on the UN Draft Declaration on the Rights of Indigenous Peoples. The UN Human Rights Council had approved the Declaration on June 29, 2006, in Geneva with Russia and Canada opposing it as reported by Wilton Littlechild. The declaration will go to the UN General Assembly in the fall where some of us in the Treaty 6 area fear that Canada will reword the draft declaration so that it erodes or weakens the version that we want. Reports from member nations were delivered.

The first Australian delegate mentioned the need for indigenous research and networking in the higher education system. The delegate said, "We are slowly losing people that were involved for many years in higher education through retirement. We are losing their knowledge. There is pursuit of indigenous epistemology as part of the research and with the help of elders in students' theses. There is consideration of research and practice of indigenous epistemology. There is a potential role of indigenous systems with members working with their institutions and universities. The high education system in Australia is currently lobbying the government for funding with the rational of indigenous inclusion in the higher education system, inclusion of indigenous courses, and for research and teaching practices." The second Australian delegate asked, "What is 'indigenous' or 'indigenous knowledge'? One definition is, it is cultural knowledge and traditional knowledge. It is known by an indigenous person with knowledge. But traditional knowledge can also be known by any nonindigenous person having knowledge as learned from an indigenous person."

The report on Sami Higher Education in Norway was delivered by Rector Mai Britt Utsi. She spoke of the situation of the Sami Language and Higher Education and the future of Sami Higher Education. She said the first argument [or basis] is the Norwegian Constitution as in article 110A that provides for the "protection of Sami, acknowledgement of Sami as one of two forming nations. With the Sami Act, language and rights are highly protected. There is also the Charter for Regional or Minority Languages with supporting references to the ILO Convention no. 169, Agenda 21, Norwegian Public Commission Reports, and the Nordic Sami Convention (not yet ratified). Samiland covers the Arctic, Russia on the right, and Alaska."

Ms. Utsi said the second argument is "the situation of the approximately fifty thousand Samis in Norway, Sweden, Finland, and Russia of which approximately twenty-five thousand speak Sami. The focus is on education and research with a Sami perspective. Sami related education at all levels is offered in certain areas in Norway. There is a right to receive tuition. The main higher education and research institute is the Sami University College (SUC) affiliated with the Nordic Sami Institute. SUC has knowledge of the Sami language as an admission requirement.

A new building called the Sami House of Knowledge is being constructed with Sami institutions under one roof. It is seventy-seven thousand four hundred square feet and costs forty-four million U.S. dollars. Education and research activities include a research center for reading and writing of Sami languages, Sami rights, reindeer herding, traditional economics, and climate change with the ACIA (Arctic Council). International collaborators are WINHEC, University of the Arctic membership, and Arctic Council on Arctic Environmental Protection. There is VERDDE exchange program between SUC and Nunavut Arctic College, Yukon College, and University of Greenland and Yakutz. The future of Sami Higher Education involves Sami political intent to organize SUC/NSI as Sami University with the main responsibility for Sami Higher Education and Research. There is also culture and academic exchange and development."

The Taiwan delegate said that "since 1996, concern on indigenous education vanished but has since revived in one university. There are bachelor's degree, masters, and PhD programs with a special focus on language as well as being a research center for indigenous students. We want to try a community college in Taiwan. Some students are struggling. There is more support for higher education bodies through scholarship, assisting students learning their language and culture, and special policy for indigenous students to achieve their level in higher education. We teach students about our songs."

The first delegate, Tim Tompkins, from Canada, said, "We have about sixty-five higher education institutions. The AFN (Assembly of First Nations) has a Chiefs Committee on Education that works on education policy issues. In the last year, social welfare was worked on. In the last year, AFN came up with Kelowna agreement where $1.8 billion was to be allocated to education. The February election came about, and the new government committed $500 million for post-secondary education. There was some support from premiers in view of the declining number of students. There is policy change occurring with INAC working on education policy guidelines. There is no reference to supporting post-secondary institutions. First Nations education policy legislation has implications for post secondary."

The second delegate from Canada reported that in late 2004, there were some major issues identified, such as post-secondary education. The delegate said, "The government struck a partnership with AFN to develop a policy mandated by the prime minister and has invited input from First Nations. The sixty-five institutions in Canada are seeking to get accreditation. There is support for students through the Indian Student Support Policy. First Nations need to have accreditation and recognize full control of post-secondary education. INAC is putting forward its policy without our input. We last communicated with them in February. We have in Canada an abundance of students wanting post secondary. What we don't have is funding support for these students." The third delegate, Amelia Clark, of Old Sun Community College from Canada, said, "Two years ago, Canada designed work with five knowledge centers. Four got off the ground. There is a centre of learning, the First Nations Adult Higher Education Centre that is co hosting a knowledge center using learning bundles to host a conference with two themes."

The fourth delegate from Canada, Laura Horton, director of Post Secondary Education Programs Seven Generations Education Institute, Fort Frances, Ontario, spoke of the Seven Generations Program. She said this program has been going for the last twenty-five years and has strong backing of elders. She said they want to bring home our own accredited programs. She expressed concern over development of our own programs and resources, which landed in the mainstream education systems. She said they considered what would be included in a master's program. She said, "We have to have cultural standards, say what your practices are, do we speak our languages, where is it do we sit and think? The only place is in the master's program where four distinguished elders sit and support. Chiefs support the accreditation of the program though they are not academics."

On Tuesday, August 8, Peter Defoe, chairperson, Fondu Lac Indian Reservation Lake Superior Chippewa, one of five Minnesota (MN) Chippewa tribes, made a welcome. He said, "As I look at the delegates' list here, I am reminded of the struggle of indigenous people worldwide. The key to our survival is education. We almost lost our language here. We're spending a lot of time in preserving that. We always stress education. It's our way of survival in this world."

Mike Rabideaux, superintendent, Fondu Lac Reservation Ojibwa School, Cloquet, Minnesota, gave a welcome. He said, "I'd like to welcome honored guests. We truly know the challenges that are ahead. We know what is going on today in the world. What it is like our indigenous history teaches everywhere [that] contact brings changes. The challenges we face today are disconnected. Here we have resurrected the elders' restorative circle. We need that focus here and in other places."

Shirley Defoe, conference coordinator, read a letter from Prince Albert of Monaco for his being unable to come to this conference. She said Prince Albert has been a supporter of indigenous issues.

Reports from each indigenous nation continued beginning with Trevor Moeke, New Zealand. Moeke said, "Māori are the indigenous people of New Zealand. The population of New Zealand is four million. The Māori is about seven hundred thousand people. Sixty percent of the Māori population is still in school. The increasing population has implications for the workforce. We are confident, as we are gifted and smart. In Parliament, we have a number of guaranteed seats. In the next fifteen to twenty years is the prospect of a Māori-driven democracy. There are twenty-eight technical institutes, three colleges, and three Wananga (equivalent to tribal colleges in the U.S.). The legacy is our Māori students have been put in standard school systems and still have failed. Our language has been spoken and has never been written down, but we are now working on it. From our descriptive, we reform our aspirations and go forward to a new day, a new way where our grandmothers teach the little ones. Three Wananga teach somewhere between forty-five to fifty thousand people. Language is broadcast on radio and TV to make huge inroads in language use. We are all singers in the language. In 1769, Captain Cook came around. The representative of the Queen of England came to sign the Treaty of Waitangi. Since then, there has been a Māori language commission. Māori is the other official language of our country. There are new Māori words coming up, for example, a word for genetic manipulation or for ecclesiastical. Twenty percent of the population who speak Māori is non-Māori. The Māori Nation own 80 percent of the fishing operations. Economics are very closely tied down with the education of our people. We have the right to participate in the world economy, to good health and a higher standard of living. This implies lack of services that contribute to a poor standard of life for our people. We are working toward balance between leadership and those who line up. Government talks to us 'we'll' talk to you what you need in the next three to five years, and we'll make an agreement. But this is debatable."

The next speaker was Verlieann Lienomi Maline-Wright, Ed.D, vice principal, Kula Kaia puni'o Avenue, Honolulu, Hawaii, and president of the National Indian Education Association. She said, "There a several reflections. Te Wananga in New Zealand are our cousins. You cannot help but feel the change through your commitment for indigenous knowledge, sustainability, and control of our own education systems. I really feel and think that it is a moral obligation of the Crown to continue to support education. The corners of Hawaii epistemology are earth corner; life-force corner (energy, humanity) of our genealogy, belly button, genitals; and embryonic (child connection with his/her ancestry) placenta corner. It is about who we are as human beings. We are trying to include these in our education. Wellness constructs are physical, mental, spiritual, and emotional. The role of accreditation is that we encourage communities to take a role at what they can do for their children. To include cultural perspective, how do we develop our school community for us to commit to do this best, to be successful, to be happier, and to be contributing to society? The ethical space question is, what does this imply? It is cultural values, which interact with tension and resistance with Western styles but which has control to function in Western-based societies. Sustainability based on our economic connection with our traditional knowledge. Building a legacy today for the children of tomorrow is why we are here today."

Executive Co chair Turoa Royal announced the consideration of a working group for academic programs are set up. Tom Davis of Fondu lac Tribal Community College made a motion that we set up a working party for academic programs, putting toward a WINHEC-accredited degrees, with clarification of master's degree and PhD in addition, with reference to a spiritual dimension. This motion was carried. Limited copies of the second edition WINHEC accreditation handbook were circulated. The handbook describes the accreditation process, which, in part, is approved by the WINHEC Board of Affirmation. The Board of Affirmation recommends an applicant member indigenous nation or institution of higher learning for WINHEC accreditation. Co chair Royal read the minutes from the meeting held on November 24 and 25, 2005. Four motions were presented; one of which was on accreditation, the creation of a WINHEC stamp, the logo has already been created, and a motion to adopt minutes, as read, was carried.

Laura Horton, director of Post Secondary Education Programs, Seven Generations Education Institute (SGEI), Fort Frances, Ontario, presented the SGEI Post Secondary Education Circle Self-Study as a submission to the WINHEC Board of Affirmation for accreditation for August 2006.

Mai Britt Utsi of the Sami University College (SUC) provided an accreditation application package. She said what is notable is "the Sami language shall be developed as academic language. Sami traditional knowledge shall be documented to the academic curriculum." The Sami accreditation application process includes an explanation of the SUC mission statement and the objective of the application. Further supporting information includes an elaboration of Sami cultural values, Sami spirituality, use of natural symbols as fire, fish, animal bones, and other valuables, research activities, education activities, language studies, natural science and social studies, Sami journalism, Sami teacher training, practical and esthetic studies, organization, Sami education achievements, infrastructure, and strategic challenges.

A first motion was made and seconded that "the WINHEC Executive Board hereby approves the self-study for WINHEC accreditation submitted by the SGEI of Ontario and congratulates them for the quality of their application and agrees to proceed with the onsite accreditation visitation." A second motion was made that "the WINHEC Executive Board hereby approves the accreditation application submitted by the Sami Alluskoval Sami University College." A third motion was adopted and carried, which said, "The First Nations Technical Institute in Tyendinaga Mohawk Territory, Canada, accepts the letter of interest to apply for accreditation."

The WINHEC accreditations in the form of an inquiry for the University College of Northern Manitoba and for early childhood and K-12 schools are pending.

The WINHEC Honors Awards proposal for various categories of recognition of achievement or education service of individuals was presented. The categories are

- WINHEC Order of the Circle of Chiefs of Indigenous Leadership for past chairs on the honorable completion of their term
- Circle of Elders of Indigenous Wisdom
- Circle of Scholars of Indigenous Knowledge
- Circle of Services to Indigenous Education

The Executive Board recommends that Dr. Lionel Bordeaux, Dr. Rongo Wetere, and Turoa Royal be recipients of the Order of the Circle of Chiefs of Indigenous Leadership.

On Wednesday, August 9, the representative for the Canadian caucus presented draft recommendations for WINHEC to support the UN draft Declaration of the Rights of Indigenous Peoples. The representative also offered to host the 2009 WINHEC in Canada with the location to be determined and that the coordinating body is FNAHEC or NAIIHL. There was mention of setting up a Canadian office of WINHEC.

Turoa Royal, executive Co chair, invited the representative delegates, if they did not already, to sign the Declaration on Indigenous Peoples Higher Education. I signed on behalf of the Saddle Lake Cree Nation. He announced that minutes of this conference will come out in about six weeks and will be on the website.

Working group reports and recommendations continued. It was said that there are two forms of recommendations. One form is recommendations from working parties or committees. A second form is some countries are asking WINHEC for any country wanting particular recommendation for support for any particular action from WINHEC.

The WINHEC Funding Committee's recommendations for action are

- Individual membership dues be $100 per annum
- Sponsorship or waiver process for organizations/nations/tribes needing assistance for annual dues and potential waiver for individuals unable to pay their dues
- National chapters should pay a percentage, to be determined, of their institute membership fee to WINHEC International for its operations.
- National chapters should provide for the relationship with WINHEC International uniformly in each of their chapters and bylaws and be consistent with that of WINHEC International.
- WINHEC should promote, facilitate, and fund exchanges for students and faculty.
- WINHEC should accredit and mainstream institutions' indigenous programs as well as those of indigenous institutions.
- WINHEC members are urged to review and comment on the draft business plan.
- The Funding Committee should complete the WINHEC business plan by November 2006.
- The WINHEC business plan should focus now on core operation and provide for later modification for expanded operations and services to meet identified needs.
- WINHEC should ensure that the business plan meets WINHEC's strategic goals.
- WINHEC should create and fund an international help fund to assist indigenous organizations in need.
- Ensure that a majority of the international and national WINHEC executive boards' membership consists of indigenous people

The above recommendations were adopted by the majority of delegates expressing their support by saying "aye."

Questions and comments were the following:

- Communities and nations who considered themselves sovereign and self-determined are provided with an option not to be affiliated with colonial states.

- The alternative is to have a sub office of WINHEC in countries in which WINHEC has a presence.

- Tasks are to amend WINHEC bylaws to include national chapters and to define the relationship relative to the drafting of a business plan with financial projection of costs and revenues.

The Language Revitalization Committee as reported by the representative from Canada recommends that WINHEC have a policy statement to support indigenous language revitalization, with a vision and mission statement, objectives and recommendations, including language teacher education, language learning at all levels, including immersion, use of current and emerging technology, indigenous language authorities, establishment of standards of fluency, and creation of new worlds to respond to new tasks and circumstances.

Questions and comments involved the importance of inclusion of elders and the use of words like "spirituality," "sovereignty." It was also noted that religious ceremonies and the services of cultural language practitioners would be good. A motion to support the recommendations of the Language Revitalization Committee was made and supported with "aye" and no "nays."

The Promotions/Publicity and Education and Cultural Exchange Committee report was provided by Marcie B. Krawll of ArrowMight International, Ottawa. She said the mandate of WINHEC should be to be a vehicle for information exchange through use of publicity and promotional means/materials, articulate general steps for education/cultural exchange, identify institutions that conduct education/cultural exchanges, document and publish events that reflect WINHEC interests, and preview promotional materials. The committee defines publicity and promotions as information exchange and sharing that provides guidelines for education/cultural exchange, provides links about challenges in indigenous education, and provides materials that promote the objectives/goals of WINHEC. General discussion said that WINHEC not be involved in direct exchanges but be a source of information sharing and exchange for WINHEC members. The committee's actions or objectives are

- List of institutions/providers that conduct exchanges
- Identify funding sources as appropriate

- Review and edit promotional materials for WINHEC
- Develop a calendar of events
- Create process of endorsing education/cultural exchanges.

The committee's recommendations for action are

- Collapse both committees into one
- Title the change to "Exchange, Publicity and Promotions"
- Committee supports and will participate in standardizing the process for reviewing online and printed promotional materials for WINHEC
- Pass membership fees to the Fund Raising Committee
- Develop a process for WINHEC to endorse those institutes who want to participate in student and faculty education/cultural exchanges.

Activities and Deadlines

- Calendar of events for the WINHEC website
- Undertake other activities upon support by general membership
- One committee and one title

Discussion involved the creation of a website including updating of journals and documents and of an image repository. The delegates adopted the issue of putting copyrighted material for reprinting on the website and of the whole issue of intellectual property rights.

The Academic Programs and Indigenous Studies Working Group's findings were

- Defining what is "indigenous" in view of numerous indigenous peoples and variations thereof

- Being indigenous is based on a set of values and principles that connect the descendants of the original people of the land to sacred practices and customs, traditional economic structure, historical and spiritual lineage, and connected to the spiritual, physical, and metaphysical, stories, intellectual tribal/clan identity.

Indigenous means descendants of the First Peoples are the center of existence supported by traditional political institutions; spiritual, social, intellectual and cultural knowledge; having identity as a distinct cultural group; and attached to geographical habitat and ancestral territories; and having language tied to the land.

Tasks include determining what makes a good indigenous program and whether the program has demonstrable connections to the community and is responsive to its needs. Curriculum must include privileging of indigenous knowledge, epistemologies, and experiences in curriculum design, course delivery and accreditation, and detailed methodology. There must be faculty and student involvement. The goals of student involvement must be to develop and produce students who understand the experiences of indigenous peoples. Criteria for Indigenous Studies Programs come with recommendations for

- WINHEC convening a meeting

- A meeting of the Indigenous Studies Working Group be convened in Brisbane, Australia, within six months to advance business including the potential model of WINHEC master's and PhD

- Following Brisbane, the Indigenous Studies Working Group meet to advance the Australia debate on definitions of "traditional," "cultural," and "indigenous" knowledge.

Discussion included a request by the executive Co chair for the conference to move so that "each student work out their study plan for completion of their master plan and to address the issues of students having nonindigenous supervisors and that language is the foundation of indigenous peoples in the face of much use of English. Spirituality also makes up who are indigenous peoples." The delegates carried a motion to his effect.

Verlieann Malian-Wright made the Accreditation Committee report. She said the accreditation handbook is online. There was a review of the Seven Generations Education Institute Self-Study Report and application, as well as for the Sami Alluskoval Sami University College Self-Study Report and application. There was a review of the First Nations Technical Institute, Tyendinaga, Mohawk Territory supported by a letter of intent for eligibility application. The application for Key Ala Pone College in Hawaii is pending. The WINHEC Honors Award proposal was presented by naming of the three recipients of the WINHEC Order of the Circle of Chiefs. These recipients are

Turoa Royal, Dr. Lionel Bordeaux, and Dr. Rona Wateree. A motion was made to adopt the Accreditation Report and carried as presented. The delegates reviewed, moved, seconded, and carried each of motions 1 and 2 eligibility application for WINHEC accreditation by Sami Alluskoval University College; motion 3 First Nations Technical Institute letter of intent to apply for WINHEC application; motion 4 Board of Affirmation recommend that Dr. Lionel Bordeaux, Dr. Rona Wateree, and Turoa Royal be approved as the first recipients of the WINHEC Order of the Circle of Chiefs.

The Software Tools Working Party made its recommendations and report. It reported that the XMEG and IKM be distributed on the WINHEC website with appropriate documentation and acknowledgments. Action remains incomplete, however the committee recommends that this not be done, but people can still visit www.metadata.net/ICM or sourceforge.net. The license agreement between DSTC and WINHEC must be finalized. The committee's recommendations are

- That IKM report back next year on progress

- A list of all WINHEC members be listed on the website including a description of their organization and website

- Consideration by the Finance Committee of obtaining financial assistance in helping to fund this and other technology-based initiatives.

The Software Tools Working Party Recommendations and Report can be accessed at bonniemarino@taviho-wananga.mauri.nz.

The Order of the Circle of Chiefs framed certificates were officially presented to Turoa Royal, Dr. Wateree, and Dr. Bordeaux. In his acceptance speech, Dr. Bordeaux acknowledged the support and guidance from his mentors Stanley Redbird and others in his development. He also acknowledged our history and ancestry in the quest for the development of indigenous peoples worldwide through education with our own laws. He linked economic development with higher education as he stated, "So we don't have poverty in this world. There is potential for education and economic exchanges." He said various government models throughout the world must be looked at and for us to address our own models and correct them. Dr. Bordeaux concluded, "Realization of who we are today is a beginning toward a realization that we are best." Turoa Royal's message was "WINHEC has a very responsible job [which] is to maximize the human potential of all our people."

The recommendations from the delegation from Canada were reported by Trevor, the representative who stated he wanted to introduce a couple of motions for adoption or action. One is the UN Draft Declaration of the Rights of Indigenous Peoples and that WINHEC fully supports the Declaration adopted by the UN Human Rights Council on June 29, 2006. Two is the National Association of Indigenous Institutes of Higher Learning [NAIIHL] in Canada is offering to host the 2009 WINHEC. Three, that NAIIHL will examine the possibility of establishing a WINHEC chapter in Canada. Four, First Nations University of Canada, that WINHEC support First Nations University and all First Nations owned and controlled institutions' struggle to maintain indigenous control of indigenous education in Canada. Five, for the First Nations University of Canada to be accepted as a member in WINHEC (for information only). Six, that WINHEC calls upon DIAND [Department of Indian and Northern Development] to clearly articulate its support for First Nation controlled post-secondary institutions in its First Nations education policy framework and management framework; and that DIAND commit to providing secure and ongoing resources, which support the operation, capacity development, and growth of First Nations controlled post-secondary institutions in Canada.

Discussion involved the responsibility of chiefs to come up with a workable strategy. Dr. Wateree indicated that though he agrees with the substance of the Canadian delegation's plea, he said he was not satisfied with the approach of indigenous institutions of going to government with hand in mouth. The recommendations of the delegation from Canada were carried. Turoa Royal made a concluding remark, "We will be working closely with Canada as to how we will work with these [recommendations] and go forward."

The delegates from Hawaii announced that the WINHEC 2007 would be held in Hawaii on October 21, 22, and 23, 2007, at Shauna University, Honolulu. The theme of the conference is "Liko Lililehua." Liko represents the element present in every particular location of the land. "Liko" can also be a child, especially of a chief. "Liko Lililehua" means chiefly child of Lililehua.

APPENDIX N

INDIAN RESIDENTIAL SCHOOLS HEARING—OCTOBER 12–13, 2006, ALBERTA COURT OF QUEEN'S BENCH, COURT HOUSE, 611—4TH SW, CALGARY—A PARTIAL REPORT

COUNCILOR ERIC J. LARGE

I attended the above court hearing, the eighth of nine national hearings that are part of the approval process of the Indian Residential Schools Agreement. I was there to voice a partial objection to the residential school settlement and to note the response of former students. I presented my partial objection on the basis that the $3,000 per month compensation plus more should continue after the final year of discharge from residential school because of the lack of meaningful education received by myself and former students at residential school and for our lack of preparation for careers or work. I also wanted to keep informed of the hearing process and the input or objections of other residential school former students.

    A judge presided over this two-day hearing. On October 12, the first presenter was the legal counsel who said he spoke on behalf of the plaintiffs (Assembly of First Nations on behalf of the residential school former students). He gave a background of the Agreement in Principle as approved in November 2005 and of the Final Agreement of May 2006. He said this hearing is the eighth of nine applications in court. He stated today's hearing agenda includes this application on behalf of the plaintiffs, a Northwest class action handled by the Merchant Law Group. He stated a notice of motion of three remedies contingent on court approval, in part, seeking a court amendment and a court judgment settlement of the residential school agreement. Approval of the conditions of the agreement includes the payment of legal fees of which there are three types: (1) formula "regime" independent counsel, (2) law firms as part of the agreement, and (3) process fees. The plaintiff's lawyer said this hearing's application will consist of lawyers speaking and class members speaking. He said there are fifteen class objector members requested to speak by the deadline [of August 25, 2006] with a total of sixty-four objectors filed to date. He asked the judge that he [the plaintiff] would make a list of former students present who wished to speak.

The lawyer representing the Merchant Law Group made a remark that many survivors of residential schools are no longer present here.

Other related matters needing to be addressed are: settlement by court hearing; settlement by draft orders; test for certification; test for settlement approval; and objections made orally that have been received in writing.

Court documents of three volumes were referred to that contained the four main elements of the settlement. These elements are the Common Experience Payment (CEP), Independent Assessment Process (IAP), the Truth and Reconciliation Commission, and the Healing and Community Initiatives. The CEP condition states that every former Indian residential school student who resided at a residential school will receive the ten thousand dollars for the first year and three thousand dollars for each succeeding year while in residential school. A $1.9 billion is the plaintiff's estimate to cover the "ten and three." It was stated, "Day students are not eligible for the CEP, but they are eligible for the IAP for serious sexual, physical, and psychological abuse." The average length of attendance at residential school is five to six years. There are seventy-nine thousand survivors with an average expected compensation of twenty-five thousand dollars. The application for the CEP sets out a list of eligible schools. In the event a school is not listed, it can be added through courts' determining using criteria. The survivors have four years to make a claim and longer if exceptional circumstances warrant. There is a draft claim form of two or three pages requiring a survivor's name, residence, group (status Indian, Métis, Inuit), name of school attended, certain identification, for example, birth certificate or other key certified documents, and verification by the Crown. There is a list of schools with their names and location. The time limit of the CEP is four years or beyond as a result of undue hardship or being able to establish exceptional circumstances. There is a two-part appeal procedure with a National Appeal Commission/Council. The plaintiff's lawyer stated, "Any balance left in the fund will be paid out to the two entities mentioned by 2015. The CEP should and will be paid to every eligible Indian student who attended an Indian Residential School. If there is a dispute, the courts will ultimately decide."

The purpose of the IAP is an additional claim of sexual abuse, serious physical abuse, and serious psychological abuse. The application deadline of the IAP is the fifth anniversary of the implementation date. The implementation date is sometime in the spring of 2007 and be in effect up to five years from the implementation date. Resources [will be available] that will deployed that will deal with the claims that will arise. "The Crown is required to process the claims at a minimum rate of twenty five hundred claims per year. Class members will be given up to nine months within an application date. All applications will be processed within the sixth anniversary year of the agreement. There are approximately ten thousand claims in the courts and five thousand in the Alternative Dispute Resolution (ADR) process. Canada is not obligated to provide additional resources for the Agreement except for monies required for the IAP. The purpose of the IAP is for persons currently in the courts and for the IAP to eliminate the barriers that exist to make these types of claims more efficient and streamlined. If class members went to the courts, 80 to 90 percent of the class members would never receive the claims they intended to get." Stated problems of the ADR process are:

- More monies spent in administration than on compensation. Monies spent on the IAP is paid on compensation and not in administration.

- The IAP can't be dismantled by the Crown. The only way it can be dismantled is if the whole nine Courts do not agree with it.

The plaintiff's lawyer said, "There is no cap on the settlement. There is no maximum the Crown will pay. My submission is the settlement is a very fair settlement." The IAP application form is user-friendly, is a simpler form, and is for only persons whose claims can be verified. There is a section that deals with the abuse. The class member is asked to give details of the abuse. The IAP compensation is based an on grid/points system. The more serious acts inflicted on the claimant, the more compensation is payable. The adjudicator determines the maximum to be paid. In the Harms Section, points are awarded for both the harms and the acts. Class action members describe the harms they received. They tell the adjudicators in their own words. They must show they incurred loss of income and loss of opportunity. Members can ask whether they want the adjudicator as male or female. In the compensation rules, the adjudicator applies points for compensation; the more serious the acts, the more compensation. There are aggravating factors, such as loss of opportunity. The maximum in the grid compensation is up to $275,000.

The Truth and Reconciliation Commission will be established to allow class members and others to tell their stories in a culturally appropriate setting and to create an historical and archival record as to what occurred in these schools and why. The Commission will receive $60 million. A healing fund will be set up.

An administration will be set up. An oversight function will be provided by a National Administration Committee of five members to provide feedback to Canada to ensure that the settlement will be implemented according to the agreement.

Legal fees fall into

- Fixed fees for the national consortium of lawyers as named in the agreement
- Per file fee to be paid to independent counsel, to be paid for work in progress up to a maximum of four thousand dollars per file
- Merchant Law Group will be paid as per schedule B of the settlement.

Class members do not pay any legal fee, except under the IAP. Under private contract, Canada will pay legal fees up to 15 percent.

It was stated that pursuant to Draft Orders no. 1, an amendment proceeding be carried to create an amalgam of the various proceedings in the event this court approves the Northwest settlement into the "Fontaine" agreement. Draft Order no. 2 calls for approval and certification that is very detailed and defines three classes. These classes are

- Survivor class—members having attended a residential school up to December 1, 1997, and alive at May 30, 2005 (date in which the federal representative was appointed)
- Family class—parents, siblings of the member based on residence
- Deceased class—deceased before May 30, 2005.

It was stated that if eight of the courts approve the agreement, and one does not, then the settlement does not go through. A signed release extinguishes a class member's claim against the defendant in respect to claims of Indian residential schools and not other matters that arise between Aboriginal people and Canada (and on no other legal right Aboriginal people and Canada may have, for example, treaty or other Aboriginal rights). There could be a dismissal order. There can also be an opt-out order. The deadline is expected to be in 2007 from the date of court approval (one hundred fifty days from that date). The court has the authority to make an order to extend the deadline, for example, the claimant didn't know. A notice provision, assuming settlement approval by nine courts, will instruct how to opt out and how to make a claim, who the claimants can contact and what information they get. Alternatively, how the claimants exclude themselves. After the notice, Canada will report to you, that is, the administrator gives the notice.

The hearing presiding judge raised the point of the five thousand or more class members who may reject the settlement or whether Canada can reject it, but he said, "It should be survivor class members, and we will clarify any circular reasoning over lunch."

After lunch, the court heard that certification, as referred to in paragraph 244 of the factum, gives reasons why certification is necessary. These reasons, as stated, are to facilitate or access justice and the courts. To be certified, an action must have five criteria; identifiable class, residence in a residential school for certain fixed dates, class proceeding is the preferable proceeding, representative plaintiffs were incapable of representing themselves, and the representative plaintiff including the AFN National Chief's representative group who cover the major characteristics the survivors have. Whether, as a group, the class is being treated fairly, "unless the agreement is unreasonable or unfair, it should be approved." The alternatives are individual litigation or no litigation.

It was stated that an example of the test to settlement approval is an Ontario case which has been followed in British Columbia and elsewhere to date. "What is fair and reasonable is an inquiry which is fact driven based on what is before the court." Courts have come up with interrelated factors. One factor is that rights of absent class members are respected. In addition, that success depends on whether the case proceeded on a litigation stream could have succeeded, in terms of settlement monies made. Amount and nature of the discovery on examination depends on the question whether the Crown had sufficient proof. The plaintiff's lawyer spoke of the merits of the settlement and submitted this is a fair settlement, briefly summarized the salient terms and conditions, and said the negotiations were full.

The plaintiff's lawyer referred to the *Dabbs and Parsons* test to support that the settlement is just and fair, and that it should be approved. He said the test also requires the court hear from objectors in assessing those objections from a legal perspective and not from a social or political perspective. Known objectors do not determine the reasonableness or fairness of the settlement. That not enough money is being paid, said the plaintiff's lawyer, is not a valid objection. Claimants can pursue litigation. In other words, acceptance of the settlement is optional for the class member. There are approximately three hundred objections across Canada, less than half of 1 percent. The vast majority of claimants are from Alberta, Saskatchewan, Manitoba, and Ontario. Alberta does not preserve claims at death. The plaintiff's lawyer said best information is five or six class members die every day. For sixteen months, approximately two thousand two hundred who would not have recovered anything will recover under the settlement. The plaintiff's lawyer argued against compensation to family members, but that compensation be paid only to those claimants who resided at schools, and that not compensating claimants whose claims are weak, is not unreasonable.

Regarding legal fees, it was stated that there are over forty different law firms in litigation in the settlement. The hearing presiding judge said, "We are not obligated under statute to approve those fees." The AFN legal counsel replied, "You are obligated under the agreement to approve these fees."

The plaintiff's lawyer then said, "This is a unique settlement in Canada. These Aboriginal groups are very concerned that the legal fees be restricted, that they be capped to forestall collusion and to seek court approval." The judge asked what linkage exists here. He commented, "If we assume there was an agreement by counsel for the settlement, then those counsel agreed separately on the fees. If the class settled under Section 35 in the Alberta Act and legal fees are dealt with in Section 39, I need to know why this court should be doing what it is requested to do." The plaintiff's lawyer replied, "There is nothing uncommon about this settlement in respect to fees." He referred to the *Gariepy* case and said, "In exercising your discretion in determining what is fair and reasonable in payment of legal fees, of what is fair and reasonable in risk undertaken and the success that was achieved, and all the legal work was done in a contingency basis combined with achievement of successful settlement, combines with the reasonableness of getting paid for what you did. The risk goes right up to implementation, for example, five thousand or more survivors objecting to the settlement or a successful appeal. The fees sought are only 5 percent of the CEP and 2 percent of the rest."

The plaintiff's lawyer then referred to legal fees in Ontario. He continued, "Parties agreed to all of the settlement has to be approved. No one agrees with the position of the Merchant Law Group that, unless it gets paid $40 million, then the agreement does not go ahead. They were part of the agreement. In conclusion, the overall reasonableness of the fees, either the fixed amount or the process leading to the fixed amounts, should be approved." He cited support with, "unless premium fee amounts are paid then."

The presiding judge then allowed some Indian residential school former students to make their objections and also opened the court for them to make comments though he commented, later in his closing remarks, that these comments were not the intention of this court.

The first objector, a survivor of the Blood Tribe, said he attended the Standup Day School, which operated from 1952 to 1969. He appealed the federal government's decision not to include the Standup Day School as an eligible school. The plaintiff's lawyer referred to a volume in the court factum that deals with class members that criteria such as residency determine eligible CEP recipients. Day students are not eligible for the CEP. He added, "If you attended residential school and didn't live there, you can make a claim for an incident that occurred at a residential school."

A statement was made by other lawyers of the national consortium of counsel, a group of nineteen members as all supporting this settlement and that, up to this point; they have not been heard from much.

There were three test case objectors. The first objector said he has a signed affidavit stating he attended St. Bruno's Residential School situated on the south shore of Lesser Slave Lake. He said he "remembers public humiliating discipline" when he ran away from school. He recalled lack of proper care and education and serious sexual abuse of which effects led to alcoholism. He stated his support for the settlement. The second test case objector attended residential school from 1959 to 1969 and said she incurred physical abuse. The third test case objector said she attended the Holy Angels School in Fort Chipewyan from 1950 to 1959.

The next objector was a family class representative of the Mikisew Cree First Nation who said she did not attend residential school, but that her mother and father had attended. She said her mother suffered effects of attendance that led to alcoholism and being in foster homes in Alberta. She read from an affidavit of her mother relating the effects of residential school, such as lack of parental communication, emotional support, and parental teaching. She thought the settlement is a fair settlement.

Court heard statistics of the mortality rate and the citing of an affidavit of Richard Curtis in volume 5 of the joint motion materials. Specifically referred to was an exhibit report of Singer and Associates which sets out estimates of mortality. In 2001, there were 83,895 survivors. In 2005, there were 80,012. In 2006, there were 79,994. One thousand persons die per year, or three or four dying per day. It was stated that this indicates the urgency of resolving this issue through this settlement.

On October 13, the lawyer for the Crown referred to a certain judge about legal fees. He said that the judge had said the fees are fair and reasonable and was prepared to approve the settlement. The Crown lawyer reasserted that the whole settlement agreement must be approved. There was discussion of potential abuses, the rationale for paying class counsel fees and legal process fees, and that the defendant (the Crown) is paying $2 billion in fees. The hearing presiding judge said there is potential for mischief in the current arrangement.

The AFN counsel said, "Your Honor, my law firm does not stand to benefit from the legal fees under the fee approval being sought for your approval." He gave a brief background of the genesis of the settlement. He said, "Phil Fontaine, in 1990, was the first person to bring into the public view the legacy of the Indian residential schools and of painful and personal disclosure of his attendance at residential school. In 1998, there were political, individual, and class proceedings. In 2004, the AFN held a conference in Ottawa to deal with the dispute resolution process, and a report was made of the shortcomings of the ADR. In May 2005, the agreement was developed with the appointment of the federal representative Mr. Justice Iaccobucci, a common payment to address the issue of residential school, and a restriction on legal fees. On legal fees, the objective of the national chief and the AFN is on the common payout to survivors, and legal fees. Those fees should not be paid unless they are verifiable and that all survivors were to get the CEP without the survivors paying the legal fees. That is, that the CEP should not be clawed back. Four criteria determine that the fees are fair and reasonable."

The AFN counsel indirectly accused the Merchant Law Group and the federal lawyer as being conflicted in this instance, "as they are interested in ensuring filling their pocket. If the settlement is not approved, individual litigation will occur and take up to decades to settle. The approval of nine courts across Canada will ensure supervision. There are known conditions, deadlines, court supervision of the CEP and the IAP, and have unlimited resources to handle the settlement." The presiding judge remarked, "Bearing in mind, the courts do not give political and social relief." The AFN counsel continued, "On behalf of the national chief, this is the best deal possible. I am asking you, do not acquiesce to the invitation to tinker. I ask you to approve the deal as presented."

Counsel for the attorney general of Canada said, "The attorney general of Canada fully supports the agreement. The agreement seeks a comprehensive resolution of the legality [?] of the Indian residential school settlement.

Canada's view is the benefits offered are fair. We urge this court to approve this settlement as presented to you. I have been to seven jurisdictions and have heard dozens and dozens of objections." She referred to an affidavit of the federal representative to the settlement agreement. She submitted, "The benefits of the settlement go far in achieving fairness." She referred to legal fees and pleaded for the courts for supervision. The presiding judge asked, "Where does Section 39 come in?"

The counsel for the attorney general of Canada (AGC) referred to two affidavits, one sworn September 29 that "addressed, to a certain extent, how Canada will implement and meet its commitments under the settlement agreement." The first affidavit is from the supervisor of operations, Indian Residential Schools Resolution Canada (IRSRC), that referred to ADR hearings that were conducted at two and a half hearings per day. At this rate, it was found that three thousand one hundred hearings per year are needed to complete all the hearings. The AGC counsel said that Service Canada has 320 offices across Canada with twenty thousand staff. Service Canada is the department that will issue the CEP after verification of former students' application.

The second affidavit concerns the retrieval of Indian residential school records. There is some difficulty in the retrieval of records in order to verify the application. There is perception by IRS claimants that Canada is not making sufficient efforts to retrieve records. Four hundred eighty advance payments have not been paid due to absence of records. In Alberta, 2,309 claims of the eight-thousand-dollar advance payment have been made—165 have been rejected; 1,531 have been processed; 121 have been rejected due to lack of records. IRSRC had 75 percent of the records to verify the claims and intends to have 90 percent of the records verified.

The next presenter was the legal counsel for the General Synod of the Anglican Church of Canada; the Presbyterian Church in Canada; and The United Church in Canada that, he said, are referred to as the "Protestant churches." The counsel continued, "The Protestant churches submit the agreement is a fair and just settlement for the resolution of the legacy of Indian residential schools and urge approval. The first benefit is that class members will be paid and the IAP without adjudication of any liability awarded. Bilateral agreements were made that emphasize healing and rehabilitative efforts. The bilateral agreements require the churches [contribute] $23 million to $24 million toward payment of the claim and payment of grants and in kind for healing and reconciliation. The second benefit is that the time and expense saved by the Protestant churches, once the settlement is approved, [and] will allow the churches to participate in and fund healing and reconciliation programs. The Protestant churches are committed to participate and to provide documents to make the Truth and Reconciliation process work."

The next presenter was the legal counsel for the Catholic entities. He said, "I am counsel for the forty-nine Catholic corporations that have entered into a bilateral agreement with the Government of Canada. All forty-nine of the Catholic entities support the settlement agreement. The forty-nine Catholic corporations include nine Catholic corporations in Alberta." The counsel said that, among the elements of the agreement, $25 million will be made in kind to the survivors, families, friends, and their communities for healing, commemoration, and reconciliation. The counsel said, "The entities have agreed to open their archives to the Truth and Reconciliation Commission including records, photos, and other materials. The entities agreed to participate in commemoration events. The settlement is fair, reasonable, and comprehensive. Under the agreement, the former ADR where a survivor received only 70 percent of the settlement, Canada will top off the other ... It's time to put the legacy of Indian residential schools to bed."

As allowed by the presiding judge, objections by IRS former students continued. The first objector referred to the settlement made a year ago, about the 70 percent payment by the government and 30 percent from the Anglican Church of Canada, and asked, "Why did the government only pay me 70 percent when I was 100 percent abused? Why did the church only pay 30 percent when I was 100 percent abused?" She referred to a recent *McLean's* magazine article on the Merchant Law Group. The second objector was a daughter of a survivor who said she represented her seventy-five-year-old mother who is in a seniors' home. The daughter said the CEP covers too many criteria. She said her mother told her there was abuse, slave labor, lack of time for school, serious physical abuse, and time spent cleaning and cooking. She said this contributed to her mother's low self esteem and her showing of lack of care to her children.

The third objector was another former student who stated that he attended Crowfoot School and Ermineskin School in Hobbema. He said he was not in favor of this whole settlement nor of the payment to the Merchant Law Group. He continued, "I am not in favor of the IAP because people in the Reserve have not been consulted. Who authorized these people who sit at the negotiation to represent the survivors? Was it supported by the chiefs of Canada? There was no communication. There was no report by Iaccobucci."

The former student thought that "We should have a better representative for our survivors."

The fourth objector was another male survivor who said that payment of the "ten and three" was a bribe and mentioned abuse that occurred at residential schools.

The fifth objector was a partner for a former student from the Siksika Nation who said that survivors are affected by the Merchant Law Group and other lawyers in southern Alberta. She read a letter. She said the Merchant Law Group, seven or eight years ago, approached survivors with a request for their names and addresses. These survivors are still waiting for their claims to be advanced. She said, "I am very hurt by actions and correspondence from the Merchant Law Group. I find it reprehensible that the MLG will be getting $40 million. They have done little to advance our claims. We want to be released from MLG and other lawyers who will also be getting $40 million. Eligibility for compensation should be moved back to 1998–1999."

I was the sixth partial objector. I read out a three-page letter dated August 16, 2006, with an attached letter. I stated that the three thousand dollars per year payment in the CEP should continue to be paid to former students due to the lack of meaningful education and post–school employment skills and readiness.

The seventh objector was from Samson Cree Nation. He asked whether the CEP and IAP can both be claimed. He referred to the claims process in Alberta, consultation, and legal fees. He asserted that claims must [be dealt] with fairly. He said, "Every person who I dealt with has a story of abuse." He was concerned that the IAP settlement of twenty five hundred claims per year out of eighty thousand survivors will take about forty years to settle.

The eighth objector was also from Samson Cree Nation. He said he attended Ermineskin Residential School. He said the Aboriginal Healing Foundation (AHF) was given money several years ago that didn't reach the survivors. He said, "In my opinion, it was squandered." The AHF will be getting new monies under the settlement, but the AHF will not be funding any new initiatives. He continued, "This is hush money for the genocide and abuse. There was outright murder at these schools. No one is addressing that."

The ninth objector was a male elder who said, "As a personal victim, I am affronted that lawyers and others are saying this is the best deal." He referred to a certain law group and the $1.9 million for the Common Experience payment. He continued, "I have not received a single penny in four years.

The important thing is for me to heal for the abuses we suffered." The elder recalled the strapping he received and cited personal sexual abuse. He said, "Nothing in this world can ever bring back what I lost when I was in residential school. We are the people that suffered that have yet to heal. I have to relive all the anger and the hate. What I lost is priceless, the loss of contact from my parents, the culture I lost. Today, I don't practice my culture. I don't know all that. This money I'm going to get means nothing to me. I wish everything is all over. They can keep the money. I want to heal."

The tenth objector was a female survivor who said she is a nonstatus Indian. She referred to a letter dated August 2, 2006, that said no records of her attendance were found.

The eleventh objector was another female who was the daughter of a male former student now deceased. She said people in the settlement process are not being involved. She said her father was a class member in residential school who recalled his woundedness. She objected to the clause that addresses the families. She said, "My dad's sorrows and woundedness are mine. He has no avenue for satisfaction."

The twelfth objector was a former student of the Ermineskin School for 1966–1974. She said she experienced emotional, psychological, and sexual abuse. She recalled, "If you excelled in boarding school, you were beaten down. Woundedness carries for a lifetime. Fear of darkness still lives with me. There is no healing in the penitentiary system. Counsels represent the survivors of the Indian residential schools. I've never received any correspondence from the Merchant Law Group. There is disconnection of the family unit. Residential school has dispossessed my people because they removed the children from the elders. That is genocide. That is the death of societies. Our women took care of the children and the camp. Our men went out to hunt to feed the people and to protect the camp. Our men have been emasculated. They are disempowered in the streets and in the federal government system. Is it just? Is it fair? Do you have all the facts? Does the beneficiary receive healing? Who benefits?"

The thirteenth objector was a sibling and daughter from Frog Lake First Nation who said she was advocating for her sisters and parents. She referred to the Japanese victims of war who were compensated and asked, "When are we going to be compensated? You are opening the wounds, the hurt. When is it going to end?"

The fourteenth objector was a former student who said, "At six years old, the priest told my grandparents I had to go to residential school, or my family allowance was going to be taken away. I experienced physical and sexual abuse. No amount of money can replace what I lost, nor is going to ease the pain. I can't sleep at night. The Merchant Law Group didn't do anything for me. From 1998 to about a year ago, I got only a handful of letters, some saying I owe them money. Am I just a number? What about my family? I really wish they would quit using our hurts to get their money. Because of the sexual abuse, I could not trust."

The fifteenth objector was from Northern Alberta who said, "There has been very little communication on this process. This court hearing process, because of cultural differences, is very intimidating and also because of the residential school. We see people in the community living in third-world conditions. The survivors have nothing. They want something before they die."

The hearing presiding judge announced that the transcript of this hearing will be available next week by asking for it at the clerk's office downstairs.

The sixteenth objector was from Saddle Lake. She said she was a direct descendant of Chief Blue Quill whose name is used in Blue Quills Indian Residential School. She said she was sure that Chief Blue Quill intended that his descendants receive a good education. She was objecting that, under the settlement, no compensation was being made for the deceased, specifically that there is no compensation for her mother, grandparents, siblings, aunties with names Norris, Veronica, Theresa, Leo, Mary, Eva, John, William, and Clara. She requested that these names be recorded, and they are eligible for compensation.

The seventeenth speaker said he spent over twelve years in Ermineskin Residential School in Hobbema. He recalled he was three and a half to four years old, but he said, "From there, I have no memory until I was in grade 5. I suffered abuses, psychological, physical, emotional, and spiritual. I lived there from 1969 or 1970 and from thereon, moved straight to the jail system. I was given a number, 93, and was given another number in the penal system. I was comfortable there. I was full of hatred because of the treatment I received. I had no sense of identity for six years I was inside. I was so antisocial. I even hated my own kind, my father and my stepmother. It is difficult to heal. It's not my fault I am a criminal because I was taught to fight in residential school. I finally tried to realize at about [age] thirty-one or thirty-three what life was all about and to try to forgive people."

The eighteenth speaker was from Driftpile First Nation. He said he attended St. Bruno Residential School at Joussard, Alberta. He said, "I spoke only Cree. I was beaten by the nuns, priests for speaking the devil's tongue. I got beaten up for a whole year for speaking my language. I was physically, mentally, sexually abused. I couldn't understand why this nun would beat the crap out of me and then take me to her room at night. I only thought maybe she loves me. But then, the whole thing would begin again the next day. Then two nuns finally left me alone. But then I had to face the boys. I learned to be tough. The nuns and priests had so much control over us that nobody ever said anything. We don't need lawyers. Just split the money down the middle."

The nineteenth speaker was from the Blood Reserve who said he is a survivor of St. Paul's Anglican Church Indian Residential School. He recalled being abused physically, mentally, psychologically, and sexually. He said he works now as a Blood Reserve Indian Residential School liaison officer. He said there is lack of communication regarding this settlement. He said 2003 statistics show that millions of dollars was spent on administration, and there needs to be better administration by lawyers. He mentioned development of rules of conduct by lawyers is needed. He urged that Indian Residential Schools Resolution Canada should have people who can speak the language. He asked, "How does the Alternative Dispute Resolution going to be worked in the Independent Assessment Process? Is it going to end?"

The twentieth speaker was from Saddle Lake who spoke on behalf of her husband who was unable to travel as he was eighty-nine years old and is a World War II veteran who served in several countries in Europe. She said, "We both made application for an advance. They were unable to find his records. I am also a survivor. I'm asking the court if there is a way find his record."

The twenty-first speaker was from the Sarcee Reserve. She said, "I am a survivor. I attended residential school from six years to seventeen years old. I suffered in physical beating."

A lawyer recommended that clients who have left the Merchant Law Group "be allowed to leave debt free. The Merchant Group will be getting $40 million, and that should be enough. What is the Merchant Law Group getting paid for? If it's work on the CEP, it would be a very small amount. Also for the consortium, they are getting paid $40 million." The lawyer pleaded, "For Mr. Littlelight and for the hundreds of other survivors that have received letters saying they owe Merchant and other lawyers [should] be let go."

The AFN counsel said, "When the settlement is approved, all the outstanding work in progress, the work in progress, will be paid."

A lawyer from the audience asked, "Will the claimants be given an opportunity to verify the payments of legal fees?"

The presiding judge replied, "No."

AFN counsel said, "The AFN and the national chief have to ensure that payment of legal fees will be verified."

Some of the lawyers that were present discussed the issue of the lack of former students' records and the verification of the advance payment. It was said that as of June 2007, ninety percent of the claims will have been verified and that "if an individual is denied the advance payment, they are still in a position to apply for the CEP."

The AFN counsel spoke of the tension from the objectors, which is part of the negotiation of the settlement. He said, "The AFN is the only national body. It is the 613 chiefs who have elected Phil Fontaine and by virtue of a number of resolutions passed by the assembly by consensus, beginning in 1990 and coupled with that, that Phil Fontaine was himself a survivor. The AFN is committed to the settlement agreement and has to live within the budget. It has conducted national and community meetings plus a database of thirty-five thousand names and more by the day. There has been ground level input. It doesn't mean every individual has been consulted. There will be a notice program. It will be very extensive and culturally sensitive notice. The Indian Residential Schools Resolution Canada also funds communication programs."

The lawyers continued discussing the verification of legal fees that no lawyer is paid twice for the same work and that other claims resulting from residential school can be applied for under the Independent Assessment Program.

The above report is not complete. It is intended to partially paraphrase some of the proceedings and to show some of the input and responses of speakers, presenters, and objectors of the Indian Residential Schools Settlement Agreement. The implications and impacts for the short and long term of the residential school experience are complex and intertwined. There are some elements of the settlement agreement, such as whether day school students are eligible for benefits that need clarification. First Nations or their agencies will need human resources to assist the residential school former students and their families in providing accurate and timely information and form filling when the settlement agreement is approved by all the nine court jurisdictions.

APPENDIX O

FIRST NATIONS CONFEDERACY OF CULTURAL EDUCATION CENTERS ANNUAL GENERAL ASSEMBLY, OCTOBER 20–21, 2006—RADISSON HOTEL, WINNIPEG, MANITOBA—A REPORT

COUNCILOR ERIC J. LARGE

On day 1, October 20, Carol Beaulieu made opening remarks on behalf of the Manitoba Cultural Centers, and Gilbert Whiteduck, President, made remarks on behalf of the First Nations Confederacy Cultural Education Centres (FNCCEC). Whiteduck said there is increased role of elders in the cultural centers. He said this year is his last year as president. He said, "We're in a critical stage. It cannot be another task force but action in united voices. We need talk about the present and the future for our youth. Without that, no wonder we are in trouble today." Claudette Commanda, the national coordinator of the FNCCEC provided an introduction to the Annual General Assembly. She thanked the Manitoba Cultural Education Centers for hosting this year's AGA on a short notice. She also thanked the commitment of Gilbert Whiteduck and the support he gave to her and her staff.

Chief Morris Shannacappo, of Rolling River First Nation and the Chair of the AGA, welcomed delegates to the Treaty No. 1 territory. He announced that Robert's Rules of Order will be followed and that each speaker will be allowed a time limit of ten minutes. He requested if there were any changes to the agenda, such as the election for the new president of the FNCCEC. Delegates requested meeting in caucus by regions. A suggestion by one delegate was that one person is selected for president by consensus not elected, as we need to work together. I suggested a rotating spokesperson be appointed by delegates from the east, south, west, and north. A different spokesperson would occupy the presidency each term. Claudette Commanda reminded the delegates that we are incorporated, have a charter and bylaws that determines an election process. Rachel Mitchell was finally appointed as the electoral officer with volunteers coming forward to form the resolutions committee. The minutes of the 2005 AGA and the Audit Report 2006 by

KPGM were reviewed and adopted. I moved that KPGM be appointed for 2007 which motion was adopted unanimously.

The first speaker was Allan Clark, Director General, Canadian Heritage, Aboriginal Affairs Branch, who said, "Canadian Heritage is kind of a department of culture to some extent. [It deals in] official languages, sports, program support, and friendship centers. There is a treaty based language policy, for example, the Aboriginal Languages Initiative (ALI). There is support for Aboriginal specific that is inclusive of First Nations, Métis, and Inuit. We support the National Gallery and have an Aboriginal representative in the Canada Council. Language and culture is important to identity, well-being, and the treaty relationship. There is a strong correlation between revitalization and retention of culture and language. The language program of Canadian Heritage is the Aboriginal Languages Initiative. A $5 million provides support for First Nations languages in Canada. As you are aware, very small amounts goes to communities to build their language programs. The focus is on administration. The ALI is trying to improve funding that makes sense, using money on projects and the results of the program, federal government concerns on issues of accountability, accepting and approving applications. It is more focused on the people communicating across Canada and the staff. The turnaround of funding, on average, is three months. Last year, we renewed ALI for one more year. The Minister of Heritage Canada is Bev Oda. We, Heritage Canada, met with the Confederacy and other organizations on how a new language program [can] look like and on how the money can be allocated. This requires a political decision. Canada has a role and duty in supporting, but it's First Nations that [must commit]. ALI is going to be community driven. We're looking for more funding, better access to funding, and better and more equitable access to funding. [In looking] at regional and national projects, we heard there is an appetite for best practices. We have to accommodate a long-range strategy. It is also a broad-based issue, [affecting] peoples' lives in areas such as education and early childhood development. We have communicated with the Chiefs Committee on Languages of the AFN and the FNCCEC in the last year. We've moved ALI and the reporting. These are things we are changing."

Questions and comments from delegates were the following:

- What happened to the Regional Language funding and also the Critical and Endangered Languages initiative? Will it go to the national organization?

- Request for support for permanent funding to support language programs as well as protecting early language learning along with $300–$400 million to support our language initiative programs. The French language is given that much permanent funding.

Mr. Clark's reply was "We have been meeting for AFN for distribution of the Critical Language Funding."

I asked, "Will our program funding be decreased if we sell pens, caps, etc. to show where our museum is located?"

Mr. Clark: "No. The $8.5 to $8.7 million is for the Cultural Education Centers Program. I cannot change the guidelines for museums."

I noted that of the $8.5 million, $4.5 million goes to the FNCCEC for distribution to cultural education centers, and $4.2 goes direct to other cultural education centers.

Gloria Wells of the Alberta Caucus said that for 2008 access to Education Policy Program is to go the AFN through Canadian Heritage. "Alberta wants to remain independent."

Delegates from Alberta and Saskatchewan then discussed the process of choosing potential candidates for the national presidency. Delegates said they didn't know who is all running, what the role of president is, and whether the position is full time or not. I suggested that the potential candidate be chosen by consensus of the Alberta and Saskatchewan caucus. Alberta and Saskatchewan were ready to nominate me. However, after reconsideration, the caucuses asked Gilbert Whiteduck to stay another year due to the transition in cultural education center funding and to retain stability. Whiteduck agreed to remain for another year as president on the condition he wants support like ideas and phoning him, saying, "Look, here's what I've done in this area regarding language and culture."

Back in the plenary session, Claudette Commanda, reminded the delegates that "the Charter states that the candidate for president must be directly involved in the cultural center in the community level."

The electoral officer, Rachel Mitchell, called for nominations. Gilbert Whiteduck was nominated by Barry Ahenakew of Atahkakoop. Whiteduck declined. Chief Keith Mathew of the Thompson Band, BC, was nominated and accepted by acclamation to be the president of the FNCCEC.

On day 2, October 21, Chief Tyrone McNeil of Sto:lo First Nation, BC, delivered a message from Chief Cranmer who sits on the AFN Chiefs Committee on Languages and who represented National Chief Phil Fontaine.

Chief McNeil said, "The AFN is trying to engage Canadian Heritage in a collaborative approach for a one-hundred-sixty-million-dollar funding initiative. The ALI was extended to 2006–07. In 2005, the AFN devolved administration of ALI. Six regions received direct funding, and four regions remained with the existing process. For 2006–07, we are working on direct funding. Research and development consists of a proposed First Nation Languages Act and research. In 2006–07, the AFN initiated a National First Nations Language Initiative and requested a funding contribution from Canadian Heritage. The Chiefs Committee on Languages will coordinate this. A national research plan will consist of the collection of baseline data. A national clearinghouse online will assist individuals and communities in lifelong learning of languages. There will be a conference in January 2007. There is a proposed First Nations Special Projects Fund that will be national in scope. The short term goal of the AFN is to access commitment of funding for communities and First Nations control of programs and funds." I asked for clarification of the funding mandate and flow of funding to the community where the preservation of language and culture are needed rather than spent on administrative levels with layers of approval.

It was announced there will a "Preserving Aboriginal Heritage: Technical and Traditional Approaches" Conference at the National Archives and Library in Ottawa September 24–28, 2007 to help people preserve their heritage and objects.

Regional cultural education centers reports were presented. The Northwest Territories representative reported that there was a Dene National Conference in Yellowknife. A Dene elders' "Restoring Balance" project that was funded by the Aboriginal Healing Foundation was held and whose focus was on the residential school impact. A report was produced. There was also a "Dene as a Second Language" project for adults, which was successful so that schools are now using the project. The Arctic Health Research Network looks into traditional and Western health. There are two cultural awareness workshops. One is for NWT medical professionals. The AGA will be held at the end of October 2006. There was a twentieth anniversary celebration at the end of July 2006. There were four videos produced on moose hair tufting, spruce basket making, and two others. It is hoped that a traditional knowledge conference for 2007 will be sponsored.

Becky Paul of Chilliwack made the BC regional report. She said there are eighteen cultural centers in BC. Their concern is lack of funding. There is an annual elders' gathering. She said, "There is concern that the cultural centers in BC are becoming very insignificant to our leadership. We are hoping to meet with provincial leaders of political organizations, planning to get together in November 2006. We want to organize as a more formal provincial organization to get more representation in the BC Chiefs' Summit. We are concerned about INAC's education policy. Most of the cultural education centers are still involved in language and culture. We are concerned that INAC requires BCRs [Band Council Resolutions] of support, that funding application should be based on a nonprofit society's standing."

Gloria Wells, the Alberta representative, said Alberta representatives met twice with Canadian Heritage regarding the Task Force on Culture and Language. The Alberta delegation had four suggestions:

- That there should be one layer of administration
- Concern that the role of the FNCCEC has been diminished
- Misrepresentation resulting in organizations having many mandates but no one specific to preservation of culture and language
- Community-based projects, administrative model inefficiency of networking, and ensuring funds reach communities.

[The Alberta delegation raised the issue of improvements, requested for a meeting and proposed an MOU [Memorandum of Understanding] with the new AFN Regional Chief, Wilton Littlechild. We said we wanted regional status of the nine Alberta cultural education centers.

The representative for Manitoba said there are fourteen centers in Manitoba. The representative reported that Norway House Cree held a youth camp and that the Rolling River Education Program held a homecoming in 2006 and is working on a Cree dictionary. The Winnipeg Cultural Education Centre is working on a library, new software, videotapes, books, DVDs, etc. Though cultural centers are participating in consultation workshops, they are feeling neglected.

A representative from the Akwesasne Mohawk Nation made the Ontario report. She reported that there are nine cultural education centers in Ontario. She stressed the need for more communication and regional strategies that focus on cultural and language events. The cultural centers support developing curricula for classrooms and conducting interviews with elders. They also see the need for ongoing advocacy, working to deal with stereotypes and improving race relations. Language training also needs to be encouraged.

The Quebec representative was Stephen Bonspille, as the outgoing representative, and Donna Goodleaf, as the new representative. They reported that the newest program developed and referred to as the "New Rosetta Stone" is used in classes in their communities. The language program is in its fifth year. Their cultural education center asked for core funding for an immersion program that would involve bringing in indigenous and Haudenasaunee speakers in workshops and speaker events. They produced two TV shows and one children's puppet show for children and schools. They hire students coming out of adult education programs to be hosts for language conferences as one effort in language preservation and informing people about where they are going. They are enhancing and teaching who they are as Haudenasaunee people. There are productions on radio and in newsprint as well as DVD. Kanestake is another community that voiced urgency in a search for funding for projects to support language and culture. The representative from Kahnawake voiced support for a language law is in place and that elders have a central role in First Nation language development. The coordinator of the Kitiganzibi Centre said his center offered tourism/cultural workshops, is always seeking funding, and is trying to establish new programs. An Innu elder from the Innu Cultural Education Institute said they got little funding and face much accountability from government. He said they use festivals and radio to transmit language and said they are about to develop a high school curriculum in their language.

The representative from New Brunswick reported that there are no cultural centers there, but there are programs. There is lack of funding. They question the Aboriginal Languages Initiative coming in.

The representative from Prince Edward Island said there are languages classes in schools. They have seven people that speak Micmac who have a working relationship with Parks Canada. The work has a video and interpretation on a Micmac cultural center. They also have workshops for children involving the Department of Fisheries and Oceans, Education, INAC, and other different capacities of government. There are basket demonstrations by an elder. The center also works with tiny tots through singing and dances. There are interpretive trails of ancestral homeland.

The representative from Nova Scotia reported that there are Treaty Days celebrations involving the Micmac and the federal and provincial governments. They are working with Algonquin University in an archival program for a degree. The Cape Breton University has a cultural program. From May to October, ships come into port, and the Micmac are putting together an exhibit and gift shop. The Micmac Tourism Committee is working a strategy for tourism. The Atlantic Policy Congress of Chiefs is considering a program by residential school survivors for an archives and museum. The Membertou Cultural Heritage Centre is working on a proposal by a committee for workshops on how to market and package. They are working with a Parks Canada interpreter.

The Yukon representative reported that the Tlingit Council has a language program in a heritage center. He reported they have organized a language symposium with two other Tlingit communities, identified new initiatives such as immersion camps for elders, and hope to organize camps that are more seasonal. He said there is need for less spoken English in their training. The new direction is that they just hired a full-time language instructor in their day care.

The representative from Saskatchewan reported that there are a number of things they are focusing on. They are bringing together elders and observers in the Cree language, and *oskapewsak*. There are language groups, Swampy, Woodland, and Plains Cree, as well as Saulteaux, Denesuline, Dakota, Nakota, and Lakota. The representative reported there is desire for cultural and language retention that is supported by strategy. There is recognition for the strengthening of linkage to community and focus on actions targeting language retention. There are plans for a language conference on November 22, 23, and 24, 2006. There is concern on how to ensure revitalization of language in our community. They are working with youth who do not really identify with their own culture.

The representative said, "We need to find a way for them to identify with their own culture through the use of elders on how we can reach the youth." They have a "Keeping House Project" for the past thirteen to fourteen years or more. They are considering multimillion-dollar projects that require partnership with one other community. They are working on how to revitalize language and culture with youth, parents, and adults. They see a gap there and are seeking ideas on how [language] immersion is working. The representative said, "We want to work more closely with political leaders in the eight linguistic groups, where their priorities are, and getting their support for accessing funding. We are developing capacity in all areas, finance, human, and infrastructure, from a holistic perspective. We [are concerned for the] protection of sacred areas and protection of sites so there is more respect and protocol is ensured. We are going to endeavor to get our resources and materials more accessible through technology to attract and perhaps engage youth, for example, in modules with games, teaching through history and culture as support for language and cultural retention, and looking at basics as to where we come from rather than from the Eurocentric perspective."

Angie Bruce, development manager from the Aboriginal Healing Foundation (AHF), made a report. She said the AHF began in 1998. She said the AHF cannot fund direct language programs, but funding can be used for healing. The AHF has funded 1,300 projects in the last seven years. A $125 million is to be allocated to the AHF under the Residential School Settlement. There is a six-month waiting period in the Common Experience Payment. She said there is probably another seven to eight months before the $125 million becomes available. The AHF program took about ten years to be developed. The $125 million will best be spent on existing AHF programs that focus on direct healing for survivors, one-on-one healing circles, and with elders and traditional counselors.

Six resolutions were to be dealt with by the delegates. However, I had to leave, so I could catch my scheduled flight back to Edmonton, Alberta.

APPENDIX P

UNITED NATIONS EXPERT SEMINAR ON TREATIES, AGREEMENTS, AND OTHER CONSTRUCTIVE ARRANGEMENTS BETWEEN STATES AND INDIGENOUS PEOPLES—HOBBEMA, ALBERTA, NOVEMBER 14–17, 2006—A PARTIAL REPORT

COUNCILOR ERIC J. LARGE

I attended the above seminar on Tuesday, November 14 and Wednesday, November 15, 2006. Elder Norman Yellowbird of Samson Cree Nation said the invocation. The welcome was said by Chief Victor Buffalo of Samson Cree Nation. Chief Carl Rabbit of Montana Cree Nation welcomed delegates as well as Acting Chief Rick Lightning on behalf of the Ermineskin Cree Nation.

The international delegates introduced themselves. They were from Guatemala; Oscar Hodgeson, Moskito from Moskitia, Nicaragua; Kuna Nation, Panama; Bill Means, Oglala Lakota, South Dakota; Andrea Carmen, Yaqui Indian Nation and Executive Director of the International Indian Treaty Council (IITC), and Francisco Cali; Southwest Africa; Rikitangi Gage and two others from Aotearoa, NZ; Charmaine White Face, Clifford White Eyes and two other delegates from the Tetuwan Oyate (Great Sioux Nation). *Tetuwan* means "dweller of the plain," the Buffalo People.

The representative of the United Nations High Commission for Human Rights read a three-page opening statement. She extended a welcome to the Second Expert Seminar on Treaties to the representatives of governments, the Government of Canada, indigenous representatives and elders, treaty experts, participants from nongovernmental organizations and academic institutions, and the people present. She said the High Commission Office organized a First Expert Seminar on Treaties, agreements, and constructive arrangements in Geneva in December 2003. She said the purpose of the seminar "was to provide an opportunity to consider the study of this theme of the Special Rapporteur of the Sub commission on the Promotion and Protection of Human Rights Professor Alfonso Martinez, and in particular the studies, conclusions, and recommendations. I would like to remind all of us of results of that meeting, as I believe we should, at this seminar, build on the work that was done at that time. The 2003 seminar considered the impact of the legacy of historical treaties and looked at how treaties, agreements, and other constructive arrangements can play a role in reconciling indigenous peoples and States.... There is space in the agenda for a discussion on the international and regional context and, in particular, the role of the Declaration on the Rights of Indigenous Peoples, adopted by the Human Rights Council in June this year and currently before the General Assembly, and human rights treaty bodies and regional human rights mechanisms. You will know that a preparatory meeting on indigenous nations' treaties was just concluded yesterday. The preparatory meeting covered a number of important themes, including some to be discussed during the United Nations seminar in the next four days."

Continuing, the UN representative said, "What I wanted to do is underline the importance of the Declaration and acknowledge the efforts made by indigenous representatives coming from this community who have been active negotiators on your behalf over a good many years." The representative then declared open the UN Expert Seminar and invited the participants to nominate a chairperson/rapporteur.

Sharon Venne was nominated by William Means to chair the seminar. The agenda was duly adopted. Miguel Alfonso Martinez, UN Special Rapporteur, made introductory remarks. He said, in part, "Today is a special day. Why is it? In 1999 was the submitting of the completion of the Treaty Study to the Working Group on Indigenous Populations and to the UN Sub Commission. My study is the result of a collective contribution of many people, especially indigenous people, and a number of governments including the Government of Canada. The submission of my final report was not the end of the learning and understanding of treaty, but to have gatherings and seminars such as this one. We have unique opportunity to follow up first on the study, and, second on the study of 2003 of the importance of treaties of indigenous peoples to consider the best way to study and advance treaties. Treaties have an intrinsic value and the treaty-making process. Negotiations start by recognizing. This is an opportunity to stress and understand better why indigenous people have been successful. You have a great responsibility now how to continue to advance the task of Martinez Cobo in the 1980s, and all those who have an understanding of these rights will have a place along with the indigenous peoples." Martinez acknowledged the seminar as first of its kind in indigenous lands.

Wilton Littlechild then presented agenda Item 1, Recommendations of the Expert Seminar on Treaties, agreements, and other constructive arrangements. He referred to an eleven-page document titled E/CN.4/2004/111 dated January 2004. This document, on page 2, lists six conclusions of experts and fifteen recommendations: two by governments; one by the Commission on Human Rights; seven by Working Groups, treaty bodies, and special procedures; three by UN bodies and specialized agencies; and two by the Office of the High Commissioner on Human Rights. The document notes that this Seminar on Treaties, agreements, and other constructive arrangements between States and indigenous peoples is "to explore ways and means to follow up on the recommendations included in the final report of the Special Rapporteur, Mr. Miguel Alfonso Martinez (E/CN.4/Sub.2/1999/20)."

A three-page statement on behalf of the Government of Canada was made by Ms. Victoria De LaRonde, Director, Treaty Policy Directorate, Indian and Northern Affairs Canada, Ottawa. She said Canada recognizes seventy treaties signed between 1701 and 1923. She said, "Treaties we continue to make, treaties are important Canada believes, for two very important reasons. One, they are recognized in our Constitution. Two, they are a significant part of what Canada is today. It is important we keep alive the relationship formed by treaties. In any relationship, there are different perspectives. Canada has been working to reconcile perspective on interpretation of the treaties. [In] the past ten years, we have established treaty tables. A Treaty Commission was established in Saskatchewan and now in Manitoba. Canada hopes to set up other Treaty Commissions across the country. In 2005, Canada and Treaty 9 commemorated the one hundredth anniversary of that treaty. Year 2006 commemorated the signing of Treaty 10. Treaties are part of the whole curriculum in the classroom. In 880 schools, thirty-five hundred teachers have been taught how to teach on treaties. In 2005, Canada agreed with Treaty Nations in Saskatchewan to start a study on treaty implementation. Canada recognizes the basis of very strong partnership on treaty for today and into the future." In regard to the UN Declaration on the Rights of Indigenous Peoples, Ms. De LaRonde said that the Declaration's treaty provisions were recognized as important by Canada but she said "however, especially within the Canadian context, the Declaration's provisions on lands, territories, and resources are broad, unclear, and capable of a wide variety of interpretations. These provisions could also hinder our land claims processes in Canada, whereby Aboriginal land and resource rights are premised on balancing the rights of Aboriginal peoples with those of other Canadians, within the Canadian Constitutional framework."

There was discussion and input by the treaty experts. Mr. Martinez said, in reference to Document III [E/CN.4/2004] that he will limit his comments in reference to Canada's input. He said his recommendations "should be understood in the context of the entire treaty study, its conclusions and recommendations." He commented on paragraph 7 and paragraph 9, in the first and second section, regarding the "establishment of an effective mechanism for conflict resolution, that prevention and conflict resolution should be part of the recommendation of this Seminar. The important thing is the effectiveness or potential effectiveness for prevention and conflict resolution depends on the participation of indigenous peoples, either a permanent forum like the Waitangi Tribunal or some commonly agreed mechanism to be abided by all the parties concerned."

Martinez said the word "effectiveness" is the problem because it depends on the participation of indigenous peoples. He questions the effectiveness of existing mechanisms of conflict resolution. He continued, "It is in the best interest of all parties, both States and indigenous peoples, to accommodate these disputes within the domestic process. But if this is not the case, there is the international arena. [There must be] capability of thinking in terms of establishing a new jurisdiction to deal with indigenous issues in an indigenous jurisdiction [in a judicial capacity]. [We are] inviting projects in various areas possibly of effective domestic conflict resolution mechanism. [Regarding] paragraph 9, what can we do to fully implement the process of treaties? Treaties are not contracts. Treaties are agreements . . . have by definition, an international connotation. Paragraph 9(d) [mention of the] International Court of Justice could be an advantageous position at some point. The recently established United Nations Human Rights Council is subordinate to the General Assembly."

Ron Lameman of Treaty No. 6 said he was glad for the presence of the representative of the Government of Canada. He said, "The people in Ottawa need to hear of the UN. They need to be reminded treaties have not been respected, and lands are being taken from indigenous peoples as we speak. In reference to Conclusion 3 of Document III, that harmony, justice, and more positive relations is not the case in Eastern Canada. Indigenous peoples were not consulted in NAFTA and CAFTA. We consider our right to practice traditional activities. In dispute resolution mechanism, we have a long way to go in that regard, for example, Caledonia. The collective nature of our land is lacking. Certainty accomplishes the same things as extinguishment. Treaties being part of the [education] curriculum is not there yet. It is different from inviting people to speak on treaties to First Nations people and non-First Nations people who are part of the treaty and are the biggest beneficiaries."

The representative from the Kuna Nation, Panama, spoke in Spanish and referred to pueblo (home), indigenous, America, Mexica, Panamania, punto, Latin America, and Internationale.

Andrea Carmen of the International Indian Treaty Council said the recommendations and comments in point 7 are not happening. She implied that indigenous peoples' rights and interests must be protected by international bodies through the establishment of a unique mechanism of monitoring of treaty provisions. She said there must be consultation on food security and food sovereignty. There must also be, "Compliance through indicators or benchmarks in this area and in other areas, such as land. Indigenous peoples began working on conflict resolution and prevention in 1994 with a call for a permanent forum to be an effective mechanism for prevention and conflict resolution. The ability to intervene or prevent conflict is very important. Required is treaties being included in the Permanent Forum meeting [agenda] on lands to be held in 2007. [It is] very important for the creation of a specific body attached to the new Human Rights Council to address violations of indigenous peoples' human rights and the compliance of Treaties, agreements, and other constructive arrangements."

The African representative said, "We, as the Africa delegation, we were absent from these consultations since 2003. The Masai and some other tribes in Mali, since 1920, signed agreements. The rights of indigenous peoples must be the foundation of these negotiations."

Wes George, of Treaty No.4 and Federation of Saskatchewan Indian Nations (FSIN), read from a prepared text. He said, "Our presence here is to assist in this process [regarding] the Government of Canada's document and the difficulty of getting it on the internet. The Canadian government marginalized our indigenous peoples' rights while ignoring international law and instruments. Canada's version of Document III 2004 only points to marginalization. Canada's document is a racist position and is contrary to First Nations' position. [We recommend] that E/CN.4/2004 Document 111 be rejected and that proper representatives from Canada, the governor general and the prime minister, be here and meet with our chiefs. This seminar is an opportunity to correct those deficiencies."

William Means spoke on the terminology of "Treaties, agreements, and other constructive arrangements." He said, "The use of 'agreements and constructive arrangements' were developed in the early 1980s to deal with dictatorships and the formation of new constitutions. Issues of indigenous peoples are always about land. Citizenship was imposed upon us Lakota in 1924. Gold was discovered in the early 1860s. Treaties are peace treaties. There are treaties of accommodation, such as in Panama. There are treaties of trade and commerce, such as NAFTA. To the U.S., treaties are domestic in nature. When you signed that treaty, it is nation to nation."

Charmaine White Face, of the Tetuwan Oyate, noted the absence of the U.S. Government at this seminar. She commented on the conclusions of the first expert seminar. She referred to paragraph 2 of document III of January 2004 that mentions the loss of lands, resources, and rights of indigenous peoples. She said the 1868 Fort Laramie Treaty created the Great Sioux Reservation that included all of South Dakota and the Black Hills for the exclusive use and occupation of the Sioux. "In 1871, the U.S. passed the law that said any treaties made prior to this date shall not be changed. We were in reservation prisoner of war camps. No implementation of these treaties threatens indigenous peoples' survival as distinct peoples. Cultural genocide is forcing us to live in reservations. The late president Nixon opened our lands in Southern Nebraska to open pit uranium mines. We have been seeking redress. The Tetuwan Sioux Nation was founded in 1893. We have exhausted all domestic remedies, including the Secretary of State. Our first treaty was made in 1658 with France and the U.S. in 1868. For us, it has become more than cultural genocide but physical genocide that shows as birth defects as a result of radiation in the air and the food we need. We are all related, not just to people but to the natural world. [In reference to article 17—biodiversity] we, indigenous peoples, are the elders of the earth. We need to know how to protect without destroying the land, water, food, air, and ourselves. At the last meeting, we asked for recognition of the international status of our treaties. We need to get our treaty resolved so our people can live, for there is a direct threat from radiation from uranium mines. We are dying from cancer. I have already had cancer of the throat. We need to get this treaty issue resolved. We are dying."

Rikitangi Gage of Aotearoa said that New Zealand policies have worsened their treaty policy recognition and implementation.

Gordon Lee, Treaty 6 elder and former Chief of Ermineskin Cree Nation criticized, in Cree, the Canadian representative of how the Government of Canada has good words of the treaty relationship but how in fact Canada does not act in good faith nor recognizes the true treaty relationship which was to benefit and protect us. "The government of Canada understands that indigenous treaty people surrendered all the land. Treaty was to be interpreted the way we understood. The Supreme Court ruled that any ambiguity is to be decided in favor of the Indians." In reference to conclusion 2 of Document III, elder Lee recommended that treaties be understood and implemented in accordance with the negotiations they were made and in "accordance with the spirit in which they were agreed upon."

I addressed the expert panel by referring to paragraphs 7 and 9 of document III and the Final Treaty Study (1999) of Alfonso Martinez. I specifically mentioned the issue of conflict resolution of disputes between indigenous treaty people and States. I asked whether indigenous people have to exhaust all domestic avenues to resolve disputes or disagreements with their States and, if they are still not satisfied, whether they can then forward their disputes for redress to the international arena. I said the treaty peoples have been recently losing cases in the lower courts and in the Supreme Court of Canada, the highest domestic court. I asked for clarification. Mr. Martinez responded by saying that if indigenous peoples are not satisfied with domestic resolution, then there should be some international mechanism. He said there has been no representation by indigenous people in domestic law. Domestic judges' rulings are weighed in the judges' favor. He said, "A State can be litigating forever for they have the resources, whereas indigenous people lack the resources. There should be an effort to exhaust, not in the present judiciary or jurisdiction, but with a new jurisdiction to deal with indigenous issues and resolution of disputes. It is in the best interests of indigenous peoples and nation states to facilitate the establishment of [mechanisms to address] conflict situations."

Chief Ovid Mercredi, of Grand Rapids First Nation, said First Nations in Canada had exhausted all mechanisms domestically.

Mr. Martinez responded, "In my report, I recommend a new jurisdiction. Existing systems of States are not sufficient. [There must be] a new jurisdiction with the full participation of indigenous people in the resolution of conflicts and finding an international forum for resolution."

The five-page River Cree Declaration was circulated. It was to be dealt with first thing in the morning of November 15.

I went back to the Seminar in the afternoon of November 15. Item 3—Implementation of Treaties was being discussed.

The first presentation was a ten-page presentation made by Sandra

Ginnish of Indian and Northern Affairs Canada, Ottawa. She referred to the UN Seminar of 2003 regarding, specifically, the negotiation of modern treaties and the recommendations made in the seminar. Ms. Ginnish said her presentation today was an update on progress achieved since 2003 by Canada. She said modern treaty making in Canada was (1) negotiated land claims resulting in modern-day treaties and, (2) negotiated self-government agreements that were either standalone or part of land claims. She said, "Aboriginal and Treaty rights are affirmed by the Constitution Act, Section 35, [that deals with] reconciliation between the Canadian State and Aboriginal peoples plus Supreme Court of Canada [rulings]." She recommended that the use of these two avenues "is not just a one-time event but requires an ongoing process." She said between 1973 and 2003, fifteen modern treaties were made and that an additional five modern treaties have since been ratified. She gave the example of the Decho Agreement that recognized a land claim and Constitutionally protected thirty-nine thousand square kilometers of land, both surface and subsurface resources, and harvesting rights. She mentioned the Labrador-Inuit Agreement of December 1, 2005, that involves 5,840 Inuit, land ownership, and resource sharing.

Ms. Ginnish said there were three Yukon Final Land Claim Agreements and self-government agreements. There are sixty-three active self-government agreements on the national table. The Supreme Court has recognized Métis constitutionally protected rights, for example, the *Powley* decision. She said since 1996, implementation of obligation plans have formed the implementation policy in stages. One is the evaluative assessment of sources and collection of identification (research). This is complex and considers the unique aspects of each agreement. The Specific Claims Process is there to address past grievances of Indian lands, other assets, and treaties. She continued, "Canada has settled 205 specific claims since 1973. Canada is resolved to resolving grievances by addressing past injustices via partnerships on Aboriginal lands and surrounding communities. Lessons learned there is a sound body of constitutional law that is a prerequisite to the balance of rights. Treaty negotiations are a generational process of about fifteen years with about ten years of preparation. There are implementation plans of obligation with a time frame. It also requires finding a way of more effectively managing disputes. There is no guarantee of success."

Andrea Carmen, of the IITC, asked, "I would like to know how Canada defines 'modern Treaty'?"

Ginnish replied that "modern treaty" is used to "describe those negotiated agreements, such as comprehensive land claims process and self-government process."

Ron Lameman said, "When we go to Geneva, one or two [representatives of the Canadian government] always describe how wonderful things are. Our treaty rights don't come from Section 35 of the Constitution but from the negotiated treaty by my ancestors. What's in this document is not true. The status of all this land is [based] on certainty and extinguishment and taxation at the end."

William Means questioned the definition of "treaties" by Canada as "arrangements and agreements." A delegate from Saskatchewan asked, "Why does Treaty Land Entitlement [TLE] settlement take so long? Are these modern-day agreements recognized as international treaties?"

Ms. Ginnish replied, "The government of Canada is very well aware we have a significant backlog. There is need for a great deal of research to substantiate the claim. The minister has asked the department to pursue the claims process."

Mr. Martinez: "A province does not have international standing to negotiate treaties."

Charmaine White Face: "The international understanding of treaties is not the same as governments' understanding. Would Canada be willing to enter a treaty with the Great Sioux Nation?"

Ms. Ginnish: "The Office of the Treaty Commission in Saskatchewan has been discussing with Dakota-Nakota. The issue is being reviewed. We have a number of exploratory treaty discussions."

Mr. Martinez questioned the present state of affairs in Canada and remarked that this requires an effective domestic process to oversee the state of affairs. He referred to paragraph 7 that refers to the use of "improved processes."

Tommy Monias, of Cross Lake Cree Nation, said, "We started in 1994 on the self-determination process, which Canada doesn't recognize. The Northern Flood Agreement [NFA] is not recognized as a treaty by Canada. Canada recognizes only the chief and council, but we have a self-determination process. But there is poverty, people on welfare lines. The eradication of poverty is in the NFA. Canada will be very afraid when one day the Cree will be one nation, under one law, one God, one constitution, and one land."

Chairperson Sharon Venne cautioned the questioners and commentators, saying, "This is not a complaints process. There was a preparatory session earlier in the week in Enoch Cree."

William Means: "Can you elaborate on the role of the provinces in the new treaty-making process?"

Ms. Ginnish: "We'd like to table a document, which speaks to the land claims processes."

Andrea Carmen commented on the standing of oral history understanding and role of the indigenous version.

Ms. Ginnish: "The Supreme Court of Canada has examined historic treaties. It has considered, in several cases, oral history, for example, in the *Marshall* decision and in work being done in Treaty 6 to compile oral history and in Saskatchewan.

The Kuna representative from Panama spoke in Spanish with references to terms, such as pueblo, indigenous, territorial, Panama, Kuna, epagniola, and de Colombia, among other terms.

APPENDIX Q

ASSEMBLY OF FIRST NATIONS SPECIAL CHIEFS ASSEMBLY, DECEMBER 5, 6, AND 7, 2006, WESTIN OTTAWA HOTEL/ OTTAWA CONGRESS CENTRE—A PARTIAL REPORT

COUNCILOR ERIC J. LARGE

I attended the above meeting. On day 1, Tuesday December 5, chiefs, proxy chiefs, elders, and veterans made a grand entry. The Co chairs were Luc Laine and Roy Whitney. Chief Stephen McGregor of Kitigan Zibi First Nation said welcome remarks.

The AFN National Chief Phil Fontaine made the opening address. He said, in part, "Good morning to all. First of all, I want to join Mr. Elder Courchene to express thanks to the drum group. Mr. Courchene is absolutely right, we're about our children. This is our house, our gathering. When people come to us, we treat them with kindness and respect. Strong words will be spoken on a number of issues. There's a lot to represent on. There are a number of important issues to be dealt with in the next few days.

"Last Tuesday, I co chaired the Aboriginal Health Summit along with Premier Gordon Campbell in Vancouver. Premiers, First Nations leaders, and others reaffirmed their commitment to First Nations' health, to agree on a First Nations Action Plan and to close the gap. Everyone recognized the current health crisis must be seen as a crisis. The Minister for Health Tony Clement, I hope recognized the need for collaboration. Minister Clement will be here to sign an agreement. During last week's summit, Premier Doer of Manitoba agreed to hold next year's summit. I want to compliment BC for signing a commitment on health. National initiatives are also critical for First Nations access to health.

"[We've worked on the] First Nations Residential School Settlement Agreement. There were nine public hearings at the Superior Court level. Upon approval, there will be a comprehensive community campaign to ensure that each of the approximate eighty thousand survivors is well aware of their rights under the agreement. Nine thousand four hundred elder survivors have already received their eight-thousand-dollar advance payment. The deadline for filing claims for the advance payment is the end of this month. The oldest known survivor is 102. This eight-thousand-dollar advance payment and the common experience payment for all survivors is only payment for loss of language and culture. No amount of money can make up for the residential school experience. The agreement provides for enhanced resources. The Truth and Reconciliation Commission can provide a lasting legacy. Stories must be told, so we can educate the Canadians what the residential school was about and what it was trying to do.

"Last Tuesday, a major blow was dealt to the recognition of indigenous rights. A motion was passed to delay the passage of the Declaration of the Rights of Indigenous Peoples. Canada was opposed to this aspirational document. Over the past several months, we have seen our government in Canada oppose the passage of the Declaration. Yet Canada has worked previously to support the UN.

"We met yesterday with Minister of Heritage, Bev Oda, on language cuts of $1 million to $2 million. I pressed our case aggressively and asked questions I thought needed. But we failed. There is an article that pertains to language and culture preservation. Thanks to Willie Littlechild, Rick Simon, Ken Deer, Ted Moses, and officials like Roger Jones for working many years at the UN in securing support for the Declaration of the Rights of Indigenous Peoples.

"An economic update was made by the government last month. Of $13.2 billion announced, we were told $800 million was given to First Nations. The Residential School Agreement is not a program or services. Funding levels have been set for $400 million over two years, $150 million this year, and $300 million for the next year for northern housing.

"We simply cannot be silent. We must voice our concerns of issues that are blamed on poor First Nation leadership, but we have inherited through the Indian Act and chronic under funding. Our traditional customs and laws is where the answer is, not in a revision of the Indian Act. A federal election is coming in a few months. I am glad to see two additional Aboriginal members of Parliament. The RCAP made 440 recommendations."

At 11:00 a.m., the assembled chiefs, chiefs' proxies, elders, some First Nation children, and observers went to rally at Parliament Hill. This national protest, organized by the Chiefs of Ontario and the AFN, called "To Save Our Legacy," was to remind the Government of Canada's failure to act, that it fails First Nations peoples, and for First Nations to highlight their goal to seek justice and our fair share. Specifically, the rally was held to remind Canada of its cuts of $160 million in language funding, the cap for core funding for First Nations that has been imposed since 1996, the growing gap between First Nation communities and non-First Nation communities, and that Canada cannot continue to ignore this fact. I carried a placard that read "First Peoples, First Nations, Where is the honour of the Crown?"

Government representatives present at the rally were NDP Leader Jack Layton, NDP MP Pat Martin, Liberal MPs Tina Keeper and Gary Merasty, a Bloc Quebecois MP, and Indian and Northern Affairs Minister Jim Prentice. AFN National Chief and the Bloc Quebecois MP addressed the rally. Mr. Layton said, in part, "Is it right for the banks of this country to earn $10 billion a year and tax breaks, while First Nations live in poverty? It is not right for First Nations language and culture [support should be cut] when the money was in the bank. The RCAP should be implemented." Mr. Prentice's address to the rally was booed, and he was unable to be heard. He managed to say, "The first budget included $3.7 billion for Aboriginal peoples. The government is working with First Nation leaders in housing. The First Nation language money earmarked in 2002 was never spent." Another MP said the Kelowna Accord was supported by three opposition parties who are urging the government to implement it.

The Special Chiefs Assembly resumed its meeting in the afternoon with a four-page PowerPoint presentation called "Make Poverty History: The First Nations Plan for Creating Opportunity" presented by Bryan Hendry, Acting Director of Communications at the AFN. He said this work is based on three strategic sessions and is a "campaign to generate public awareness and support to position First Nations poverty as an important issue that must be addressed in the next Federal Budget and Election (p. 1)." The First Nations Plan also seeks to capitalize on the following key points and dates:

- UN Declaration vote
- Ten-year anniversary of RCAP
- One-year anniversary of First Ministers Meeting on Aboriginal Issues
- National Aboriginal Health Summit.

Some of the accomplishments to date are collaboration with national Make Poverty history campaign, over eleven thousand signatures on an online petition, briefings to two opposition parties, a reception to launch a ten-year RCAP Report Card, and participation in the release of Campaign 2000's Child Poverty Report Card 2006. The First Nations plan "is based on

1. Governing Our Lands, Resources and Communities—Asserting Rights and Jurisdiction
2. Achieving Justice and Our Fair Share—Implementing Treaties
3. Strengthening First Nation Communities—Alleviating Poverty, and
4. Securing Opportunity for First Nations in Canada and internationally."

An announcement was made there would be a national economic conference in January and a national treaties conference in March of 2007.

An AFN report on the "Royal Commission on Aboriginal Peoples (RCAP) 10th Anniversary" was presented by Regional Chief Angus Toulouse, ON. He said the RCAP Report "was the most extensive study on Aboriginal people. It called for immediate unequivocal action. It related the continuing legacy of poverty, suicide, the residential school experience, etc. It outlined a blueprint to restore the original relationship between First Nations and Canada based on trust and sharing. It recommended nation building that primarily rests with the local people. It recommended control of resources and the establishment of First Nations government, structural changes, and commitment to dialogue."

The next report was from Georges Erasmus, President of the Aboriginal Healing Foundation (AHF) and former national chief of the AFN. Among other things in the RCAP Report, he said the report offers opportunities as models of self-government, healing that is just beginning, to move away from the paternalism of the past and for us to continue on our efforts. He said that, aside from the Aboriginal Healing Foundation and the Residential School Agreement, little has changed, and emphasized healing.

During the questions-and-comments session, Chief Terrence Nelson, of Rousseau River First Nation, said, "We need our own action, our own agenda, and control of resources." Chief Billy Joe de LaRonde of Pine Creek First Nation said, "RCAP Report has a fundamental flaw, that the French and English are the founding nations of this country." Chief Ron Ignace, of BC and former chair of the AFN Chiefs Committee on Languages, said, "I recommend a principled, common, united front on preserving languages based on elders' advice. We got to reach to Canadians and others, even go internationally. We need action now, engaging internationally to protect and promote First Nation rights. Last week, the United Nations made a motion, through an amendment by Namibia, to set aside the Declaration on the Rights of Indigenous Peoples to allow more time for further consultation. I believe this will be a delay of at least five months. In the next nine months, we need to stand with other indigenous peoples that we cannot agree with governments' [delay]. We must remind countries that opposed the approval of the Declaration are talked with until they see our position." Grand Chief Ed John, of the BC First Nations Summit, said, "Australia, New Zealand, U.S., and now Canada have consistently opposed the Declaration. The Declaration does a number of things. It addresses ongoing racism imposed on indigenous peoples, and it provides for minimum standards in upholding the dignity and well-being of indigenous peoples. What will happen? No one knows. But Canada is proposing an action plan. Of the African group of fifty-three countries, forty-seven supported the Namibia amendment." Chief John read Canada's statement on its reasons for opposing the Declaration, which says that any statement in the Declaration must include the State's domestic or territorial position(s).

On day 2, Wednesday, December 6, a report on the Dene Tha Court Ruling was given by Regional Chief Bill Erasmus, NWT. He said this was a very important case with recent results. He said, "The case talks of the need to have our people participate and to have meaningful consultation. It's still in court." Chief James Ahannasay, of the Dene Tha First Nation, said the Dene Tha won the court case, but Indian and Northern Affairs announced after it wants to appeal. There are implications for First Nations. Chief Ahannasay said the decision ruled that "First Nations have to be consulted in environmental review process including the right of being informed of decisions made in the review process that may affect the Aboriginal and treaty rights of First Nations. Justice Phelan [referred to the] environmental impact and cumulative effect of facilities proposed now and into the future. The ruling applies to all treaties in Canada. Consultation cannot be meaningful, is inadvertent, or cannot be viewed narrowly but must consider Aboriginal and treaty rights. The funding issue must be the topic with links to adequacy of remedial action. We need to think carefully how we deal with each other historically and in the usage of overlapping areas."

The next report, "Resource Revenue Sharing," was delivered by Lawrence Joseph, new Regional Chief, Saskatchewan, whose AFN portfolios include economic development and resource sharing. He said this area is called resources revenue and benefits sharing. He said, "RCAP celebrated ten years. Self-government without an economic base will be an exercise of illusion. Now very little has been achieved. Canada has reached a failing grade in a recent report card in closing the gap, with it, unwillingness to implement the Kelowna Accord. It stalled efforts to recognize and implement self-government. A call to action is affirmed in Section 35 and Supreme Court decisions. $200 billion is to be invested in the First Nations traditional territory in the next ten years. [We need] to ensure adequate consultation occurs, that First Nation resource rights [are assured], and that there be responsible management. [Regarding] the NRTA in the Prairie Provinces, First Nations need to come together as to how they can get their fair share. What Saskatchewan chiefs have done on the UN Declaration on Indigenous Peoples Rights is, Saskatchewan First Nations have made their own Declaration and tells citizens of Canada. Saskatchewan First Nations will be presenting a resolution that calls upon Canada to adopt the Declaration on the Rights of Indigenous Peoples. Also, the chiefs of Saskatchewan, in unity, support the passage of the Kelowna Accord."

Chief Terrence Nelson said First Nations want action, not wait around for the government to act in our best interests. He said he would put a resolution before the assembly, planning for a one-day national railway blockade for June 29, 2007. This blockade of CN railroad will lose $27 million in Manitoba according to Chief Nelson. He also estimated the resources in Manitoba are extracted for $27 billion per year there. He called for the establishment of a planning committee and to go back meeting as nations as we have treaties.

Resolution no. 1—FSIN support of the UN Declaration on the Rights of Indigenous Peoples was adopted with one opposed and no abstention. Resolution no. 2—Indian Residential Schools Composition of the Truth and Reconciliation Commission was adopted. A roll call of the chiefs and proxies was held that indicated ninety-one delegates present. Resolution no. 9—Support for the National Railway Blockade was adopted with six opposed and three abstentions. Resolution no. 3—FSIN Chiefs in Assembly Declaration of Support for the Implementation of the Kelowna Accords was adopted.

The next agenda item was First Nations Drinking Water and was presented by Regional Chief Rick Simon, Yukon. He said in November, INAC announced that eighty-three First Nations were on a boil-water advisory. He mentioned a five-point action plan that deals with capacity, regulations, accountability, and sustainable water treatment. This also calls for the formation of an expert panel and public hearings conducted this past summer. He said there is need to address resources capital and development of new standards for water treatment.

Merrill Am and S. Phare presented a review of the Final Report of the Expert Panel on First Nations Drinking Water. This review includes of a summary of recommendations to the chiefs in assembly. The main recommendations consist of three options or regimes. The first option involves the federal regime, which has the same standards that apply to all First Nations across Canada but respects customary law. The second option is the customary law regime developed by First Nations based on customary laws. The third regime is the provincial regime. This involves the adoption of provincial regimes. It faces an inconsistent and inadequate patchwork of rules and regulations. It may compromise First Nation rights. All three regimes are impacted by Section 35, federal legislation, federal jurisdiction, and First Nation water rights, including irrigation, etc.

An alternative approach assumes all levels of government already possess jurisdiction over, for example, water manufacturing. It is based on upon the RCAP approach to implementing self-government. It is a cooperative approach to defining roles and responsibilities. It suggests the making of a memorandum of agreement of the federal government and First Nations to adopt interim standards for services. This approach must consider immediate risk reduction, negotiation processes, and the cooperative implementation of an eight-year plan of regime implementation. It requires the cooperative implementing by all three levels of government of water management, framework and regulatory regime.

An update on the First Nations Housing Strategy and water was provided by Earl Commanda, Director of Housing Operations, with a seven-page PowerPoint presentation. Commanda said the vision to the housing report has not changed. Critical housing is needed as well as a call for action. There are key principles as well as the formation of the First Nations Housing Institute. Commanda said that the minister would be releasing the report on water tomorrow in the House of Commons. The report will state that the oversight of operations of local water treatment centers was unclear. A First Nation may be under third-party management. Commanda said, "We would like First Nations provide that for themselves."

Resolution no. 13, Water Consultation—AFN Mandate was to be postponed to tomorrow after the minister's announcement. A comment was made that INAC only currently funds 8 percent of water systems.

Chief Katherine Whitecloud, Regional Chief, Manitoba made the report on education. She congratulated BC on the passage of an education bill yesterday. She said this is "integral to making poverty history, it's important. Part of that is having proper, adequate education. The prime age for learning for children is one to four years old. Funding provided for education for our children today has been capped at 2 percent since 1996. $6,563 a year provides education. [We need] to ensure that our children receive adequate education. The cost of a child welfare facility for one child is forty-six thousand dollars, which will go up to $112,000. Thirty-five percent in Winnipeg are of First Nation descent. A non-First Nation child receives eight thousand dollars plus. Education for our children is very important, as they are our future. The Chiefs Committee on Education and the National Indian Education Council urge the unity of First Nations when dealing with the Minister of INAC."

Resolution no. 8—Joint Assembly of First Nations and INAC "Plan forward for First Nations Education" was moved, seconded, and adopted.

The next agenda item, "Urban/Off-Reserve Representation," was reported by National Chief Phil Fontaine. He said, "We had struck a Renewal Commission and went across the country and came back with a report of forty-four recommendations to better organize ourselves and our people no matter where they live. We've circulated an article on the *Hill Times* by Mr. Brazeau, Congress of Aboriginal Peoples. He's misrepresented this organization. It has done harm to First Nations leaders. We represent all of our people, those away from home and those at home. We can define our constituency. We know who we represent, and we know the numbers. Sixty-two percent of our people live in our Reserve communities. Thirty-eight percent of our people live in towns and cities. We need to educate and inform Canadians about the AFN and the responsibility this organization carries and who we represent. We're not a services organization. We don't build houses, hire teachers. That's the responsibility of First Nations governments. We're a political organization. We negotiate on your behalf. We do research. We provide political organization. We recognize the important work that the friendship centers do on behalf of our people. They are not a political organization. They are a service organization. We want to formalize a relationship. There are unresolved issues."

Kathleen McHugh, chair, made the AFN Women's Council Report. She said the council performs an advisory function to the executive of the AFN. The council was "established in 2004 to ensure the First Nation women's interests and perspective are represented." Some of its roles are

- accessing resources for issues, health, education, and support equality of men and women;
- the alleviation of poverty among women and children;
- working together toward the elimination of gender inequality;
- supporting achievements of First Nations women;

- elimination of inequities;
- support for women's shelters, including resources;
- effort to reduce family violence;
- addressing socioeconomic conditions that make First Nations women vulnerable to conditions of poverty; and
- promoting awareness of issue of disabilities, fetal alcohol syndrome.

National Chief Fontaine made the following statement on Matrimonial Real Property, "We need to control the outcome from this very important issue and other issues of our communities as recognized by the Constitution Act, and requires dialogue and processes."

Kathleen Lickers made comments as part of the AFN Regional Dialogue Sessions Report on Matrimonial Real Property. She said there were discussions over the last four weeks regarding property custody and access. One of the tasks is to redefine for the federal government the terms of what issues to be looked at. She said the "sessions were on principles and remedies for people who decide to live off-Reserve and remedies that a province has. The AFN drafted two legislative-type options involving recognition of First Nations jurisdiction and other options for other types of issues. The AFN still has to hear from First Nations in Alberta and Quebec. Six months is the time Prentice [Minister of INAC] has set out, to the spring of 2007." Commonality needs to be found and as well as the need for more discussion and dialogue, design of communities of a solution, and the identification of resources. Also needed for discussion is the preservation and protection of land base and guiding principles. Lickers said there "needs to be recognition of looking at this issue from a restorative justice based on our laws and customs. We are not starting from a position of legislation but from Treaty Section 35 recognition. We need more work and analysis. The work needs to be prepared, for example, what other First Nations have been working on, and be it bylaws or other processes."

Chiefs' comments were the following:

- "This will lead to loss of our lands. We cannot allow provincial law to control us. To have something imposed on us is dangerous, the imposition of non-Indian and non-First Nations law. Our law provides for the individual as well as the collective law of our people. We need to have a community-driven process. We don't need a consultation process at the broad-based level. There is capacity within us. We are

First Nations, and we have our own laws, including women, children, and men too."

- "We govern ourselves. We want to look after ourselves."

Resolution no. 21—Matrimonial Real Property was moved by Chief Doug Kelly, Sto:lo First Nation, BC. This resolution was made in reference to community-based processes and consultation as a condition, prior to the introduction of any federal legislation. There was discussion on amending of some clauses in the resolution.

On day 3, December 7, a representative of the Downtown Eastside Women's Center in Vancouver requested the chiefs' support for the homeless First Nation women, elders, and disabled living in downtown east side Vancouver. The representative said these are the chiefs' people and that Phil Fontaine was invited to visit east side, which he did, and he advocated for a health and wellness shelter. A resolution was moved and seconded for support for a health and wellness center. This resolution was adopted by consensus of the chiefs in assembly.

The Honorable Tony Clement, Minister of Health Canada, addressed the chiefs. He said, in part, "The new government is absolutely committed to working with you to get things done to improve the health of First Nations. Last week, we signed an MOU [Memorandum of Understanding] in BC at the Health Summit for a pilot project aimed at reducing wait times. [The federal government] supports prenatal care for First Nations moms and babies, a national strategy to fight cancer, and is willing to work collaboratively." Minister Clement and National Chief Fontaine then signed a joint work plan for a task group to address First Nations health. With the signing of the MOU, the minister said the government is "committing to starting, as a first step, a work plan consisting of five key areas:

- To identify cross-jurisdictional agreements,
- Examination of existing programs,
- Focus on accountability,
- Performance management ensuring getting results, and
- Examination of the legislative base to improve health matters, for example, drinking water."

Last, the minister mentioned the formation of a Health Canada First Nations Task Group along with AFN national chief.

National Chief Fontaine responded by saying there is an eighteen-month delay of the $700 million promised in 2005, that fiscal cuts results in less health benefits and sustainability in the long term. He said sustainability is key and willingness to ensure meaningful plans. He mentioned long-term funding commitment, partnership and benefits to First Nations, monitoring of closing the gap, fiduciary obligation in protecting First Nations health, inherent, Aboriginal and treaty rights, nation-to-nation relationship recognized in treaties, and that the 3 percent cap must be lifted.

The Honorable Jim Prentice, Minister of Indian and Northern Affairs, addressed the chiefs in assembly. He said, "I'm pleased to be here in the traditional territory of the Algonquin people. Collaboration between the Government of Canada and the AFN has sparked a number of key issues: drinking water, matrimonial real property, education and economic opportunities. I have delivered on every promise I have made in the last while. The Indian Residential Schools Settlement has taken decisive action. The May 10, 2006, Settlement Agreement was reached by all parties. Details include collective and individual settlement for eighty thousand former Indian residential school students and advance payments. Court processes proceeding are quite high.

"We must agree to disagree about the Declaration on the Rights of Indigenous Peoples. Naturally, it would have serious repercussions in this country including First Nations. Canada is one of few countries that entrenches treaty and Aboriginal rights. This needs appropriate wording to consider this. To say that this government has changed its position is patently false. Tackling Aboriginal poverty is important. We deliver on what we say. We say what we say. We do what we say. What I have promised upon, what I have delivered. [We want] to improve education. We signed an agreement in BC for a First Nation controlled [process] and driven in cooperation with provincial education authorities. Bill 34 BC Education passed this Tuesday. I promised I would improve the quality of on-Reserve drinking water. We fund over two hundred Reserve communities that were at risk, or worse, reduced from 196 to 131 communities, have put action plans in place in high-risk communities. On March 21, we signed an important protocol with the national chief for a safe drinking water regulatory framework and recommendations.

"I promised to deliver on treaties. I have done so. [For example] in

BC, seven First Nations succeeded with three agreements, initialed and reached the first final agreement. [Regarding the] Specific Claims Process, we are waiting for the Senate Report expected over the Christmas period. [There is progress in] Nunavut, Saskatchewan, Quebec, and Songees, BC. I've intervened personally to make sure negotiations are going forward. I am determined to identify ways to accelerate the Specific Claims Process, retooling the process. [There is] is a backlog of eight hundred specific claims. I promised the national chief to improve economic opportunities for First Nations people.

On December 1, the government [transferred] the Aboriginal Business Corporation from Industry Canada back to Indian and Northern Affairs Canada. The first step is to leverage human capital to financial capital [and the formation of a] board. There are twenty-five thousand Inuit and First Nations students enrolled in post-secondary institutions. Education of people is [the] key to a sustainable economy. Young Native students must be encouraged to contribute to the economy and to take advantage of the prosperity of our country. Human rights of Aboriginal women [are being addressed by] the Matrimonial Real Property consultation, is the right thing to do, my friends. To further protect First Nations' rights, we are committed to repeal Section 67 of the Canadian Human Rights Act. To focus on our disagreements is a mistake. Our overarching goal is to ensure the best quality of life for Aboriginal people today and for years to come. In partnership and in partnership alone, we will deal with all the issues in which we are concerned and in which you are concerned about."

Comments by the chiefs and proxies were the following:

- Concern of rights, territories now and into the future
- Necessary measures will be taken to protect these common interests in relation to the Conservative government motion in support of a Quebec Nation.

Minister Prentice: "I don't think there is anything in the Quebec Nation motion that affects First Nations."

Chief Lonechild, FSIN: "Why is government unwilling to provide the Aboriginal Healing Foundation an advance payment? A $40 million cash flow is one year's funding from the $125 million."

Minister Prentice: "I expect the court process to be made very shortly.

[Information from government lawyers], it is to be made imminently. If the court decision is not made imminently, I will deal with your request."

Other Chiefs: "Due to the language funding cuts, are you willing to increase funding? Also regarding the education cap, how are you going to improve education?" "We get unequal funding for our students on-Reserve and non-Native students."

Minister Prentice: "We put in the budget, $3.7 billion for First Nations with $2.2 billion for Indian Residential Schools. We are spending significant sums of money. Funding of education is extremely important. A $1.2 billion is spent for First Nations students across Canada. There is no cap in education in the sense you are describing. All studies show if our First Nations students continue to post-secondary, they succeed better than non-First Nations students do. We want to see collaboration. That is the way to the future. There was no cut by the government. There was no program. We are committing $5 million to look at a real program—at a real program with real dollars. We started late for this meeting. I have to go back to Treasury Board. There are issues that are germane to the people in this room."

Barbara Wardlaw, of the National First Peoples Party of Canada [NFPP], addressed the chiefs in assembly. She said, in the last election the NFPP of Canada ran five people, has registered with Elections Canada, and is planning the first convention. The party intends to run thirty seats in the next election. Five potential candidates have come forward. Noeline Villebrun will run in the NWT and another one in Toronto. She said the party has a shared vision.

Stephane Dion, newly elected leader of the Liberal Party of Canada; Michael Ignatieff; Gary Merasty, a member of Parliament for Churchill River SK; MP Tina Keeper; and MP Lloyd St. Dumont presented themselves to the chiefs in assembly. Dion said, "We are a team. We want to work with you as a team. It's my commitment. Canada needs to succeed. We want Canada to be in the land, in the revolution for sustainability, better than any country in the world. We cannot succeed if part of our population is left behind, facing unacceptable barriers. Aboriginal people will be able to give their full skills and potential. We want to build Kelowna [Accord] first, but something more. Kelowna addressed basic needs, housing, health, education, and sustainable infrastructure. We want to build on that an independent land claims body, in quick settlement. Second, capacity, when people are ready. And we want to get out of the Indian Act. It is a straightjacket for you. Third, for any Aboriginal student to get post-secondary education anywhere in

Canada. Fourth, the federal government will not limit its role to economic development to on-Reserve but will have an integrative economic approach. Fifth, to have environmental standards or better for Aboriginal Canadians as other Canadians including water. [We want] to offer the best platform in the next campaign for Aboriginal people. We will help you much more [than] as opposition, as a government."

The First Nations Child Welfare Report was given by Regional Chief Katherine Whitecloud in a six-page PowerPoint. She focused both on child welfare and the family, saying, "Anything that happens to our children is our family responsibility."

Resolution no. 7—First Nations Child and Family Services with amendments was moved, seconded, and adopted. The resolution allows the submission of a joint complaint by the AFN and the First Nation Child and Family Caring Society of Canada to the Canadian Human Rights Commission regarding the unequal levels of child welfare funding provided First Nations children and families on-Reserve. The final resolution is to be distributed in the next chiefs' assembly as stated by Co chair Roy Whitney.

At 1:05 pm, concern was raised again whether there is a quorum present for decisions and resolutions. It was found that there are sixty-two voting delegates present. Eighty-six are needed for a quorum. There was discussion, frustration, and mention of the AFN Renewal Commission and that the deadline for resolutions for this Assembly was December 5, 2006.

An update on International matters was provided by Wilton Littlechild, AFN Alberta Regional Chief. He said the UN General Assembly is meeting in New York, the UN Human Rights Council is meeting in Geneva, and the Organization of American States is meeting in the Americas. He said, on Friday there will be a joint statement made of the Human Rights Councils in support of the adoption of the Declaration on the Rights of Indigenous Peoples. Littlechild said, "There is concern that some States are attempting to exclude indigenous people participating, and indigenous people are urging the Human Rights Councils to ensure indigenous people are heard." He gave a heads-up of the Sixth Session of the UN Permanent Forum on Indigenous Peoples. The session will deal with lands and resources. He suggested presenting the inaction of the RCAP recommendations.

In his closing remarks to the chiefs in assembly, National Chief Fontaine said, "I'm very disappointed but not discouraged of being unable to finish discussing. We've received very clear instructions on a number of issues. For example, on the matrimonial issue, we have a resolution that sets out a direction that the executive will follow. We will be very mindful of what we heard here of not compromising. We'll do the best we can. We'll make every effort not to undermine the interests and rights of the people we represent. The Renewal Commission Report came about because of the difficulties, problems, and impediments. The Commission was formed to deal with these challenges. It went across the country, which resulted in forty-seven recommendations. Unfortunately, we focused on the process of electing the national chief. There are other important areas. We need to take decisions on the Renewal Commission Report. Also, want to remind, we're a transparent organization. Our proceedings are being webcast. People see how we conduct our business. They have seen how we were unable to finish our business.

"The minister today was saying, 'Canada never changed its position on the Declaration on the Rights of Indigenous Peoples.' I was disappointed on that and on a number of things he said. Whatever happens, we will have a respective, productive relationship with him. Also our people are getting angry and frustrated. But we cannot accept the status quo. We're a First Nations political organization, and that's how we're trying to conduct ourselves with Parliament and parliamentarians. As we did in the last federal election, we'll go out and encourage our people to participate in every riding to influence the outcome. We just published another public relations campaign with Elections Canada. We're doing much better than Parliament in terms of representation by women. We have at least 112 women chiefs, better than Parliament. We have hundreds of women councilors. We are going to have a women chiefs' and councilors' meeting as soon as possible."

APPENDIX R

"BREAKING THE SILENCE: INTERNATIONAL CONFERENCE OF THE INDIAN RESIDENTIAL SCHOOLS TRUTH AND RECONCILIATION COMMISSION OF CANADA" AT L'UNIVERSITÉ DE MONTRÉAL, SEPTEMBER 26–27, 2008, A BRIEF REPORT

ERIC J. LARGE, IRS COORDINATOR, SADDLE LAKE CREE NATION

The conference notice indicated that the discussions in this conference would support the work of the Truth and Reconciliation Commission (T&RC). The agenda topics were Reconciliation: An International Perspective; the Ethical Challenges of Reconciliation; Media, Ethics, and Reconciliation; and Memory, Truth, and Reconciliation.

On September 26, 2008, a welcome prayer was said by Delbert Sampson, Shuswap Nation, Salmon Arm, B.C. (Mr. Sampson is a residential former school student). The master of ceremonies (MC) announced that the formation of the Truth and Reconciliation Commission is the first time that Canada has established a truth commission. He is there is an aspect of healing to the work of the commission. The conference is a part of the public debate that is expected to support and accompany the work of the commission. The MC announced that there were services for people uncomfortable with Indian Residential School (IRS) impact. There were two male and one female Resolution Health Support workers present.

The conference plenary presentation was made by Eduardo Gonzalez, deputy director, (Americas) International Center for Transitional Justice (ICTJ). Mr. Gonzalez said the focus is on the complex question of national reconciliation after serious violation of human rights, on a few questions of the role of reconciliation through examination of ICTJ, and on specifics of the challenges of Canada's T&RC. The issue of impunity for abusers/perpetrators arises, as in South Africa, Chechnya, and East Timor. This issue brings cynicism. Mr. Gonzales asked if reconciliation is possible, "after a long time, to entire segments of the population." He said he is a former staff member of the Peruvian T&RC and said, "To abandon the concept of reconciliation is to abandon the concept of a fair and just society." He asked how we can build mutual trust and whether there is need to take the concept of reconciliation "off the shoulders of the perpetrator. We cannot be a true society when we deny persons who are victims the dignity, nor can we, when we prevent perpetrators from facing the consequences of justice. Trusting each other again can be nurtured with truth searching and truth telling. Reparation policy is the responsibility of the State." Mr. Gonzales related experience of the Peruvian T&RC, which involved the Chaga community, the prosecution of perpetrators, and the facilitation of civil trust.

In regard to Canada's T&RC, Mr. Gonzales said that First Nations, Métis, and Inuit are in the best position to identify recommendations and offer insight. He said impunity [of perpetrators] must not be allowed. In regard to the Indian Residential Schools Settlement Agreement [IRSSA], he said that unspeakable acts were committed in Indian residential schools, and there must be opportunity for the victims to be heard. In his view, the role of the T&RC is:

1. Removing of the veil of the legacy of Indian residential schools

2. Reconciliation must go beyond the Royal Commission on the Aboriginal Peoples and that the victimization of children and families was part of a process, which later served as a guide to the T&RC and Supreme Court of Canada decisions

3. Gather in strength the legacy of residential school students, consider the mandate of deceased students, and establish opportunities for them to tell their truth without cumbersome parameters.

Mr. Gonzales concluded by saying that the T&RC must reach out to the youth and "should envision a country where very few can say this did not happen."

The panel discussion of the first topic, "Reconciliation: An International Perspective," was chaired by Peter Detch, professor of Philosophy, University of Montreal.

The first panelist, Jeff Corntassel, of Indigenous Governance Programs, University of Victoria asked, "What does justice look like in the light of truth telling, genocide, and the raising of consciousness?" He said, "Truth telling is part of a larger process [and asked], how is this played out in other countries and in the context of Canada?" He listed three aspects of this process: truth telling, restitution, and justice. He said the process involves renewing the relationship and a commitment toward renewal. He said it becomes rhetorical if there is no action and that there is no justice without meaningful reconciliation and restitution. Corntassel continued, "We have to talk about reality and of restoring ourselves as indigenous people." He described the Cherokee Corn Mother story in which a long memory is kept alive in the Cherokee people. He cited the work of truth and reconciliation in Guatemala, Peru, and Australia that overlooked meaningful restitution and notions of indigenous justice. He mentioned the 1991 Council of Reconciliation in Australia in which it was hoped that reconciliation would unify the country. He said Prime Minister John Howard refused to apologize on behalf of the Australian Government.

Corntassel briefly mentioned the Inter-America Reparation of Human Rights, that intergenerational effects are not being looked at, and that cultural rights have been stripped. He said a United Nations Resolution [11/295 September 7, 2007, Declaration of the Rights of Indigenous Peoples] states in Article 28 that when indigenous peoples have been dispossessed of their lands, territories, and resources without their free, prior, and informed consent, they have the right to redress or just, fair, and equitable compensation. Additional questions Corntassel raised, related to truth and reconciliation commissions, are indigenous concepts of reconciliation are lacking, there is lack of consideration of the harm caused to communities versus individuals, and to what degree is there restructuring of the indigenous and State relationship.

The second panelist was Paige Arthur, Deputy Director of Research, of the International Center for Transitional Justice. She presented a PowerPoint on the following questions:

1. What is the relationship between truth and reconciliation?
2. What is the role that identities play in truth and reconciliation?
3. How do you engage the unengaged?

She briefly mentioned the South African Truth Commission where more than twenty-six thousand South Africans gave statements and where full amnesty was given to perpetrators for full disclosure.

In regard to the question of the relationship between truth and reconciliation, Ms. Arthur said the general aim is to find out facts to counter the State narrative, to better understand the State in abetting abuses, and to use facts and narrative to validate victims' experience. The generation of political will to transfer views of institutions is also important. Arthur stated reconciliation is "creation or recreation of bonds of trust between citizens of a State"; specifically, it is "reconstruction of interpersonal relationships with more of a restorative justice approach." It involves a process of decolonization. She briefly cited the South African T&RC that found correlation between truth and reconciliation through a complex and varied means of reconciliation.

In regard to the question of the roles identities play in TRC, Ms. Arthur gave the example of the Balkans (1990s) case where identities may foster a competition of a hierarchy of victimhood and the example of Iraq reparations where there is competition within groups. The Balkans trials showed denial of the atrocities of a group.

In regard to the question of "How do you engage the disengaged?" Ms. Arthur said that a TRC should not demonize and that there should be consistent and adequate funding. Different modes of outreach should also be considered and must be started early. She mentioned the education outreach in Peru and Sierra Leone and the bridging of the gap in Belgrade where community groups such as nongovernment organizations (NGOs) can act as trusted mediators. She concluded by saying she is not recommending that truth be watered down.

The next presenter was Cynthia Milton, Canada Research Chair in Latin American History, Department of History, University of Montreal who gave a PowerPoint on "Reconciling with the Past : Peru Fifty-four Months After the CVR." Milton said the tensions began with the regional spread of Sender luminosa (Shining Path) and act of violence from 1980 to 2000. The Peruvian CVR (TRC) provided a national narrative of harm done. The path to societal reconciliation, contingent upon knowing the past, was considered. The CVR had a broad mandate, a wide scope, and it investigated assassinations, disappearances, and other grave violation of people. A final report was produced on August 28, 2003. The CVR recorded six hundred thousand refugees and found that 55 percent of the atrocities were committed by the Shining Path and 35 percent by other (government). Three out of every four victims were non-Spanish victims.

Milton said TRCs are indispensable yet insufficient. She gave a pictorial representing a TRC as political formula versus wedge. In response to a TRC, a church reaction might be, "Never again to abuses and atrocities" while a banker's response might be, "That it never happened", and a military response might be, "No, so we can never speak of it again." A wedge created by a TRC is space for other public spaces. Reconciliation is a term with many possible definitions. It does not mean forgiveness or impunity. It is between citizens and their past. Reconciling with the past involves macro- versus micro truths. Micro truths involve silence, emphasize indiscriminate violence of the state, and do not necessarily make it to the macro narrative. Milton said, "One positive of the TRC is the formation of public hearings, hearing and making heard the victim of human rights violations. The Peru TRC cannot be compared with Canada's TRC. The Peruvian model had an authoritarian trajectory with truth based on a political formula. With Canada's TRC, what are the transition, the expectations, and the wedge that will create the space for other public spaces?"

The rapporteur was Daniel Weinstock who summarized themes in countries when a TRC was completed with attendant problems and obstacles, such as:

1. Clarity objectives—There is a need for clarity regarding reconciliation.

2. Inflation—to repair in a year everything that has gone on for centuries

3. Risks being a process being co-opted or managed by the elite (the oppressors or were oppressors), that the TRC becomes a talk shop where people just listen. "We can't assure those fundamental injustices will just go away."

4. Population indifference—"Will the TRC be accompanied by a transformation of segments of the general community?"

5. To focus on the work on the past is not enough, but also defining and addressing those institutions that are still there.

Questions and responses from the audience and the panel included:
Meaning of transition as in "transitional justice" and not be caught up in the term.
Forgiveness versus discussing and addressing the question of "How the T&RC would be used as a wedge for healing?" A panelist's response was "You can't demand forgiveness without having this discussion."
Who benefits from this process? Who benefits from the political process, the apology we heard from Prime Minister Harper last summer? How do we

engage the communities, their cultural protocols of the community? The response was "There probably are going to be many beneficiaries. Political, morally problematic groups do not nullify the benefits to others, such as the victims and unexpected beneficiaries. Civil societies are also 'watchdog' in their role."

How do people benefit?—Response: "With dedicated funding and staff."

Is the T&RC in Canada more symbolic as it doesn't take the perpetrators in court?—Response: "These processes are very much unpredictable."

"Democracy in Canada is indoctrination of my people, for example, the Indian residential school and the legacy of 'star light tours' in Saskatoon. There is subtle genocide developed over centuries. This IRSSA, primarily, is the T&RC going to be recognized globally as in other international processes or be preempted by the influence of the U.S.?" A panelist's response was "It brings related issues of how countries can learn from each other. In some cases, it is easier to learn. There is very fluid communication between the TRC experience in Peru and in South Africa."

The next topic was "The Ethical Challenges of Reconciliation" presented by Christian Nadeau, Department of Philosophy, of the Université de Montréal. Mr. Nadeau asked, "Is reconciliation possible at all? What is it we want? There is a responsibility of an agent toward another. There are two schools of thought. One is punishment to the wrongdoer. Two is restorative justice. Stakeholders to an offense must get together." There is a role for an apology. Nadeau gave a brief history and intent of the Indian Residential School. The racial crime was that there is one Canadian nation and that there were major human rights violations. There must be a form of community justice to State crime victims. Wrongdoers and State authorities need to engage as individuals with a conscience within a community system and the establishment of dialogue. This is where parties reason together and recognize what was done and why. There must be community response to both wrongdoing and reconciliation with the intent of preventing a similar wrong in the future. There must be apology, commitment, and the prevention of wrongs.

The next panelist was Val Napoleon of the Faculty of Law, University of Alberta. She stated consideration for a healing journey be depoliticized. She said there are assumptions about health, healing communities for the past and future, and on who, why, and how one is being healed? "Aboriginal people have been burdened by colonialism, must talk which is therapy. Self is a Western self not an Aboriginal self. It is an imported self and emotion. Self is a cultural concept, the way we understand. There are major differences. Appreciation of differences and similarities is important. There are challenges of power-based education, age, and of powerlessness, not getting your own way. What are the consequences of defining people as victims, for example, victims of crime, Aboriginal women?" Napoleon said, in part, that politicizing healing "means contextualizing individual circumstances within communities" and asked, "Can the community help people not be trapped within the IRS experience?" To assist healing, she recommends

- calling on community resources
- recognizing the politics in ceremony, that ceremonies have cultural context
- recognizing deep pain
- recognizing the responsibility to ourselves and the community and,
- staying with the difficulty as, that is when one learns.

The next panelist was Dale Turner, of Government and Native American Studies, Dartmouth College, Hanover, New Hampshire. He stated the ethical challenge of reconciling what the commission [T&RC] will hear from the public policy in relation to Section 35 rights. He said the findings of the T&RC must be useful to the IRSSA and lead to renewed relationship. He cited the text of Section 35 and its application to *the Delgamuukw* decision of 1997. He noted the sub summation of Aboriginal interest to the State with the unilateral assertion of Crown sovereignty. He said Aboriginal rights are *Sui generic* [of one kind] and cited *the Vanderpeet* decision of 1996. He said the "Court and States must take into account the perspective of Aboriginal people understandable to the general legal and Constitutional system." He mentioned that the Royal Commission on Aboriginal Peoples Report [RCAP] lacks in public policy and though there are two hundred feet of archives in the RCAP Report and that the T&RC will also end as a huge pile of information. Turner recommends that the work of the T&RC will say "never again" to residential schools, "is used to level a historical field," and will result in narratives as being a political value in relation to Section 35 rights.

At coffee break, a male former IRS student collapsed to the floor in the foyer but was able to get up and announced that he was all right. I quickly went over to see if I could assist and ensure that he was all right.

Back in the conference during the questions period, not wanting an answer as I said I was only sharing the questions and had to take ownership in dealing with them, I asked, "Is it ethical for any individual or institution to focus only on the IRS former students who are the main financial beneficiaries of the IRSSA? Will reconciliatory strategies not only help heal the deep emotional and psychological harms of IRS former students, but lead to the healing of attitudes and historical misperceptions of institutions (schools, universities, the legal system, churches, other professions, governments, the media, entertainment industry, etc.), and the general public? What is healing? Can it be measured? At what point in time can healing be said to have occurred, if at all? Can the financial and emotional cost to the former students, their families, their community, and to the Canadian Government be calculated? Is healing a journey or an ongoing process, rather than an objective? Can catastrophic harms of the mind, body, and emotions ever be healed?" One panelist's response was "We need to have different kinds of conversation on power structure, violence, the need to have space and conversation that can change attitudes of the State and intellectuals."

Another question concerned the Aboriginal concept of justice. The response was "There is a gap. There is little recognition of indigenous legal concepts and norms."

Another question concerned inequity in knowledge, and those indigenous libraries are in our elders who are our knowledge. Our language is healing. Another related question was "How is the T&RC to deal with loss of language and culture?" Panelist Turner responded, "I think speaking a language from knowing a language."

Question: "Is the statement taking to occur in the T&RC a repeat of the RCAP [Report]?" Panelist Turner responded, "I think there is some value. Canadians don't know, next to nothing, of Aboriginal people or their own history. People need to read RCAP and bring it to the classroom. Chapter 11 of RCAP deals with Aboriginal people within Canada. It is important that the T&RC be aware of past Acts [legislation] in Canada, to appease, and so the meaning of 'Aboriginal peoples,' to remind the federal government, is the form [that] is not derived in the language of the reports but is rooted in rich cultural venues of Indigenous people."

Mathew Coon Come, former National Chief of the Assembly of First Nations, made a statement. He said, in part, "The language of the Constitution and the previous TRCs is not the language of the Cree. There are stories of atrocities and the removal of children from their families. What have we created with the limitations of the T&RC? Frustrations and expectations are raised. Perpetrators will not be subpoenaed. Have we learned from the past? Will the T&RC [Report] collect dust somewhere? [He expressed hope that] academics and civil rights groups will be able to intervene. People who have been victimized will have their day and will tell their stories in Cree." The response from panelist Ms. Napoleon was that the RCAP Report produced twenty thousand pages, and the *Delgamuuwk* decision produced fifty thousand pages. She mentioned the challenge of engaging the next generation of people who are not connected directly to IRS. She said it "was hoped that one of the court cases would generate interest, but unfortunately, the session was simplified due to language difficulty (terminology)."

On September 27, the topic "Media, Ethics, and Reconciliation" was dealt with. The Chair was Lance Delisle, morning host of K103 Radio in Kahnawake.

The first presenter was the Executive Producer-east for APTN, who spoke on the "Role of Media in Society." She quoted Knowlton Nash, formerly of CBC, who described the role of media is "to provide raw material for intelligent public debate." The media is gatekeeper engaged in a subjective process. It requires the understanding of issues of people who make decisions. It involves the concept of balance, for example, making the experience of IRS former students understandable. It is a process that needs to move forward and to move an agenda forward, such as healing. It involves choosing or makes availability to share your story with a reporter. The presenter advised being prepared for interviews. She said media cannot play an advocacy role. She was asked, "As a survivor, why take a chance to tell my misery and be laughed at?" The questioner said perhaps that she can tell her story in a book for her story to have full effect, for her story needs more than two minutes. The presenter responded, "Unfortunately, there's a lot of discrimination and racism out there. It's a choice. You are not obligated to take part."

The next presenter was Mike James, of the Department of Political Science, University of Victoria. He said the international aspect surrounding the T&RC is a powerful discourse in its website. There is capacity for the T&RC in Canada to move the country for understanding from the settler society. James said, "Canada's T&RC is different from the TRC in Uganda and other TRC hosting nations. It has some strong similarities with key countries who are [characterized by]:

1. Political context surrounding the T&RC
2. Kind of injustices the T&RC is dealing with

3. Nature of the T&RC's mandate, and
4. What are the motivations that the players have?"

James said, "The situation in Canada for hosting a T&RC is inauspicious." He talked about a few important barriers in Canada that require media strategy and engagement that may result in some success. There are political context indicators. He asked, "Is the T&RC being held under the same regime that committed the abuses? Or has there been a change? Or is the regime investigating itself? Are groups affected politically marginalized? In Canada, the regime continues. The Indian Act is still in place. Settlers are the majority. Government policy is paternalistic. Indigenous communities are politically marginalized."

James discussed the nature of injustices that a T&RC addresses and that will likely impede the commission. These are:

1. "What is the level of social complicity in the injustices committed? What is the time frame of the occurrence of the injustice? The more social complicity, the more resistance to the revelation of something really wrong with the basic structure of the society. It is easy to gauge complicity over one or two decades where there is a temporary period of madness that affected everyone and makes it easier for a commission to accept a T&RC. But in Canada, we are talking about a one-hundred-year period of IRS. The longer the social complicity, the more stonewalling and resisting."

2. Who or what is the major actor to disrupt a T&RC? It was the army in Latin America, while the civil population in Canada has potential to stonewall.

3. Mandate of the T&RC. In some ways, it's the kind of mandate where the regime and its marginalized victims intersect. There is "more robust focus on naming names." In Canada, there is intent on putting events in the past behind but weak on naming names.

4. Motivations—survivors most directly affected from federal government are very different according to a survey.

James said the priority is a public inquiry to engage the public in social change, for self-determination for indigenous people, which are not motivations of the Canadian government as indicated in its refusing to apologize. He summarized his topics as regime continuity, politically marginalized survivors, high level of social complicity, social complicity over a period of time, and government opposed to change. In regard in the role of media, James concluded, "Media, in some way, share in common mode of perception, of an eventful gaze, managing complexity that uses a spectacular, cataclysmic event and explanation of events to convey certain impacts. Media love to engage viewers and listeners in a lively debate. Some debates on historical injustices are borderline hate, for example, in letters to the editor, talk shows. The factual is becoming less and less tenable."

The next presenter was Ellen Gabriel, President of Quebec Native Women's Association. She said, "It is important that we look at the goals of the T&RC. Its mandate should be "to provide a culturally appropriate forum for survivors. The T&RC's mandate is awesome. They have a big mandate. The role of the media is to address truthfully the work of the T&RC and with cultural sensitivity workshops. The view of media and the public is from colonizers' viewpoint. Media must engage the public. There is continued vulcanization of Aboriginal people with cigarette selling and being a drain on the Canadian taxpayer. In my eighteen years with media, there is a lot of racism still out there. Do we need to feed more of it? Most media are privately owned and do not subscribe necessarily to ethics. It is so important that the media be educated on the true Canadian story, such as the picture of the little boy who enrolled at IRS with his braids and when, later, he is shown in his school uniform without his braids.

"In 1847, Edgerton Ryerson did a study for the government on industrial school training. Indian education was really that. [I hope] with the T&RC report, a gender-based analysis be done, that it record the continued discrimination of Indian women and record the taking away of the rites of passage of girls. I want journalists to do their best stories when they tell our stories. The Government of Canada failed to recognize that the IRS experience was an act of genocide, as it had a policy of targeting an identifiable group. I want the media to remember the IRS children lacked nourishment, love, and [experienced] physical hurts, and the parents, grandparents were not there to comfort their children.

"I want the government to realize that we are nothing without our land and communities. Harper's apology has a long way to go and that the media sit down again with us. Society needs compassion. This is one hundred years of history we're talking about, that it be taught in schools, and that Canadian children be taught what happened there. Racism is not acceptable. The T&RC's like coming up a Pandora's Box, and the media has a role and that you academics also be [an] alliance to Aboriginal people. Make research that can be shared. Indigenous knowledge is just as valid as nonindigenous knowledge and hope that the T&RC Report will not be just a weed growing somewhere."

The rapporteur, Renée Dupuis, Chief Commissioner of the Indian Claims Commission of Canada, summarized the presentation of this morning's panelists.

Jane Morley and Claudette Dumont-Smith, Truth and Reconciliation of Canada Commissioners were introduced. Commissioner Morley clarified that this conference is not a T&RC event but is an academic conference. She said, "A report will come after two and a half years in our mandate. The T&RC in Canada is different from South Africa. In Canada, we are dealing with a minority. In South Africa, there was a majority. Ownership of the process by survivors plays a central role in the T&RC. The mandate [is] of reconciliation, of changing relationships, and changing attitudes. [It will involve] telling a story, recognizing its relevance, it's healing of survivors, families, and Canada needs healing. [Regarding] the role of media, we need to engage is key in social networking. The apology does make a difference, [it's] a major settlement approach. [The IRS experience] happened because of a policy of elimination. Polling [after the apology showed that] 80 percent of Canadians were aware of the apology. [With] the T&RC mandate, somehow we need to recapture that, what survivors want, what they want in a change in power relationship, and from dominant/subordinate relationship but one of interdependence."

Questions and comments from the floor included:

"In many countries, violations by perpetrators are protected by a veil of silence, a veil of euphemism. In Canada, certain harms and abuses is an issue. The challenge of the T&RC is to go beyond euphemism. [There's] need for certain standards, parameters, that is absolutely essential. The challenge of the T&RC is when survivors want to tell everything including identifying abusers. [There is] need for protocols within the community and the media."

Kathleen Mahoney said she was the chief negotiator for the AFN in the IRSSA. She said the naming of people is impacted by legislation. She said, "Privacy Act in Canada limits to some extent. We were told by survivors that survivors did not want a court/trial approach. In Ireland, naming names did not work. Survivors want a safe cultural environment. Survivors [in Canada] did not want to be cross-examined. The IRSSA is a court agreement and court-supervised agreement. Documents can be called by parties. There is recourse to the courts when churches refuse to [release documents]. The T&RC's challenge [is review] of how Indian residential schools were created, who, and why they ever [existed]. The T&RC is not a public inquiry."

Claudette Dumont-Smith, T&RC commissioner, said there is the "issue of safety and health concerns. Recollection of stories brings forth all kinds of issues and is being recalled. There is a Health Canada IRS Regional Health Support Program, works 24/7 and refers [survivors] to psychologists and counselors. Aboriginal people have to be there in everything we do."

Questions and comments were the following:

- Filling survivor needs to criteria, for example, cultural help. It is important to get down to survivors and what they need. We have a key to our own destiny
- The issue of trust is a challenge
- Because of victimization, the spirit of people needs to be rebuilt
- The T&RC must include the Inuit in the process, and
- Healing of intergenerational impacts.

National Chief Phil Fontaine of the Assembly of First Nations gave his plenary presentation. He said he has ten years of residential school experience, is a survivor, and comes from a family of twelve. Ten of his siblings attended residential school. His mom and dad attended, while his grandfather on his mother's side attended an industrial school. He said that twenty years ago, he went public with his abuse experienced at residential school. He said, "Canadians need to know, that it become part of the public record and to engage in healing to make ourselves better. Government and churches, the perpetrators, had to acknowledge their experience and at some point, that they had to apologize. I am hopeful that what I have to say is useful to the challenge before us. To understand the T&RC, people should be, at least, [to] understand the history.

"The idea of T&RC did not come by accident. We had to fight for everything that we have, the IRSSA, apology, T&RC we fought for that, every inch of space. No one came to us to say you need that. It is so important to thousands of people, many of whom suffered abuse that is unimaginable.

The T&RC is important to those people, and no one has the right to take that away.

"In 1998, Minister [of Indian and Northern Affairs Canada] Jane Stewart presented the Statement of Reconciliation. It is significant that we advanced this issue. We knew it wasn't enough that the government had to go beyond this; that Canada was responsible for what happened. There was $350 million for healing. We knew it wasn't enough. We knew one of the results would be floodgates, filing civil suits, claims, charging perpetrators of criminal acts. There were twelve thousand claims before courts. The government was struggling. It came to me for ideas. We met on a process other than courts. There was concern that survivors would be revictimized. The Alternative Dispute Resolution (ADR) emerged through dialogue session. Government provided $1.7 billion, which was bogged in spending on maintaining the system. The government spent four dollars to one dollar in compensation, and that compensation would take fifty-seven years. We realized we needed something else, that it [ADR] was flawed, deeply flawed. We met in Calgary. There were two hundred and fifty people, experts, church representatives, elders, survivors, and AFN. We looked carefully at ADR. It was obvious we needed something other than ADR. I told Mario Dion, ADM, [that] we go out and study across the world. We studied the Irish experience, and a report [produced] became the basis for the May 2005 political agreement with the previous government.

"The elements of the agreement were the CEP, commemoration, additional support for the Aboriginal Healing Foundation, apology, T&RC, and an improved ADR. We felt alone. We couldn't capture the country's interest. We were supported by the survivors and the chiefs. In 2005, we signed the agreement in November. Prime Minister Martin made a commitment there would be compensation. We put a business case together that led to signing of the agreement on November 21, 2005. It was a complicated process. At one meeting, there were eighty lawyers around the room. It was an achievement, the CEP of $1.9 billion, IAP, and T&RC. The only other interest group that supported us was the churches: United Church, Presbyterian, Anglican, and Roman Catholic. The T&RC is so important because we knew when all the money is gone, this will be a lasting legacy, and this will be forever.

"On the apology, we were in the House of Commons in our own right. The apology sets the stage for reconciliation, so real healing can be achieved. The T&RC is about writing the missing chapter in Canadian [history]. A survey found that 83 percent of Canadians were aware of the apology and that 73 percent supported the apology. The T&RC is not a public inquiry, nor naming names. It does not have subpoena power. It is so broadly based. Churches and government have opened up their records and their release. The thing that guided us, in personal disclosure, was survivors saying, 'We don't want to go to the courts.' Survivors wanted to be assured of their safety, not to give in to Canada. The details of the abuse are in the IAP. It is a very painful process. We see the T&RC, as an incredible opportunity, become part of Canadian history and that real healing happens. The T&RC has to be truly independent. It's a survivors' commission for both national events and commission-based initiatives. Government must not be allowed to control the commission. The commission will preside over truth sharing. The commission has to be partial to the survivors. We support 100 percent of the T&RC and the commissioners. Justice Laforme, at present, is not well, and we hope he recovers."

The next topic was "Memory, Truth, and Reconciliation." The first presenter was a PowerPoint presentation on "Who Can Share Memory?" by Sue Campbell, of the Department of Philosophy, Dalhousie University. She dealt with memory, how people share in a political context, and how change can be made. She said, "T&RCs are a lot about memory, of former students, and Canadians." She talked about the values of memory, about who has the power, and different ways of sharing memory. She said nonindigenous Canadians played a role and still play in assimilation. She cited the apology and closure from a throne speech of Prime Minister Harper. She asked, "Who can share what kind of memory?" She said, "Part of the legacy of IRS is the stereotype of the 'frozen past,' a dehumanizing stereotype and that [people impacted have] to get over it is another form of assimilation." Campbell advised that our conceptions of memory are of political conceptions, and therefore "our views of memory are not politically impartial."

APPENDIX S

TRUTH AND RECONCILIATION COMMISSION—SHARING TRUTH: CREATING A NATIONAL RESEARCH CENTRE ON RESIDENTIAL SCHOOLS CONFERENCE, MARCH 1–3, 2011, VANCOUVER, BRITISH COLUMBIA—A SUMMARY REPORT

ERIC J. LARGE

On March 1, 2011, Justice Murray Sinclair, Chair of the Truth and Reconciliation Commission of Canada (TRC), provided the welcome and overview. He said there were five hundred registrants of the conference, and one hundred fifty survivors registered. He mentioned the intent of Indian residential schools as an assimilation process, Christianization, and that it was both successful and largely unsuccessful. It was successful in that language and culture were taken away. It was unsuccessful in that assimilation did not succeed. Justice Sinclair said significant abuses occurred with lawsuits filed in the 1990s. The Supreme Court of Canada found there was government and church liability. A class action settlement agreement was court created with compensation for residential school former students and the creation of the Truth and Reconciliation Commission. In the mandate of the TRC was the creation of a National Research Centre. Justice Sinclair mentioned that speakers from sixteen countries would relate reconciliation processes worldwide in the areas of document collection, archiving, and protection of records. He added that the legacy of Indian residential schools (IRS) and much about IRS was hidden from both Canadian and Aboriginal people. The T&RC's task is to ensure that the National Research Centre will contribute to a permanent memory of IRS. Justice Murray said that T&RC's mandate "calls on us to gather documents on Indian residential schools and placed in the National Research Centre, that statements also be placed in the National Research Centre, and that access to history is made available."

Brad Morse, Dean of Law, University of Waikato, Paring, New Zealand, and University of Ottawa, Faculty of Law, gave a PowerPoint overview of the TRC mandate. He said the T&RC mandate is in Schedule N of the Indian Residential School Settlement Agreement [IRSSA] that gives the T&RC

a five-year term with three commissioners and staff, regional liaisons, and an Indian Residential School Survivor Committee of ten members. Morse briefly outlined the tasks of the T&RC as:

1. Facilitate the gathering of the "truth" through individual statement taking, truth sharing by former students, their families, communities, and from those involved in the residential former schools
2. Support the holding of seven national events and community events to contribute to truth, healing, and reconciliation
3. Foster public education about what happened in the Indian residential schools and legacy
4. Aid in the development of regional, community, and national commemoration initiatives
5. Encourage reconciliation, and
6. Create as comprehensive an historical record as possible.

Morse cited article 1(e) of Schedule N of the IRSSA that creates the National Research Centre [NRC] as "records shall be preserved and made accessible to the public for future study and use." In addition, article (3[d]) authorizes the T&RC "must establish a research centre and ensure preservation of its archives." Morse said the NRC would continue to grow after the T&RC is closing and final report [completed] and that the NRC will be open to receive statements with no time limitation, and from the Independent Process Payment (IAP), litigation, and dispute resolution processes. The purpose of the NRC is to ensure that "all materials are created or received with a purpose and tradition in keeping with the objectives and intent of the commission's work." He said the NRC must reflect the openness of the T&RC work to move forward. He stated the NRC's collections "must be accessible to former students, their families and communities, the general public, researchers, and educators who wish to include this historical material in curricula."

With regard to subjection to privacy legislation, Morse asked, "How to maximize access?" He continued saying that preservation of documents require a place for repository but does not mean only one place for access. There must be consideration for modern technology strategies, regional access, and mobile TRC displays. The management of the NRC would also consider a standalone center, perhaps be a branch of the Library and Archives of Canada (LAC) with an oversight board, linking with the LAC and the Canadian Museum of Civilization with participation with survivors and Aboriginal organizations, linking with the Canadian Race Relations Foundation or the Aboriginal Healing Foundation, and links with others ensuring permanency all established out of the T&RC's budget (article 12 of the IRSSA).

In concluding, Morse said there are questions regarding the scope of the T&RC that need clarifying. Some of these questions need elaboration, such as the T&RC is not a federal commission like the Royal Commission on Aboriginal Peoples (RCAP) or all others. T&RC's source is the IRSSA that is an out-of-court settlement binding all parties to it and subject to judicial scrutiny. Morse ended, "The commissioners carry the yearning for true recognition of the horrendous harms done, the desire for healing of generations, hope for reconciliation and renewal shared by millions in Canada, and the goal to always remember that it never, ever happens again."

Trudy Huskamp Peterson, author of *Final Acts: Guide to Preserving the Records of Truth Commission, USA*, spoke of challenges and considerations that need review. Among these are what happens to records after a commission ends? What principles are used to evaluate to the role of human rights? Questions needing to be asked relate to the temporary nature of truth commissions established to inquire into and report on a path of abuses committed by a previous representative regime and usually during and immediately after a regime change. Peterson said commissions that were completed by early 2006 were nine in Central and South America; six in Africa; and four in Asia. She said there are two record types. The first is physical records that includes paper, electronic, audio-visual, and some objects. The second is functional, which has the aspects of function (administration), program (decision making, final report, and statements), and investigation. Sources of information include government records, records of nongovernment organizations, commercial and noncommercial records, and records of international and intergovernmental organizations. Custody of commission records needs to be considered as well as access to the records. Will there be records laws controlling access, or would there be special interventions?

Peterson mentioned the United Nations principles drafted by Louis Joinet, and adopted in 1997, against impunity of perpetrators. Peterson said Diane Orentlicher updated these principles in 2005. The Joinet principles are based on the right to know (by the person and collective) and the duty to remember (responsibility of the State). The State's role is to "ensure the preservation of and access to archives covering violations of human rights and humanitarian law."

Peterson said interarchival initiatives must consider descriptive standards, code of ethics, and draft principles of access to records. These initiatives must also provide for the selection of a successor repository and consider the legal aspects, such as the application of existing law, confidentiality, and access issues. There must also be political consideration. Is there reputation and reliability of the custodial institution resulting in access and where records should be deposited inside or outside of the government? Archival work is based on the nature of the records, existing capacity of archives, financial and secure situation, and experience with public and access services. Is the archival work sensitive to the research needs of the communities? Peterson concluded that archivists as duty bearers for human rights, appreciate, secure, preserve, describe, provide access, and promote use of the archival records.

DOCUMENTING AND MEMORIALIZING HUMAN RIGHTS ABUSES IN AFRICA

Doudou Diene, chair of the Board of the International Coalition of Sites and Programs of Conscience, former United Nations Special Rapporteur on Contemporary Forms of Racism, Racial Discrimination, Xenophobia, and Related Intolerance in *Senegal*, reported that children have been taken and are being abducted recently in Chad when one hundred children were taken to Europe. He said central to truth and reconciliation is the issue of memory, which is one dimension of justice. He said memory as facts raise the question whether the National Research Centre is going to focus only on facts. What of the silence and invisibility of the victims and survivors? There is also silence in the current history books. Crimes can be documented in written form or in the oral traditions, in the memory of the victim. Memory is carried in cultural expression, paintings, dance, etc. that provides information on the tragedy one has lived. Mr. Diene said, "The impact of silence occurs when historians have manipulated what happened as in Indian residential schools. Silence is the focus today, on what is currently happening, not what happened. We are wondering what to do with memory, of the facts and trying to provide historical truth. There is the ethical context in which violence happened and to try to investigate the human values that were the basis at the core of the Indian residential schools. What are the values today? While factual memory is important, living memory is absolutely important." Mr. Diene proposed three ideas. One is investigation of the specific situation of victims and the universality of the practices of victimization. The second is to investigate human values. The third is to look at the impact on the present day by linking facts, living memory, and the human values of today.

Freddy Mutanguha, executive director, South African History Archives, *South Africa*, gave his presentation in French. One important development he related was the establishment of the Kigali Memorial Centre.

Catherine Kennedy, Executive Director, South African History Archive, *South Africa*, talked about independent archives, not national archives. She said the South African government between 1948 and 1994 imposed apartheid. The South Africa Truth Commission was established in 1995 to record the memory of the past, to attain justice, and to promote national healing. Over twenty-two thousand victims made statements, and more than seven thousand perpetrators applied for amnesty. Ms. Kennedy stated there are unfinished reparations. The final version of the Truth Commission report is in German. The materials produced uncovered human rights violations and covered part of the transition process. There are gaps and unrepresented histories. Ms. Kennedy said the commission had a narrow scope of mandate. There was no consideration of violations that occurred prior to 1960. There are also no records taken of abuses in other countries where apartheid was in effect. In a form of revisionism, all three South African parties challenged the findings of the Truth Commission report. There was loss of records through theft. There was a need to guard against purging of memory. Access or lack of access to records needs consideration. Kennedy briefly outlined the South African History Archives mandate and some of the challenges it faces, such as privacy concern.

Tom Adami, Chief of Archives and Records Management of the United Nations Mission of *Sudan*, gave a PowerPoint presentation called "Setting the Scene." Mr. Adami began with the idea of intersecting of archives with the process of reconciliation and how process management can inform decisions about Indian residential schools. He said today, March 2011, inequality and abuse of rights continues. Technology also is very critical. It does not follow that accessibility will occur. There is also accessibility of records by people and illiteracy. Mr. Adami's PowerPoint photos were of images drawn by children affected by conflict in Chad in 2009. He spoke on the role of archives in justice and in the accountability of legal bodies. He said forgiveness is an individual concept, of individual human beings that is an important part of reconciliation. Technology used in accessing information is necessary but is expensive. Adami said knowledge management could have a techno central approach, an ecological approach with people and the environment, and a holistic approach with the creation of interface of all the stakeholders. He asked, "Is there a best practice model for a T&RC?" He concluded, "Maintaining archives is ensuring that human rights are preserved."

Questions and comments from the audience and previous presenters focused on memory and memorials, memoria, and memorializing. Doudou Diene said that knowledge, facts, ethics, values have a role in personal and collective transformation.

Stephen Smith, Executive Director, Shoah Foundation, *USA*, was the lunch keynote speaker. His message is the value of an archives as an archives of conscience not just an archives of collections.

DOCUMENTING AND MEMORIALIZING THE HOLOCAUST

Joanne Rudof, Archivist, Fortunoff Foundation, Yale University, *USA*, said the New Haven Area Survivors began producing video tape documentaries in May 1979 of one hour each of four survivors of the holocaust, and, in June of 1979 a Holocaust Survivors Firm Project began at Yale University with professors and staff that later included other states. Ms. Rudof said the project expanded and systematized. Recordings are called testimonies. There is team approach, attentive listening by two listeners, and emotional support. Survivors introduce themselves rather than being prompted or made script ready before. Listeners and interviewers are prepared. The background, history, geography related to concentration and displaced persons camps are considered. Survivors and witnesses state their experience at their own pace. Rudof said this process is a painful recollection not for healing. The pain triggers are spontaneous. She concluded that many pieces are still missing after sixty-five years since the Holocaust. Links are www.neworbis.library.yale.edu/testimonies and www.library.yale.edu/testimonies.

Dr. Susanne Urban, Head of Historical Research, International Tracing Service (ITS), *Germany*, began her PowerPoint of the mission statement of ITS, which is to serve victims. She described the working relationship of the UNRRA, IRO, and ITS. She said ITS is responsible for preserving documents of the fate of the victims/survivors of the Holocaust and the Nazi persecution and supports historical research. The website is www.itsarolsen.org.

Kim Simon, managing director, USC Shoah Foundation Institute, University of Southern California, *USA*, presented the topic, "For Visual History and Education." She stressed the importance of the duty of care, concern over intellectual property, privacy, context, and potential misuse.

She also expressed the need to widen access to records to benefit teaching, research, learning, and policymaking. She mentioned the work of the "I Witness" educational project whose focus is with Holocaust and genocide survivors and that witness video testimonies should be made available online. The link is http://college.usc.edu/uhi/aboutus/.

ARCHIVING FOR ADVOCACY

Kate Doyle, Senior Analyst, National Security Archive (NSA), George Washington University, *USA*, stated that NSA is a nongovernment organization founded in 1985 by activists for fighting for people's right to know in the United States and worldwide. It uses the Freedom of Information Act (FOIA) to obtain declassified government and agency documents. She said one benefit of Canada's T&RC is the transfer of its skills of collecting, documenting, and archiving. The link is www.gwu.edu.

Grace Lile, Director of Operations and Archive Witness, New York, *USA*, said her organization is involved in human rights, advocacy, and activism. She said it is also involved in training and collaborating in the recording in video documentaries human rights advocacy. The recordings hold five thousand hours of video developed since 1992 of events or abuses. The link is grace@witnessforchange.org.

Marijana Toma, of the Coalition for RECOM [Regional Commission], told of the real war in Croatia and Serbia where there was ethnic cleansing. In Serbia, there was conflict between Kosovan Serbs and Kosovan Albanians. This conflict had widespread atrocities. Ms. Toma said RECOM found about forty thousand missing persons and is still looking for about sixty thousand missing persons. War crimes were committed with many victims. There was denial, minimization, or justification for the crimes. Ms. Toma said research was conducted and documents collected for the prosecution of war criminals and for raising indictments. One of the challenges faced by the Human Law Centre (III.C) in Serbia was the government and a hostile public. Ms. Toma said the III.C conducts credible documentation, which it also preserves. This documentation includes witness statements collected since 1992. She concluded that there is desire for a regional T&RC supported by a coalition of the European Union, the President of Serbia, and one other support body.

Ramon Alberch, Director of the School of Archivists and Document Administration, Autonomous University of Barcelona and former President of the Archivists Without Borders, *Spain*, reported that his organization is concerned with original and reliable documentation, fighting impunity and collective amnesia, ensuring access to information, establishing resolution, protecting human rights, and restoring confiscated assets. Mr. Alberch reported ASF (Archiveros sin Fronteres) [Archivists without Borders] is involved in the protection and restoration of archives in countries of dictatorships. He said ASF works in training and working with families of the disappeared, for example missing children.

Alberch highlighted the construction of the Democratic Memorial of Catalonia as a homage to "A Future for the Past." He said there was collective amnesia for the period 1976 to 1990 when silence was a pact. Another challenge he reported is political policy, and the need for a review of the past is advisable. He said collective amnesia is not conducive to reconciliation. He said the Law of Democracy Memorial established by the Parliament of Catalonia in 2007 has main goals of promoting democratic memory, preserving memory as a civil right, identifying people who disappeared during the Spanish Civil War and during the Franco regime, attention for former prisoners, tributes, conferences, and an information and documentation center.

On March 2, the keynote speaker, Georges Erasmus, Chair, Aboriginal Healing Foundation (AHF) and Co chair of the Royal Commission on Aboriginal Peoples (RCAP), referred to the IRSSA and said the T&RC's mandate, within budget, is to record Indian residential school material and documents. He related RCAP's and AHF's work in hearing survivors at gatherings and the publication of stories. He said a story is a powerful thing. [Provided it is believed—my comment] a story can bring about a political revolution and has the potential to bring about cultural and spiritual transformation. Erasmus commented that the "Indian problem" and the breakdown of trust is the story of Canada and in the settlement of the West. The treaty mentioned education where the transfer of useful European skills [is taken] as a necessary supplement to traditional life. Churches served as an economic supplement for missionary work. Government influenced the treaty that resulted in the loss of the spirit and intent of the treaty. Erasmus said "Aboriginal people became the objects of the Christian campaign of a State-supported school system that was painful and violated the trust relationship. Treaties, on the other hand, were based on mutual respect and dialogue and endeavored to create an environment based on the concept of the wholeness of life. Indian residential schools misplaced and abused trust".

Mr. Erasmus said the AHF conducted research on the Common Experience Payment, prisons, HIV/AIDS, Inuit, healing Aboriginal men, resilience, historical trauma, FAS, and other subjects. He said all these subjects have a demonstrable relationship to the IRS experience. He said these subjects link with the child welfare system, adoption, and day schools and that all of these developments must be part of the T&RC National Research Centre. Mr. Erasmus said it is a conceptual, technical, and creative challenge to find new ways to engage the community. There is neither analogy nor precedent. Narrative or storytelling is one way to evoke this legacy.

Mr. Erasmus stated that there is the potential of stewardship of this legacy with non-Aboriginal people and the use of technologies. He said, "Indians are the product of diverse, complex, and singular institutions. In addition, there are those Indian institutions, such as the Indian Act, prisons, child welfare system, IRS system, and economic and cultural institutions. There is need for creative brainstorming that ensures this project goes beyond archiving to where Native people engage with the public through access to their voice in participatory narrative and research. We must step into the twenty-first century in a new kind or relationship." Erasmus concluded that the National Research Centre values archiving and its access by all people including street people.

Karen Busby, founding director, University of Manitoba Centre for Human Rights Research, said most Canadians are still willfully blind or oblivious to the work of the T&RC and Indian residential school experience that is best described as genocide. She said that the NRC must be a sacred place for learning, teaching, and that it must create the conditions for social transformation she hoped this conference would achieve.

DOCUMENTING AND MEMORIALIZING HUMAN RIGHTS ABUSES IN LATIN AMERICA

Otilia Lux de Coti, parliamentarian, former member of Historical Clarification Commission, former Vice President of the Permanent Forum on Indigenous Issues, *Guatemala*, delivered his presentation in Spanish. Lux de Coti *said Mapu chin* is the Mayan people's language. *Guatamalan* means the home of the eagles. He advised the conference participants to have great strength, to his brothers and sisters in Canada in this work to have positive results. He related the history of Guatemala and the repression by the Spanish that led to cultural resistance that was the strategy of the ancestors of the Guatemala people. He reported that with the establishment of the Historical Clarification Commission (HCC), the world was informed of the genocide of the Mayans. However, he reported, the oppressors were governed by impunity. These oppressors were the officers of the Guatemalan army who massacred thousands of people.

Lux de Coti said 55 percent of the thirteen and a half million Guatemalans are Mayan. He said the HCC works at clarifying violent situations that occurred, of work caused by the closing of democratic spaces since 1985, and of social and cultural relationships. He said there were 3,893 forced disappearances, torture, and rapes. Armed conflict has created a negative attitude for Guatemala. He recommended there has to be truth and justice. There is no justice in Guatemala. There is legislation called the Law of National Reconciliation where Article 8 of that law deals with genocide and forced disappearances. This law is internal to Guatemala and is still not official. Lux de Coti said with the National Research program, eleven thousand files were given to the Public Ministry. Twelve thousand exhumations were conducted by a nongovernment organization but not by the State yet. Lux de Coti recommended that the T&RC maintain the [knowledge] of the IRS through technology and that it is important to teach critical history at all levels of school, training of teachers, and to eliminate racism.

Maria Luisa Sepulveda, Executive Director of the Musea del Memoria y los Derechos Humanos in *Chile*, gave a PowerPoint presentation. She said it is important to understand the value of the role of archives and human rights in Chile. Archives reveal how human rights were violated in the 1973–1990 dictatorship. Human rights organizations developed and collected testimony and other tools that helped the organizations in arriving at the truth and justice process. Sepulveda said a truth commission was set up in 1990 involving survivors and the disappeared. There were 3,195 persons identified. Human rights archives were provided to the Truth Commission for analysis, but Chile had to wait thirteen years for the dictatorship to end. In 2003–04, the Truth Commission worked with the Process of Justice in Democracy. A government program provided legal assistance for missing detainees. Sepulveda said that in 1990–2006, over two hundred remains of victims were found. Also in 2006, identity errors were confirmed. Individual reparation was considered as well as missing detainees and political executions.

Sepulveda said symbolic reparation was conducted in the form of memorials in Santiago, such as the Calama Memorial. There are 180 memorials in total. Sepulveda said a memory and human rights museum was conceptualized in 2000 from the reports of the Truth Commission but that its establishment is a presidential decision. She said there are demands from organizations of victims of gestures of memories, detention places, etc. Sepulveda said the Institutional Framework for the Process of Implementation Foundation was created, with State and HHRR organizations participating. Its task is to build collections, elaborate exhibit script, conduct public perception studies and interviews with actors, and to define and install museology. Sepulveda said "An Archive Collection and Document Centre will deal with museum patrimony and will also express dignity for the victims as well as the defense of human rights and denounce oppression. The role of education is to be a resource addressed to distinct audiences with a special emphasis on the young and children and to promote and foster reflection". In concluding, Sepulveda said, "Painful words must be acknowledged" and that it is important to take charge [so] that legitimate aspirations of truth, justice, and reparations are valued. She said we must learn from the events and draw conclusions that go beyond generations and to build a more fraternal society. "Taking charge of the past will strengthen democracy in Chile."

Christina Correa, representing the International Centre for Transitional Justice NGO, New York, *USA*, said it is important for societies to look at their past, to make efforts at truth, justice, reparation for victims, to look at structures for learning injustices that occurred in the past and at what happened to the power structure that allowed these policies to happen. She said few Truth Commission recommendations are adopted. Human rights violations are a message by perpetrators that the victims are worth nothing. Ms. Correa said however, "Victims have dignity and are members of humankind." There is a need of change in the power relations between victims and the State."

Ms. Correa displayed photos on screen she referred to as "More than just a memory" that recorded historical memories of communities in Peru where there was a T&RC for internal armed conflict that was fought in the Andes and the Amazon. Seventy-five percent of the victims spoke Quechua or another mother tongue. Correa said archives of the communities are with the Office of the Ombudsman. A Museum of Memory is under construction. The link is http://lugardelamemoria.org/. Ms. Correa said the recovery of the memories in fifty communities is contained in a nine-volume T&RC Report in Spanish that speaks little to rural communities. The solution, she said, is building a common approach or process that builds trust. She also recommends integrating a multicultural approach and recognizing differences as a political statement.

Ms. Correa emphasized working with the communities and leaders is important. She said "The process must be respected and not push for results. Fear must be dealt with such as well as recognizing displacement as a break of the order and legacy as in losing one's parents. An approach may deal with the conspiracy of silence of victims and perpetrators". Ms. Correa briefly described the Historical Memory Working Group that is an autonomous academic team that is part of the National Commission for Repatriation. She said "The risks in memory recovery are revictimization, dividing communities, and silencing victims. Workshops can open questions to stimulate memory. Maps can be used to encourage dialogue as well as walks through signature places. Time lines can be made as well as drawing one's body and individual interview conducted". Ms. Correa concluded that the present and future must be looked at, but to realize the most important is "memory as contribution to healing and a resource for recovering control and power to be actors."

Elizabeth Silkes, Executive Director representing the International Coalition of Sites of Conscience (ICSC) said ICSC, founded in 1999, works with a network of museums. The work involves changing the role of museums and historical sites from static to evolving awareness. ICSC now has 250 members. It helps publish case studies, host websites, conducts an online member forum, and a human rights campaign. ICSC's work begins with a power of place (site of memories), fosters dialogue with various stakeholders, and provides awareness for visitors to take action. Work is in the U.S., Africa, Europe, Russia, and in Latin America (Argentina, Chile, Peru, Salvador, and Uruguay). Ms. Silkes said ICSC's role is to influence political culture, inform on totalitarianism, and work with other human rights organizations networks.

EXAMPLES OF CENTERS IN BC

Robert Banno, founding president, National Nikkei Museum and Heritage Centre, and President, Nikkei Place Foundation, said he is involved with three facilities (a seniors' residence; a fifty-nine-unit care home; and the National Nikkei that houses the Canadian Japanese Museum). He said twenty-one thousand Canadian Japanese were uprooted in WWII. There was internment of families and fishermen that had economic impact to Japanese Canadians. In 1998, a Redress Settlement provided compensation of twenty-one thousand dollars per person. A $12 million fund was divided. Japanese Canadians bought land from the Japanese Canadian Redress Fund in Vancouver for $3 million for the Nikkei Care Home and the National Nikkei Museum.

Frieda Miller, Executive Director, Vancouver Holocaust Education Centre, said this center is a museum that promotes Holocaust education, hosts symposia on the Holocaust, and supports school programs and teaching material, such as the Nuremberg Student Mock Trial and with teaching resources. The center also supports professional development for teachers, Holocaust commemoration events, public programs on topics such as anti-Semitism and fascism in Canada in the 1930s and the 1940s, and Open Hearts-Closed Doors and The War Orphan Projects. It works with prime sources. There are outreach speakers. Survivors are best. In working with museum collections and archives, artifacts are important as they give weight to identification of survivors as people.

The lunch keynote speaker was Phil Fontaine, President of Ishkonigan Consulting and Mediation, and former National Chief, Assembly of First Nations. He gave a background and development of the Indian Residential School Settlement Agreement from abuse lawsuits, the Alternative Dispute Resolution, and the negotiations and challenges for the IRSSA of 2005 and 2006 to its implementation. He noted that this agreement is more than relating and getting compensation for abuses but is also about human rights. He gave his unconditional support for the T&RC's mandate and activities.

INDIGENOUS COLLECTIONS FROM NORTH AMERICA

George Nicholas, Director, Intellectual Property Issues in Cultural Heritage, Simon Fraser University, *Vancouver*, said that part of the problem is for Indian people whose cultural property has been most commodified. Indian people are indigenous people who have non-Western customary law.

David George Shongo, Tribal Archives Director, Seneca Nation, and member of the Society of American Archivist Native American Archives Roundtable: Protocols for Native American Archival Materials, *Seneca Nation, USA* mentioned deer skin archiving. He said archiving is nothing but a trustworthy information system. He referred to living archives, such as dancing to a standing quiver song before a hunt. Arrows quiver around in anticipation of a hunt. Shongo said the Seneca language is an archive of words. He concluded there must be a road map or guidelines for the security and protocols for Native American archival material.

Richard West, founding Director of the National Museum of the American Indian (NMAI), Smithsonian Institution, and member of the Society of American Archivists Native American Archives Roundtable,

Confederated Tribes of Grand Ronde, USA, said collection should involve mutual collaborators. Research should be inclusive, community based and defined, be direct and continuing, address the emotional effects of IRS, and address all aspects of the issue. He said developing sites of conscience is a work in progress. Principles serve as a guide in healing, addressing additional contemporary issues, inspire people in making change, and make the legacy of IRS responsible of both Natives and non-Natives.

Jennifer O'Neal, Head Archivist, National Museum of the American Indian (NMAI), Smithsonian Institution, gave a brief history of the NMAI, including the mission of the Archive Centre. She said there are media archives, online resources, and cultural stewardship. O'Neal said no T&RC exists in the U.S. There was a Native American Apology Resolution in 2008. NMAI activities include the Harvest of Hope Symposium, publications, exhibits, events, the White Bison Inc., Ancient Ways of Knowing (2009), Forgiveness Journey, and interest in the United Nations Declaration of the Rights of Indigenous Peoples.

Joanna Sassoon, Manager, Forgotten Australians and Former Child Migrants Oral History Project at the National Library Bringing Them Home Oral History Project, *Australia*, referred to a paper, "Giving History a Nudge." She spoke of the power of archives, stories, and the purposes for which the stories may serve. She said there must common desire to rebuild histories and new futures. It was confirmed, in 1997, a stolen generation of fifty thousand Aboriginal and mixed peoples. Care of children is a State responsibility in Australia.

Ms. Sassoon said it is difficult to access church records due to fear of litigation. With the work of the Australia Institute for Indigenous Studies, the truth about what happened to children is a form of cultural genocide. The Australia Archivist Act covers records of inquiries. Oral history projects, such as the "Bringing Them Home Project," provide children an understanding of the experience of what removal actually means. Archives, education, and dialogue give the nation a new future. Ms. Sassoon concluded there must be a national framework to balance national stories with local stories. She said the challenge is to balance what constitutes an archive and to include community empowerment.

Modifu Hogue, Trustee and Secretary of the Liberation War Museum (LWM) in *Bangladesh*, said the LWM opened in March 1996. Bangladesh, a part of the Indian subcontinent, emerged as an independent state in 1991. Hogue said there were massive violations of human rights with almost three million killed out of a population of seventy-five million. There was struggle against military dictatorship and secular versus pan-Islamism. In 1975, the military came into power. There was distortion and denial of human rights and justice.

Hogue said, "An eight-member trustee board was formed to establish a museum. Memorial sites were identified to commemorate killing fields. Education activities and collecting of eyewitness accounts by students of the events of 1971 from senior family members were conducted. These accounts are compiled into the museum's archive of memory". Hogue said LWM has a mobile exhibit and LWM has brought more than seventy thousand students into the program. The interviewer and interviewee know each other very well in the telling of past accounts. This promotes confidence and the stories are forwarded to LWM. LWM publishes the *Wall Magazine* that is sent to the schools. There is a proposed site and design of the new museum. Hogue concluded there is continuing work on bringing perpetrators to justice. Memorialization is important in the involvement of the young generation.

Patrick Walsh, Senior Advisor, Post IRC Secretariat, *East Timor*, gave a brief history of East Timor, which is located in the Indonesian archipelago one and a half hours northwest of Darwin, Australia. Walsh said East Timor has a population of one million with half under eighteen. He said "It is one of the poorest countries with subsistence lifestyle focused on the here and now. However, it also has large oil and gas resources. East Timor suffered violations of human rights. Beginning in 1975, there has been truth seeking, statement taking, and public hearings. Media and books have recorded the terrible damage done to survivors if impunity is allowed. There is community reconciliation for minor crimes". Walsh's work was part of East Timor's Commission for Reception, Truth and Reconciliation (CAVR). He said post CAVR saw the establishment of backup storage in London, England, library and Internet access, a bookshop, dissemination, a comic book, video *Dulan ba Dame* (The Road to Peace) East Timor 1974–1999. There is also a walkthrough exhibition. Walsh said unresolved issues include the role of the churches where support is minimal, and draft legislation to institute programs of reparations and institutes of memory to implement CAVR recommendations.

Judge Stephanie Milroy, Deputy Chair, Waitangi Tribunal, *New Zealand*, related ancestry history. She mentioned the establishment of the Waitangi Tribunal, which can only make recommendations. She said the purpose of the tribunal in 1975 was to inquire into contemporary claims that the Crown is in breach of in modern times. In 2004, the Maori decided to make a claim for the return of a national park. In 2011, a report was completed that indicated the end of negotiation was near, but the prime minister said there would be no return of the national park. There is a deadline for histories claims filing. The link is www.waitangitribunal.org.

PERSPECTIVES FROM CANADA

There was a panel presentation of four individuals. Ann Stevenson, Information Manager, UBC Museum of Anthropology (MOA), *Vancouver*, gave a PowerPoint that revealed the MOA was established in 1948 and houses the MOA Centre for Cultural Research. MOA renewal projects include the building and a multiversity gallery. The Collections Research Enhancement Project includes collections access, language, and expert knowledge. There is an Oral History and Language Lab and Reciprocal Research Network (RRN). The RRN is a three-year project and is a development process with open source tools and a contribution/integration system. Stevenson recommended engagement with primary users and the building of long-term relationships. The link is http://www.rrnpilot.org/.

Stuart Murray, president and CEO of the Canadian Museum for Human Rights (CMHR) in *Winnipeg*, said the CMHR "will nourish national discussion for a more equitable future for Aboriginal people in Canada." He said historical incidents were violations of human rights, for example, Indian residential schools. He said Canadians need to look at the State and church policies geared to Christianize, civilize, and assimilate Aboriginal peoples in Canada. Murray said the physical and sexual abuse will need to be looked at, as well as missing children who are buried, and the sterilization of Indian children. There must be creation of space, dialogue, and perception. Human rights must be achieved through agency and collaboration while earning the trust of Canadians, First Nations, Métis, and Inuit people. This is central to CMHR's mandate. Murray said, "Building trust is our obligation through one, continuing partnerships with Aboriginal communities, and two, for museums to ensure the [documenting of] IRS experience with first person accounts, maintaining original versions in their own language." Murray advises support for the development of the T&RC and the National Research Centre. He said CMHR would collaborate and make available shared resources.

Dr. Daniel Caron, Librarian and Archivist of Canada (LAC), *Ottawa*, said the history of Canada's IRS has left a deep scar on Canadian Aboriginal and non-Aboriginal peoples because of the removal and isolation of First Nations children and to assimilate them on false assumptions, such as inferiority. Dr. Caron said stories and truth must be told. An enormous challenge remains: the lack of knowledge. He said the "LAC can play a role and guard against future injustices, memory is kept in communities, organizations, and engender national and international understanding." He emphasized it is crucial that the most important documents are preserved in digital and analogue documents. Access to records is indicative of open and accountable governments. It is important that a shared understanding be created in the broader society. Dr. Caron said the LAC collaborated with the Aboriginal Healing Foundation in a traveling exhibition of Inuit stories in *We Were So Far Away*, with letters, photos, and other documents. He concluded LAC has legislated responsibility and that no single institution can go alone and make available. Going digital gives access to information without place or time limit is desirable. He asked for help for LAC in "learning our past and guiding us to a better future."

Ernie Ingles, Vice Provost and Director of the School of Library and Information Studies, University of Alberta, *Edmonton*, and President of the Canadian Association of Research Libraries (CARL), said CARL is made up of twenty-nine university libraries including LAC. It expends about $900 million annually, houses about eighty million volumes with one hundred fifty miles of archival material, and involves eight thousand individuals (archivists, librarians, and technologists). He said the challenge of the T&RC is preserving those stories in frameworks of five hundred years dealing with the grandchildren of the grandchildren for an enormous amount of time. Ingles recommended that the role of the T&RC is to ensure there is honor, respect, learning, remembering, and "adding value to those kinds of activities, willingness to assist in going forward with the National Research Centre." Ingles said "In addition, there is a need to consider models of centralization and decentralization of community involvement. Going digital does not ensure long-term preservation unless there is intervention. CARL is exploring with LAC in ensuring trusted repositories of files and images are held in perpetuity, however, this is expensive". In concluding, Ingles said that CARL could offer the T&RC the expertise of five thousand individuals to assist the expertise to those in regions of the country and to make available "discovery tools to the Aboriginal people and to the people of Canada to show who we are and what we want to be."

Questions and comments from the panel and delegates related to:

- Protocol and archiving of First Nations material,
- Legislation in relation to privacy and consent,
- Digitization,
- Accessibility,
- Analogue (paper records) and,
- Video presentations.

Madeleine Redfern, Mayor of Iqaluit, former Executive Director, Qikiqtani Truth Commission, presented a PowerPoint with photos and excerpts of the experiences of relocatees in the forced relocation of Inuit families from ancestral homes to another faraway location in 1950–1960 under threats. Ms. Redfern said that the effects of this relocation are alcohol use and the disruption of family ties and good relationships, being forced to work as servants to colonizing authorities, restricted from hunting wildlife, and the shooting of dogs. Trauma was silenced. People that were affected did not tell anyone of what happened, not even to their wife or family. Redfern recommended that the T&RC records be accessible and available to hear the stories of survivors, which were never told.

Stephen Augustine, Curator of Ethnology, Lantern Maritimes, Canadian Museum of Civilization (CMC), said the CMC began as the Geological Survey work in the mid-1800s. He described the CMC holdings, collections, productions, documents, photos, and audio-visual material. Archival records include field notes, letters, research reports, maps, conference reports, legends, stories, songs, films, videos, sound collections, and audiovisual records from more than one century. The Exhibition of Residential Schools Canada First Peoples Hall honors the history, continuity, and diversity of Aboriginal peoples. The hall opened in 2003 and has several galleries. There are two thousand artifacts and images that illustrate the history of Aboriginal peoples in Canada. The hall has more than two thousand square meters of space. It records the contributions of Aboriginal communities, achievements, origins, creation stories, challenges, and ancient archeological evidence. It also records how land and resources changed over time and shaped Aboriginal ways. A small area of the hall was devoted to the IRS experience of Aboriginal people in a presentation called *Conversion*.

Augustine said the CMC does not have a plan to produce a separate exhibit on IRS. He said CMC could assist by sharing potential facilities. He recommends the taking of steps to determine the volume and type of information involved, a collaborative governance structure, and autonomy.

He said there are various sources of support funding, such as churches and the private sector. Augustine said there needs to more public consultation, awareness, multimedia education programs in Canada, and for Aboriginal organizations to commit to partner in establishing a National Research Centre.

Nika Collison, Associate Curator, Haida Heritage Centre (IIIC), gave a PowerPoint presentation with color photos of the Haida Gwaii Museum at Kay Linagaay. She said their archives are in their oral histories that record their stories and origins. She stated the first European documents in 1774 were Spanish and the arrival of Captain Cook in 1778. Smallpox resulted in the deaths of one in ten Haida survivors out of thirty-five thousand in the nineteenth century. Missionaries arrived. Thousands of ancestral graves were desecrated, bones stolen, cultural treasures stolen, sold, or given under duress. Collison said "The purpose of the Indian Act was assimilation. Ceremonies, such as the potlatch, were outlawed. Reserves were imposed segregation. The IRS system was imposed to segregate First Nations people". Ms. Collison recommends to the T&RC community representation to go back to the communities and not nationalize the process. "This means also to let researchers and academies to come to the First Nation to identify each and every First Nation in their territories in Canada. Urban Indians need consideration and partnership with existing museum and research centers. There is need for money. Objects and photos need to be repatriated to First Nations". Ms. Collison concluded, "True healing and reconciliation will happen when cultural genocide ends."

Observations and Reflections from the Parties to the Indian Residential Schools Settlement Agreement (IRSSA)

Julie Roy, legal counsel representing Justice Canada, said she is one of a team offering discussion to the T&RC. She said Schedule N of IRSSA requires disclosure and sets the mandate of the T&RC, including the establishment of the National Research Centre (NRC). She said there were common themes for the NRC in the last three days of this conference. These themes are:

- Need for survivors input,
- Need for public access, and
- Need for public and private interest.

Ms. Roy emphasized educating youth. She concluded that one hundred twenty-five thousand documents have been disclosed to the T&RC.

James Scott, representing the United Church of Canada (UCC), said he is the lead person for the UCC in the IRS issue. He said the UCC operated fourteen IRSs mainly in Western Canada. He acknowledged the IRS has been a basic element of the Canadian system from Confederation. He urged the National Research Centre "must be a striking and visible signal to all Canadians of the ugly themes of the IRS." He said there is need to memorialize and listen to survivors and families for their wisdom. He concluded that churches want to work with others and with survivors with a vision with what this country needs, a witness, and transformation.

Nancy Hurn, the Archivist representing the Anglican Church of Canada (ACC), said the ACC administered IRSs from 1920 to 1969. ACC is working on records for use for healing and reconciliation. Hurn said the "ultimate home for these records will contain copies of those we are forwarding and held in a trustworthy record-keeping system, ensuring access and for use in commemoration." Records will also be available to survivors and families. Hurn advised caution on the triggering of survivors' burden of memory and encouraged the use of a research center in understanding our collective history.

Pierre Barbeau, representing fifty-two Catholic entities, said the "speakers here made me aware of my ignorance of the work of truth and reconciliation commissions, the forty-five truth and reconciliation commissions in forty-five countries." Barbeau said the National Research Centre is the establishment of a permanent memory of the IRS system and experience in ongoing memory. NRC has to preserve records and be accessible to survivors, their families, and the public, and doing this for the coming generations. He advised the Canadian public to join this goal and that "we have to ensure that the Indian residential school records are protected, preserved, and made accessible."

Barbeau said there is a duty to remember and that the Canadian government fund the NRC, as there is a duty to the public that there is sufficient funding. He said there are private archives of Catholic entities, which have to be accessible to the T&RC. He said the "doors of the Catholic entities are open, and have told the commission publicly and privately our full cooperation. We want to solicit private archives, the Oblates in Ottawa and the Grey Sisters in Montreal." Barbeau elaborated on the value of standards and ethics in archives and in the NRC. He advised, "Basic principles have to be applied and have been applied." He urged, "The application of a code of ethics, clear access rules, trustworthiness in relating the painful history of Indian residential schools, privacy of people, and fair treatment for former religious members, accessibility, and use of electronics is good." In conclusion, Barbeau advised that pressure be applied to this duty, that pressure come from the public, the Assembly of First Nations, and Métis groups to benefit living survivors.

Charlene Belleau, representing the AFN, said compensation is not going to heal the pain we [survivors] suffered. She said it is important that the T&RC facilitate the IRS impacts on our people. Facilitation can be conducted through community events, a report to government, commemoration, and collecting of records. She stressed the importance of truth in setting survivors free. She related tribal work in her First Nation, which held the first national IRS conference, established a provincial project, and investigated fourteen IRSs in BC with the help of the RCMP. Belleau said, "Don't relegate me to another number in some archive like in Indian residential school. Don't freeze my time and experience. We don't want our children and grandchildren to carry the burden of the Indian residential school. We need to move on." She advised that the T&RC deal with related issues, such as the loss of language and traditions, loss of education opportunities, and the health of our people that are all linked to IRS. She stressed the need to engage the broader public to look for partnerships in addressing funding to create archival facilities and holdings, to ensure there are health supports, especially for the IAP, persons of interest, student on student abuse, and to restore with funding, our culture and language that were lost through IRS.

Observations and Reflections from the members of the Truth and Reconciliation Commission National Survivors Committee

Joseph "Barney" Williams, Committee member from BC, said, "We, as survivors, we are scarred for life. That hurdle is so difficult to overcome. We journey not only for ourselves but for friends and relatives less fortunate than us."

Rebecca Williams, Committee member from Nunavut, said, "I had to continue experience in residential school in Churchill at fourteen years of age in the late 1960s and early 1970s. Stories are made up, experiences are real. They happen by people. The Truth and Reconciliation Commission, with help and advice, have a very wonderful, big job from the Indian Residential School Survivor Committee. First Nations and Inuit should strive to have statements and experiences and should have control and ownership of those statements and experiences."

Terri Brown, Committee member from North West Territories, said traditional stories of Aboriginal people are realistic and show our strength and resiliency as survivors. She said, "The things we did with our soul intact reflect something, gave us the energy to get up next day, and continue." She said, "That's what I want to know, how we did it, the systemic racism that happened to me, but what continues to happen today. I want to know about genocide. I want to see my vision in those buildings to be built, to see those little shoes and the closet I hid in. I want to preserve some part of the building where they imprisoned us. I want to hear from the settlers, the settler mentality that led to behavior so we can unlearn that process, the secrets, and the colonization. We'll move to a stronger society we all participate. We need to learn the mechanism of racism and exploitation. We don't want experts, academics exploiting us. We are the experts." Brown continued with "Reconciliation is:

- Equity for women,
- freedom from violence,
- that prostitution in Aboriginal culture does not exist anymore,
- when there are no more drugs, and
- when there are no more suicides in our communities.

Eugene Arcand, Committee member from Saskatchewan, said, "It's so important when people from all over the world [come] to hear us, to what happened to us in Indian residential school. It's torturous to do this. The Truth and Reconciliation Commission's mandated work is advising, to share, and to educate the world of what happened. [As for] education and archives, we have been studied and archived to death. There must be a balance. We don't want people to become experts of the Indian residential school era because of our misery. Someone said earlier in this conference, the Truth and Reconciliation Commission has no teeth. I don't agree with that. The Indian residential schools today are the teeth. With research and archives, there needs to be research with universities, post-secondary institutions, which have a major role to play. The Indian Residential School Settlement Agreement has been an exercise in futility, perpetrators are administering it. There are stumbling blocks, revictimization, and triggering. There is $60 million for the Truth and Reconciliation Commission over a five-year term. Health Canada has a $450 million health support that is expensive with therapists and psychologists. Incarceration of my people is high. That is the place for research."

[I take full responsibility for any errors, omissions, and commissions in this summary report where I have tried to paraphrase, summary, or quote. It is my effort to give the reader an idea of the conference that I attended and what it was about and not to make an exact verbatim or full report The conference is also available as a webcast in the T&RC website.]

[My observations and recommendations]

ISSUES RELATED TO A NATIONAL RESEARCH CENTRE

There is distrust of all or aspects of the IRSSA and its components by former students. There is hostility by segments of society who think they, as taxpayers, are funding this process. The IRSSA is a court-ordered agreement. There is some disbelief of survivors' experiences. There is the constant but real triggering of survivors of their IRS experience. The survivors, their families, descendants, and their heritage need respect and listening to.

Whether original hard copies or other physical records (discs or tapes of songs, stories, paintings, plays, books, or other documents) need to be housed in one facility or center needs consideration and whether copies or photos of such records can be made available through a central website for anyone anywhere to access is a related consideration.

Whether it is proper or feasible to be asking IRS former students or family members to, again, be giving their contribution or statements at their expense when so much as been taken from them. Resources should be provided the former students, family members, and their communities.

Perhaps, many First Nations, Métis, and Inuit communities may want to establish their own national or community research center, so they can have real ownership of their own experiences, stories, records, songs, stories, and other creations.

That adequate health supports be available, such as therapists, cultural support persons, and healers, and Resolution Health Support Workers to assist IRS former students, family members, and intergeneration descendants.

APPENDIX T

"DELGAMUUKW: ONE YEAR AFTER" CONFERENCE, FEBRUARY 18–19, 1999, VICTORIA CONFERENCE CENTRE, VICTORIA, BRITISH COLUMBIA—A REPORT

COUNCILOR ERIC J. LARGE

DAY 1—FEBRUARY 18

An introduction to *the Delgamuukw* decision and its legacy was presented by Frank Cassidy. Excerpts from his talk are as follows:

On December 11, 1997, the Supreme Court of Canada announced its decision in relation to *Delgamuukw*. It is the most significant judgment [to be] made in relation to Aboriginal peoples in Canada. There are implications of how the key parties: the Gitxsan, Wet' su wet'en, and the federal government have responded. There were millions of dollars spent, more so the Gitxsan and Wet' su wet'en people's lives. This case started in 1984 and before. There are implications clearly for the legal system as it does on the federal and provincial governments as it touches on Section 35. There are implications also for the submission of oral evidence to what the court terms the "Aboriginal perspective." On the issue of compensation, when the Crown infringes on Aboriginal title, the Crown must provide compensation. It may be said *that Delgamuukw* raised more questions than answers, such as "What is the meaning of 'consultation'?" It raised the issue of Aboriginal governance, or more particularly Aboriginal self-government, in relation to Section 35. The decision has social implications, for example, for youth.

Cassidy stated that *Delgamuukw* is about the meaning of Aboriginal title, about what the federal and provincial government will do with the resources. The court, while it recognized the claim for Aboriginal title, ruled that it should be sent back to the court in British Columbia.

The Gitxsan and Wet' su wet' en spent millions of dollars trying to address the errors of Judge McEachern. The court said that Aboriginal title is a constitutionally protected right. On the issue of proof of title and "occupation," only the federal government could have extinguished Aboriginal title but, after 1982 Aboriginal title can never be extinguished. The Province of British Columbia does not have the right to extinguish Aboriginal title. What will come *after Delgamuukw* is how it will affect the meaning of "fiduciary." Aboriginal title is a right to the land itself. Aboriginal people are claiming this through activities.

Cassidy said Aboriginal title is a proprietary right, the "right of possession." It cannot be more than fee simple. There are limitations to activities. Activities cannot be irreconcilable with the traditional use of the land. Aboriginal title cannot be alienated except by the Crown with the consent of the Aboriginal nation. Aboriginal title is an economic realm, very broad in scope, and has spiritual dimension. It is a collective or communal right that refers to the right of Aboriginal people to make laws and govern. Cassidy continued, "The court said all this is about reconciliation of Aboriginal rights. What is reconciliation? One view is the Crown has to absorb or conciliate Aboriginal title. What about reconciliation of the Crown to Aboriginal title? How did Crown title come about?" He *concluded Delgamuukw* is about non-Aboriginal people and Aboriginal people coexisting, basically understanding and mutually respecting each other.

The next item on the agenda was a panel presentation on "Delgamuukw: Assessment One Year Later."

The first panelist was Dan George, Chief Negotiator of the Office of the Wet' su wet'en Hereditary Chiefs (excerpts):

"We have spent three and half million dollars in 1984. The situation among our people has not changed. Fifty percent make less than ten thousand dollars. One-third feels unsafe in their communities. There is significant unemployment and drug and alcohol abuse. *Delgamuukw* is about recognition of Aboriginal title. Our chiefs are concerned for our future and children. Since 1994, we have been in negotiation process. *The Delgamuukw* decision has been buried, and there has been no change in government and practice. Industry, in many cases, has been adversarial. There has been no economic benefit from the extraction of resources. Governments and First Nations have limited capacity in addressing *Delgamuukw*. There is an uneven playing field; the talented pool is skewed. We have to find common ground. There is a lack of public education and awareness, which indicates lack of knowledge of the decision. There is a lack of trust between the Wet' su wet'en and the Province of British Columbia. There needs to be more information sharing with government and between First Nations. The treaty needs to be clarified as to its purpose. To us, good faith negotiations imply coming to the table with our interests. Our chiefs will not tolerate horse trading the things they valued before contact. We have found that the negotiations are not government to government but are co-management with the government structure. Finally, trust is needed, and flexible mandates need to be forthcoming from the governments."

The next panelist was John Langford, Chief Negotiator, Vancouver Island (excerpts):

"*Delgamuukw* is a validation for negotiations. Sixty-four percent of BC First Nations are in treaty-making negotiations. *Delgamuukw* is a validation of the treaty process. Litigation is time consuming and expensive. The Treaty Commission (TC) process in BC provides negotiation and discussion. The key challenge of the BC Tripartite Treaty Review Process is the need to get agreements quickly to ensure the viability of the treaty process. The BC process is not about title. The second challenge is the need for the enhancement of First Nations capacity. The third challenge is the effective participation of First Nations in regional decisions. This requires involving consultation and perhaps consent in some cases. It is imperative to build partnerships between First Nations and affected players."

The next panelist was Philip Steenkamp, Deputy Minister of Aboriginal Affairs (BC) (excerpts):

"These are my observations over the past year. Within a day or two of *the Delgamuukw* decision, I realized it was a very significant decision. I tried to get a handle on what it said. It raised more questions than answers. We recognize that Aboriginal title exists. It means occupancy rights apply. Infringement, when made, must be justified. The immediate effect of the decision was to raise uncertainty. We stress the importance of negotiations, of treaty negotiations in particular. We made a process response, then a policy response came later. The government has been responding incrementally to *Delgamuukw* from day one. The historic response or options have been:

1. That the provincial government [must] vacate the field, let the federal government handle it

2. Process requiring proof of title. This process is complex, costly, confrontational, uses anthropologists and lawyers. It poses considerable risk for both government and First Nations.

The initial response established a committee of ministers to provide a policy response. The government also set a mandate, guidelines, and a framework for negotiation and interim measure. This was to be under the direction of the Minister of Aboriginal Affairs with sixteen negotiators appointed. At the policy level, the province responded through the tripartite process and concluded a treaty with the Nisga. It also returned to the negotiating table with the Sechelt First Nation. Negotiating is considered the only route, but some litigation is expected. The province also signed a reconciliation agreement with the Gitxsan and Wet' su wet'en. In support of the BC Treaty Making Process, the premier met with the Six Nations Alliance in Kamloops. The government worked with the Union of BC Chiefs. The focus of the work has been with the First Nations Summit and the federal government. The discussions concluded with the Tripartite Report of which the key statement is the recognition of each party's title (federal, province, and First Nations). The BC government is responding by:

1. Consultation—Guidelines were made to provide direction for staff. More than one thousand staff has been trained on *the Sparrow* and *Delgamuukw* decisions and to negotiate consultation policy with the First Nations Summit.

2. Interim Measures—These are made as a sign of good faith and are operational tools. They allow for discussion on cost sharing.

3. Treaty Negotiation—There are fifty-one First Nations in BC that are in the treaty-making process.

A tripartite review is in place. The province focuses on land, resources, cash, and treaty negotiation. We have set aside the self-government issue for now. We have set up a 1-800 number and received twenty thousand calls, and our website received two hundred thousand bytes."

The final panelist was Gordon Sebastian, lawyer; Chairperson of the Gitxsan Treaty Society/Gitxsan Litigation Team (excerpts):

"*Delgamuukw*'" refers to a belt used by our ancestors to wrap around the head in carrying heavy loads. The Gitxsan and Wet' su wet'en are facing the disease of selfishness of the federal government and the BC government. Selfishness is about the treaty. The strength of the Gitxsan is about the family. In *the Delgamuukw* decision, the Supreme Court ruled that the rights of the

Gitxsan were not extinguished. The Gitxsan found that the court process involved about 30 percent racists, and 30 percent did not care. The disease of selfishness results in resources leaving Gitxsan territory. The conditions of the Aboriginal people have not changed, [e.g.,] unemployment. The response to *the Delgamuukw* decision from all parties has been very minimal, [e.g.,] the BC government. First Nations chief and councils and tribal councils get their mandate from the federal government through the Indian Act and not from their people who elected them. One of the outstanding issues includes the fact that the Aboriginal title of the Gitxsan and Wet' su wet'en has not been extinguished. However, there is still the artificial requirement of proof. The BC government, it seems, will deal with the Gitxsan in particular. Nine negotiating tables have been set up to deal with nine watersheds."

The concerns and questions raised by the delegates (Chiefs) were:

- The federal and provincial governments are derailing this process of treaty making. The NDP government derailed the process with the Gitxsan already, and now they are discussing how to get the resources.

- The traditional role of First Nation women was advisory. How is this being respected?

The next agenda topic was "Changing the Legal Landscape." The first presenter was Dennis de Keruzec, general counsel of the Federal Treaty Negotiations Office who began by questioning (excerpts):

"How *has Delgamuukw* affected the law? There has been no real change in jurisprudence. There has been change in one area in the sense of confirming Aboriginal rights and title. There is no presumption of Aboriginal title as a result of Delgamuukw. The Aboriginal title refers to a general interest in land beyond site specific rights. One of the prongs of the justification tests is that the Crown must act consistent with its fiduciary relationship. It has a legal duty to consult. All rights in Section 35, including Aboriginal title, do not constitute an absolute right. Governments can still infringe with justification. Chief Justice Lamer ruled that Aboriginal title is a collective right. Treaty negotiations are political and not legal in nature."

The next presenter was Rob Lapper, senior solicitor in the Ministry of Attorney General, who said (excerpts):

"We continue to look at the effects *of Delgamuukw* with uncertainty as highlighted by the following questions:

1. How *has Delgamuukw* affected the law? There are issues from last year. The Court didn't make explicit Aboriginal title as existing anywhere in BC. Subsidiary questions are: What claimants can come forward? What does the court mean by an Aboriginal nation? What's a substantial connection to the land? What's ultimate limitation? What use may the First Nations put Aboriginal title to?

2. How does the law of Aboriginal title connect with legal landscape of the rest of Canada? The notions of private property and land tenure arise as are the questions of exclusive use and occupation. Other issues involve the authority of the Crown to grant tenures of land and third-party interests.

3. What are the possibilities of further litigation on the key points of Delgamuukw? There are strong possibilities. A related question is: What do you do when First Nations have to provide proof of assertions of Aboriginal title? Most of these cases force going into trial.

4. After *Delgamuukw*, what are the differences between negotiations and litigation? One concern is the application of limitation periods imposed under statute. Also, more generally, how and when can one conclude a treaty?

The next presenter was Kent McNeil, Associate Professor at Osgoode Law School, York University. McNeil said he found that *the Delgamuukw* decision has not changed the legal landscape. He said the decision conforms generally to common law principle. However, he found the decision at odds with aspects of common law and has left many issues unresolved. On the other hand, it has resolved the meaning of Aboriginal title as being a property interest—the right to the land and the exclusive use of occupation. In *the Delgamuukw* ruling, the Supreme Court has placed a limit to Aboriginal title as it has the authority to infringe. Aboriginal title is inalienable in common law. Proof of Aboriginal title depends on proof of exclusive occupation prior to Crown sovereignty. Professor McNeil asked, why is the burden of proof of occupancy on the Aboriginal people? He said in common law that is sufficient. The Chief Justice raised some vital constitutional questions, which affect Aboriginal title lands under exclusive federal jurisdiction. Federal jurisdiction may infringe on Aboriginal title, but it has to meet *the Sparrow* test of justification, [e.g.,] forestry, hydroelectric development. In McNeil's view, this appears to be expropriation.

The next presenter was Satsan (Herb George), Hereditary Chief, Wet' su wet'en, AFN Vice Chief, BC Region (excerpts):

"It's been very frustrating to get the governments to recognize us as people with land and a government. Yet we continue to sit down to negotiate with the governments, and all we get is talk of political processes, positions that are offered and asked to sign a release clause, a certainty condition. What does government want from us? Will it result in bigger reserves and more houses for us? Why can't you respect and accept us as peoples? The provincial and federal governments have no idea of the effects of colonization. Personally, I am fed up, and you should be too.

"*Delgamuukw* was a great investment of our people. Why shouldn't we have high expectations when we own 100 percent of the land? We are a long way from the relationship we want to have with Canada and BC. We need to get organized until Canada and BC feel compelled to recognize and respect us as people, and we should not be tricked into certainty. We need to quit delaying. *Delgamuukw* is simply a tool. The real recognition of title is in our minds here and in the future."

I next attended a workshop session called "Respecting Oral Histories." This was chaired by Wendy Porteous, Chief Federal Negotiator of the Federal Treaty Office.

The first presenter was Gisday Wa (Alfred Joseph), Hereditary Chief, Wet' su wet'en (excerpts):

Mr. Joseph said, "Oral history is hard to write down, because what you were told by your parents was told over a period of time. Each clan told a segment of the activities that took place. I interviewed elders of which 70 to 80 percent are no longer here. Oral history has been very strong in Gitxsan and Wet' su wet'en legends that have been handed down from generation to generation. There was one elderly woman who sang in court, even when she was not allowed, for she was one of the people who believe very strongly in their traditions."

The second presenter was Dr. Barbara Lane, of Lane and Lane Associates, (excerpts):

Dr. Lane stated, "Oral history use in court and its admissibility raises some interesting points as well as some concern, such as the relationship between written and oral history and the weight given to oral history acceptable to court. The Supreme Court noted the crucial role of oral history:

1. Certain evidence is only available by oral history obtainable with corroborative aspects,
2. Both written and oral history can be used and are needed,
3. Oral history is sometimes transmitted to song.

I caution, just because the Supreme Court has said oral history is acceptable, it is not time to discard written history—we need both."

The third presenter was David Osborn, QC, barrister and solicitor, Ottawa; Counsel, Indian Claims Commission, (excerpts):

Mr. Osborn stated, "The Indian Claims Commission was created seven years ago. It was to get out of the arrangement where the federal government was both the judge and juror. It was to have an independent status. Its mandate arises from the Specific Claims Policy, which aims to address claims, which have been rejected. The functions of the Indian Claims Commission and how it deals with oral evidence involves assembling of documents, and it will convene. It will look whether the case should go for mediation (facilitation) or an inquiry process. It will hold hearings and those go into a report. During the course of collection of evidence in a case, we have a session in the community. There is a visit by the Commission with its mandate. It delves into issues of the First Nation and the federal government. A meeting is held with the elders and interpreters used when required. Open-ended questions are asked and the results made available to the governments and the lawyers of the First Nation. Individuals are not required to testify under oath. Cross-examination is not permitted. Indian Claims Commission lawyers pose questions, not the government's lawyers."

The last presenter was Michael Asch, Visiting Professor, Department of Anthropology at the University of Victoria.

Mr. Asch was concerned that the courts will work on establishing authority; with parties bringing forward evidence and determining what is "true"; and about what is presented and what is accepted by a judge. For example, his view is that as society organizes in the understanding of its history, it is important that the courts study a story as a whole prior to trial. He said sometimes it is important not to reveal certain facts, which may undermine the case. He urged the need to organize a conference in which we go about establishing authority, of what is accurate or not accurate.

The next workshop session I attended was "Providing Just Compensation."

The first presenter was Joanne Lysyk, barrister and solicitor, Blake Cassels and Graydon (excerpts):

Ms. Lysyk said, "How do you calculate the compensation arising from the infringement of Aboriginal title? The *Delgamuukw* decision says there must be compensation where there is justification. But,

1. When is compensation required? How long after the infringement? The issue of limitation is a very complicated one; [e.g.,] *the Stoney Creek* Case involving claims for trespass on Federal Reserve land but where the provincial limitation does not apply.

2. Who is responsible for compensation? More appropriately, who is responsible in a legal sense if there is adequate compensation? What form or forms should it take? Normally, it is money. How is compensation determined? In our Canadian system, it is largely unanswered.

There is the issue of fee simple value of land versus the issue of fee simple value of land plus spiritual and cultural value of the land to the First Nation. *The Delgamuukw* decision also mentions the economic value of Aboriginal title land."

The last presenter was Yagalahl (Dora B. Wilson), Hereditary Chief, Hagwilget Village, (excerpts):

Ms. Wilson stated, "When dealing with compensation, what should be thought about is the greater loss that we incurred in loss of traditional activities and practices on the land. How is it compensated? What is fair compensation? When you recognize infringement, there must be compensation."

DAY 2—FEBRUARY 19, 1999

A presentation was given by the Honorable Gordon Wilson, Minister of Aboriginal Affairs BC (excerpts):

Minister Wilson stated, "*The Delgamuukw* decision can be seen to present a continuing problem or an enormous opportunity. Several challenges exist of which two are:

1. *Post Delgamuukw* means government has to be much more involved through consultation;

2. All must acknowledge some measure of provision for the continuation of resource extraction.

We must set a timetable. We cannot continue to have meeting after meeting and not accomplish anything."

The concerns arising from this presentation are:

- There are many obstacles to the treaty process, and one of them is infringement.
- Some of the First Nations do not recognize the BC Treaty Commission Process.
- The First Nations need to get the governments to recognize Aboriginal title.

The next presentation was a panel on "Re-thinking Treaty-Making."
The first panelist was Edward John, First Nations Summit (excerpts):
Mr. John said, "The BC Treaty Commission is only one body. Treaty negotiations is treaty negotiating about land. The focus is in each of the First Nations Summits. The options of the treaty process are:

1. Litigation—a number of First Nations are involved. There is little progress

2. Direct action—leads to court or some form of negotiation

3. Negotiate—most viable option; negotiate treaty in a level playing field

4. Exercise the authority in our traditional territory with or without treaty. We have the authority, [e.g.,] *Delgamuukw* confirms we have Aboriginal title. Aboriginal title is held communally. Decisions are made by that community. There is an Aboriginal economic component.

During the process of negotiation, we have been talking compensation, but when we talk, we are faced with dialogue that in order for us to talk compensation, we must have proof in spite of *Delgamuukw*.

Treaty negotiation should involve protection of treaty rights entrenched in an agreement [that] future governments can never take away. *The Delgamuukw* decision means that meaningful application will apply over time."

The second panelist was Louise Mandell, QC, barrister and solicitor, Mandell Pinder, (excerpts):

Ms. Mandell stated, "When people grieve, there is denial. It is similar with the BC Government. It is still business as usual. Five percent of the land in BC is still on the negotiating table. The federal and provincial governments are still denying. My personal observation is that the situation is analogous to the Holocaust versus colonization where one society is dominating another with supposedly modern or more-advanced systems, economy, etc. The victimization of people is similar to Aboriginal people. My Constitutional observation is that the relationship between the federal and provincial government was based on certainty where they have the lawmaking authority, and there was no extinguishment.

"The treaty-making process is based on respect without extinguishment or victimization. Pretreaty studies indicate where hunting was done and traditional activities were conducted. Aboriginal people need resources, and traditional institutes need to be funded. There should be encouragement of treaties with their neighbors. Treaty making

1. Should look at territory—ask which part will consent be required and which part will require consultation
2. Ask, "What is the territory over which Aboriginal laws will take precedence and which will require shared jurisdiction?"
3. Develop joint institutions between Aboriginal and non-Aboriginal people
4. Development of fiscal arrangements, and
5. Establish capability of treaty-making to process."

The third panelist was John Watson, Regional Director General, INAC, BC, who spoke on "The Federal Perspective on Treaty Making Post-Delgamuukw" (excerpts):

"I am here to outline Canada's perspective on revitalizing the treaty-making process. I will focus on the tripartite review process and some of the ways, which are being proposed to get treaty benefits to First Nations sooner. The Delgamuukw decision is resounding support for treaty making in Canada and, in particular, BC. It endorses negotiation as the best method for resolving issues between Aboriginal groups and governments. This consistent is with *Gathering Strength, Canada's Aboriginal Action Plan*. The parties are faced with 'How can we revitalize the treaty-making process to better address the issues and expectations *that Delgamuukw* has raised and which five years of experience in treaty making in BC have brought to light?' Canada has taken steps toward revitalization in two key areas:

1. First Nation capacity. In BC, Canada initiated this work in July 1998 through the Post-Delgamuukw Capacity Panel. Canada envisioned a fund in the order of three to five million per year for BC-based capacity building projects. Through the funding of projects aimed at building First Nations' capacity, First Nations will see increased knowledge, skills, and expertise within their communities and be able to translate that to the negotiation table. I also see considerable scope for the involvement of the private sector in this initiative

2. The second initiative, which Canada has undertaken, is in the area of surplus federal Crown lands. By targeting specific parcels, we expect to achieve two goals: (1) the securing of targeted lands, which would otherwise be lost to treaty settlements; and (2) the release of the balance of federal surplus lands through the normal surplus lands channels.

"I would like to speak to three challenges identified in the report that the parties to the BC Treaty Process have concluded: overlapping land claims, accelerating delivery of treaty benefits, and governance. In BC, almost all First Nations in the treaty process share multiple overlaps. The best way of addressing this issue is for the parties to work together in the development of a mutually acceptable policy for handling overlap situations. The tripartite review also looked at ways of achieving treaty benefits sooner. It will take some length of time to conclude comprehensive, modern-day treaties.

"Two methods have been proposed in the tripartite review process: accelerated land, resource and cash offers, and staged implementation (staged treaty making). Accelerated land, resource and cash offers [have] been proposed by BC as a means of fast-tracking the treaty process. Canada's proposal is to achieve early treaty benefits through an incremental approach to treaty making. We call this staged implementation. It's the delivery of negotiated elements of an agreement before the entire treaty is concluded. A question facing the parties is whether we can accelerate the negotiation of land, resource, cash, and financial components of agreements without negotiating self-government. I believe some self-government is necessary to implement a land and resource arrangement. I conclude with a plea for your support."

The fourth panelist was Miles Richardson, Chief Commissioner, BC Treaty Commission (excerpts):

"If First Nations, Canadians, and British Columbians want to resolve the outstanding issues in the treaty negotiation option in BC, we need to do that now. The next few months [are] make or break. Treaties are no magic fix. Treaties are broad relationships, which are simply a technical instrument to set broad relationships. There needs to be trust. We give the opportunity to negotiate issues that people are suffering all over the world for. *Delgamuukw* means change on the treaty negotiation process. We have thirty-eight tables piling up. Treaty-making negotiations must start with mutual recognition that is needed in a voluntary political process.

"That recognition is necessary for an effective negotiation process. Once done, the goal in the new relationship must be made clear as well as the principles. The federal and provincial governments are very close to making a statement for reconciliation. Interim measurement statements will be seen. How do we infuse the treaty principles with good faith negotiation? Capacity is essential. First Nations need the resources. The issue of nationhood is very important in view of these voluntary negotiations. The definition of nationhood is needed in a modern context. We need to sit down as equals in a nation-to-nation relationship in these voluntary treaty negotiations. No one should be under duress in this process. It must be attractive."

The fifth panelist was Brian Smith, QC, Chair, BC Hydro and Power Authority (excerpts):

"I have a very passionate belief that we have to get on with treaties. Quite a bit of money has been lost because of this *(Delgamuukw* decision)—in the order of three hundred million according to KPGM. Business has not been involved. We should have a whole series of consultations. Business fears uncertainty. It means you don't invest, e.g., you don't invest in Alberta, so you go to Chile. Building trust will take some time. We are going to have to have some kind of shared legal systems, dispute resolution, and shared jurisdiction. Business needs to look at all this in a nonthreatening way. BC Hydro has transmission lines that run through five hundred First Nation Reserves. We will have to use interim measures. Business is a stakeholder in the process of consultation. Business got to be in support of treaties. There will be a summit in May."

The last panelist was Tony Penikett, Deputy Minister, Treaty Negotiations, Ministry of Finance and Corporate Relations (excerpts):

"There is criticism that the treaty process is slow. The province appointed me chairman of the team formed six months ago. Some of the questions, which have arisen, are:

1. Is there are any other legal instrument other than Section 35 treaty provision to give the parties a fast-track treaty possible toward the northern First Nations?
2. Was it necessary to include a lot of detail? Does such detail belong in a Constitutional document?
3. Do we need to embed all understandings in the treaty rather than agreed upon principles?
4. Are these modern treaties less open? and,
5. Is it necessary to finalize all the particulars of self-government components?

The answers to most of the above questions is no. The only answer, it seemed, was a new model treaty to expedite negotiations and compensation offers for those First Nations who were interested in fast tracking. A twenty-page draft treaty may take a year or two. A model treaty will provide a clear provincial interest. A draft treaty is intended to be a Section 35 document addressing lands and resources, self-government, transitional measures, transfer of fiscal resources, and principles. We will soon be going to Cabinet."

Questions that the delegates (chiefs) raised were the following:

1. For the First Nations who do not participate in the BC Treaty Commission Process, can they access surplus Crown lands?
2. Can First Nations be provided support to establish self-government education institutions?

APPENDIX U

PREPARING FOR THE TRUTH COMMISSION: SHARING THE TRUTH ABOUT RESIDENTIAL SCHOOLS— A CONFERENCE ON TRUTH AND RECONCILIATION AS RESTORATIVE JUSTICE JUNE 14–17, 2007, AT THE UNIVERSITY OF CALGARY—A PARTIAL REPORT

COUNCILOR ERIC J. LARGE

I attended the above conference presented by the Assembly of First Nations and the University of Calgary Faculty of Law in June 2007.

The conference began with the evening speech on Day 1—June 14 by the Honorable Jim Prentice, Minister of Indian Affairs and Northern Affairs and Minister Responsible for the Indian Residential Schools Resolution Canada. Minister Prentice spoke of truth and reconciliation as nation building. He said truth and reconciliation is "a theme that is close to my heart and whose broad themes as a government we've been working on." He referred to negotiations held in his office with National Chief Phil Fontaine and Kathleen Mahoney. He said, "In order to move forward, we have to first deal with the mistakes of the past. I want to see a file that would bring true reconciliation. I'm very moved by the experience of the former students of the Indian residential schools." He recalled Gary Lund, an MP of thirteen years, who once heard the testimony of some survivors and remarked that the testimony was the most moving he has ever heard. He thanked, first, National Chief Phil Fontaine and second, the resiliency of survivors and said the survivors need to be honored. He said Phil Fontaine championed the cause. Minister Prentice expressed the need for willingness to engage some of the difficult issues, such as resources for the implementation of the settlement agreement. He said this process is a court-driven process rather than a parliamentary process. He briefly outlined other issues his government has been working on. These issues are:

- Legislation on Matrimonial Property Rights
- Protection under the Canadian Human Rights Act for Aboriginal People

- New steps to address housing through the creation of a First Nations market housing fund providing home ownership for Indians living on the Reserve
- Employment and training with emphasis placed on training Aboriginals. BC First Nations are implementing an education program and have unprecedented control of education
- The signing of the first trilateral health agreement with First Nations in BC
- A signed child welfare agreement where Alberta is reforming its child welfare policies that will result in fewer apprehensions
- Budget 2007—This Monday [June 11], Ottawa announced legislation will be in place in September to include a comprehensive land claims process, establish a neutral body, and provide $250 million per year for the next ten years to allow the government to reconcile differences, so everyone can move forward. Minister Prentice said, "For sixty years, tribes have been asking for a neutral body to deal with land claims. Of interest is that Oka and Caledonia, among others, have appeared [before the government] in 1947."

The Minister said that when we think of nation building, we think of lawmaking and enforcement, "but it is an ongoing exercise. Citizens are in a continuous process. When forgotten, then we are at risk." He referred to the Harvard Model of Nation Building. He said indigenous nation building must develop strategies, have effective governments, and include cultural rebirth. He asked, "How does a Truth and Reconciliation Commission fit into the concept of nation building?" He recalled his own experience with the T&RC. He said he spent time in Africa studying the T&RC that allowed the country to come to grips with its past. He said in Canada, the upcoming T&RC will provide a forum where former residential school students who have been victimized will get to tell their stories on record. He said that the T&RC must be free of political parties but that it belongs to all Canadians. He said the T&RC is key for us to move forward as a nation, that courts have a role to oversee the T&RC, and that Aboriginals have a role in establishing it.

The Minister continued, "I support an inclusive process for the selection of the Commissioners and supported [by] the stakeholders." He said we need to understand where we have been and where we are going by understanding the impact of residential schools. He said the legacy is not understood, "The Truth and Reconciliation Commission will and must help ordinary

Canadians to understand where we've been and where we're going. The role of the T&RC is to develop a shared legacy and to establish a firmer foundation. It will provide for the development of an archives and a permanent repository as a source of knowledge for the future with help books to be written." The Minister referred to the residential schoolchildren who never returned home from residential school and those buried in unmarked graves. He said Bob Watts will take the lead to research this. This work will be a benefit for the Commission.

Minister Prentice said healing is another fundamental issue that is being addressed with resources in place with Health Canada and the Aboriginal Healing Foundation in a network of support services. Without mentioning his government's Prime Minister and Cabinet's formal apology for the residential school legacy, Minister Prentice mentioned the need for reconciliation, forgiveness, acknowledgment, and commemoration. He said, "True reconciliation is never cheap." He mentioned his government supporting the recent House of Commons apology for residential school experience resulting in the loss of heritage and its legacy of physical, mental, and sexual abuse. The Minister concluded, "So reconciliation can happen, which is fundamental to ... The question is for us and for the commissioners to consider. What do we pass on? Events are planned, such as a major walk in BC and other events. This is the stuff of nation building. Nation building is not always comfortable. The T&RC will [provide] a chance to participate in national commemoration events."

On Day 2—June 15, the welcome plenary was conducted. The opening plenary session was chaired by Dr. Richard Atleo, Hereditary Chief of the Ahousat of BC. Dr. Atleo referred to the language of the indigenous people they used to address Captain Cook. Understanding was difficult to attain. He said, "I had learned when missionaries came here, as told by my grandmother, of stories our ancestors lived by. Of how hard work built the civilization that was here, that was broken down and is difficult to rebuild. We have not understood each other except the fur trade."

The next speaker was His Honor James Bartleman, Lieutenant Governor of Ontario.

His Honor spoke on "The Importance of Truth Telling in a Just Society." He said, "Today is a difficult situation. I applaud this initiative to establish a Truth and Reconciliation based on moral grounds. We have to learn to live with each other." He referred to his personal humble upbringing. He continued, "It is very important to realize that people can change. Reconciliation is possible if you give people a chance." His Honour spoke of the stigma of depression and suicide that he experienced. He said he has been involved in a whole series of initiatives in reference to mental illness. He spoke of antiracism in Canada in the 1940s and noted that there has been a change in the complex society though there is casual racism that targets Native Canadians.

In reference to education, His Honour Bartleman said, "Those positive things are outranked much by negative things like in Ontario. In terms of water, 50 percent of the fly-in communities in Ontario have been on boil-water advisory for decades. For example, there are old people living in packing cases in fifty degrees below. Native kids are four to five years behind. In many of the schools, there is mold. How do you expect education when this happens? The suicides are largely children. This goes on year after year. There is violence. I built partnerships and goodwill with civil society, with the chiefs of the province, for example, Chief Stan Beardy. Those of you who will be working on Truth and Reconciliation, pay attention to the media, to not look at circumstances in a typical stereotypical way. I selected literacy and bridge building between Native and non-Native children. I adopted a nonpartisan, nonpolitical approach.

"I established libraries in every First Nation community in Ontario. I appealed for good used books. I got one million two hundred thousand books assisted by the OPP [Ontario Provincial Police] and then the Canadian Army. You have to change the attitudes of people. This year, I collected nine hundred thousand books and distributed five hundred thousand [I was involved in] fundraising for thirty-six summer reading literacy camps and other civil groups, and for a young reader program for young Aboriginal youth, kindergarten to grade eight.

"By calling it the Truth and Reconciliation Commission may be inviting unrealistic expectations, for example, producing and shelving a report. It seems to focus working with Native communities rather than the Canadian nation as a whole. We need a Truth and Reconciliation to deal with the deeper wounds of Native and non-Native people. I suspect the Commissioners will [course?] into other issues. They cannot confirm that we can deal with the injustices of the past especially the children, the impact of intergenerational aspect of the Indian residential school legacy. I also [agree] saying 'sorry' will not be enough. What has been beneficial is the healing circles because each participant can seek healing together with the perpetrator. When you lack hope, you turn on yourself. There can be no true reconciliation unless there is economic justice. The good news is, based on my efforts in Ontario, there have been tens of thousands of others in the non-Native people and Native people building bridges and working together. And I hope the commission will do its work."

The next agenda item, "Explaining the IRS Settlement," was chaired by Perry Mack QC, President of the Law Society of Alberta. The first presenter was Phil Fontaine, National Chief, AFN and conference Co chair. He began, "I consider the Truth and Reconciliation Commission as an incredible opportunity to set the record straight. We have an opportunity to write the missing chapter in Canadian history. The churches have committed to opening their rooms. We will have access to church records. The government has made the same commitment. The Truth and Reconciliation Commission has been miscast. It isn't modeled after the South African Commission. The South African Commission was a public inquiry. This one here is not a public inquiry. There is no amnesty. It is so unique. There are sixty Truth and Reconciliation Commissions throughout the world. I sincerely believe we can achieve true reconciliation, not about bringing in more hurt or shame. In 1989, I decided to speak about the residential school experience because it compromised me in so many ways, as it made me less than I wanted and deserve to be. I found that we could never deal with the Indian residential school experience without telling about it. I never claimed to be the first one to talk about this. We're all in this together. This is a common experience and challenge we face together. Every person is important and deserves respect. That's what's important about this. Everyone deserves the utmost respect."

The next presentation, "Seeking Reconciliation: Challenges in Negotiating the Most Comprehensive Settlement in Canadian History," was delivered by Honorable Frank Iaccobucci. His Honor began, "This topic of the Truth and Reconciliation Commission is the central component of the settlement not only of the past but of the future. Without a doubt, on a personal level, the Indian residential school process was the most difficult I ever encountered as a lawyer and judge legally, society standpoint, and emotionally because it gave me a glimpse into what happened to so many people. It made me somewhat ashamed. The file was also the most satisfying. The challenges were many.

Previous to 2005 at what happened, the national chief was the one who took leadership and that brought national attention. A number of claims started. Many more followed. The legal system played an important role. There were individual and class actions. [It involved] getting the support of the Canadian Bar Association. Courts are not the system to deal with something so important as the Indian residential school issue. The message going out was not just dollars, but healing and truth and reconciliation must occur. Do not be afraid of the truth. Other elements of the settlement agreement are the advance payment and protocol maintained. There were challenges of getting an agreement—the challenge of getting approval and the challenge of getting a court-approved agreement and implemented, which is still there. There was no intention of punishing the churches. No one was getting indicted. The AFN was the lead organization. But there were other Aboriginal organizations.

There was pressure on all of us to move expeditiously with the advance payment to the sick and elderly. [Former students] were dying at four or five a day. We also had court abeyance orders. We also had to have confidentiality in our process. It is important to get lawyers involved, but it is not enough, and it was necessary to get the settlement negotiated. There was complexity, court hearings, nine jurisdictions, a voluminous report agreement, negotiations, and legal fees. [With] the Agreement in Principle [November 2005], we had to get the new government to approve the final agreement. We now have the challenge of settlement agreement implementation. The settlement agreement was successful [due to]:

1. Assembly of First Nations—Phil Fontaine and his leadership and his colleagues at the AFN
2. role of lawyers taking the early cases to the courts
3. advance payment was important to show good faith of the government and giving people hope
4. willingness to settle on all [counts]
5. realization that this was an opportunity, and
6. We did not insist on perfection but a fair and honorable agreement.

As a lawyer, I hope and pray [there is] justice and truth, so we can live in harmony and mutual respect."

The next presenter, Professor Kathleen Mahoney, conference Co chair, and chief negotiator Assembly of First Nations, addressed the topic, "The Negotiated Mandate of the Canadian Truth and Reconciliation Commission." Professor Mahoney began, "The Truth Commission wasn't a given. Ironically, the other parties, supporting a Truth and Reconciliation Commission, were the plaintiffs and the churches. We were not considered a party by the other party until Chief Fontaine filed a class action, filing on behalf and or on behalf of his family and descendants. Why did the AFN settle? Because survivors wanted one. The AFN received input across the country and the AFN support through resolutions.

"The most important things were survivors to heal, and who wanted to know of the abuses and the intergenerational impact of Indian residential schools. There is the unexplained mysteries of the deaths of children, who and what was responsible, and what happened to the remains. We wanted to ensure that a similar thing does not happen again. There are the sexual, physical, and mental abuses. We wanted a system change. We wanted better education opportunities for the children. There was the forced cultural component and language loss and meaningful restoration of language. The AFN negotiated a very broad mandate to investigate and make an overall comprehensive approach to healing the residential school legacy. The specific mandate is schedule N of the Settlement Agreement. The Truth and Reconciliation Commission is not a public inquiry. Survivors told us they wanted a safe, secure environment. There is voluntary commitment by government and churches to release documents.

"The principles of the commission work came from survivors, such as do no harm, accessibility, etc. The goals are to look at the past, deal with the present, and restitution through the Common Experience Payment, Independent Assessment, and the advance payment, looking to the future, and dealing with impacts. The membership of the Truth and Reconciliation Commission will be three Commissioners and many regional coordinators. It will be a double-pronged commission, a national-level commission and representative survivors telling their stories to the world and the use of media. There is community level work to be done. It will be open to any First Nation/Aboriginal community. There will be a secretariat and community-based events over five years. Telling the truth will go in perpetuity. There will be an archive and research center for the recording and archiving stories of survivors."

In the questions and discussions, elder Roy Littlechief said, "There is need to tell the truth about the communities. At the community, nobody knows what's going on. It's a mess. People at the community are catching on the ADR, and the IAP and the other components are confusing. The survivors want the ten and three, the ADR, and the IAP. The other three components we don't understand."

National Chief Phil Fontaine responded, "I said earlier my experience was not unique but was a common experience as other survivors."

Other delegates' comments were:

- attendance at Indian residential schools resulted in the loss of culture and the taking away of our way of worship, ceremonies, land
- shame is going to taking a long time to go away
- Is there something done to gain our culture, burial ground?
- Everything that Roy Littlechief said is true.

The next agenda topic, "Why a Truth Commission is Needed," was chaired by Justice Harry S. Laforme, judge, Ontario Court of Appeal. The first presentation, "Rebuilding and Healing Aboriginal Communities, Families, and Individuals," was delivered by Professor Cora Voyageur, University of Calgary, Department of Sociology. Professor Voyageur gave a brief background of the Christianizing of Indians. She then asked, "What does it mean to lose all the children in a family as children represent hope? The Truth and Reconciliation process will provide a safe and cultural place. The people who operated residential schools must take responsibility and not deny or be saying they were just following orders, doing what's best for us, or say this was the way things were done then." Professor Voyageur then made reference to Article 1 of the United Nations Universal Declaration of Human Rights, and five factors in relation to the Truth and Reconciliation Commission.

The next presentation, "The Limitations of the Common Law in Discovering Truth," was delivered by Honorable Murray Sinclair, judge, Manitoba Court of Queen's Bench. Judge Sinclair spoke of the nature of perpetrators of violence, that violence is cyclical, and that children need to understand. He said, "Documentation of stories has to be sensitive to the very nature of the Indian residential school experience. The adversarial process, trial process in common law, is very destructive. The accuser confronts the accused. Truth is, one, accuracy of what is happening, and, two honesty, reflection, and honest testimony. Reconciliation [denotes] the whole process of resolution in the Truth and Reconciliation. [It means] the use of individual spokespeople and translating the survivor's story. There is the option of sentencing circles. Truth and Reconciliation requires protection of individuals speaking perhaps in-camera and nonrelease of names unless convicted. [There are] standards of proof or consideration of alternate truth telling and of where and how the hearings will be held, [as well as] format."

The next presentation, "Rebuilding and Repairing Relationships with First Nations Communities," was delivered by the Archbishop for Keewatin District, Most Reverend Sylvain Lavoie. Most Reverend Lavoie said,

"Changing attitudes is important. This is the ministry of reconciliation we are faced in the church today. There is the challenge of hearing the truth of all parties. They must be allowed to do so in safe environment. An apology must not be premature. It takes listening. Getting parties together is most effective. There must be reconciliation, forgiveness, and healing that involve teams crisscrossing the country, and be community based. Follow-up should be arranged. [I was at] four, five days of fasts and ceremonies in Saddle Lake in 1998–99. Archives are invaluable to the whole process, in bridge building, and healing. There will a diocese team to work with the Truth and Reconciliation Commission."

The next agenda item was the guest speaker, Honorable Michael Ignatieff, MP. His topic was "Limiting the Range of Permissible Lies: The Importance of the Record." Mr. Ignatieff referred to the Indian residential school system of abuse as a failure that was systematic right until 1996. He said it was based on assumptions of racial superiority leading to cruelty and neglect. [The purpose of the] Truth and Reconciliation "is to empower, to remember, and to deal with the challenges of the future. It must not widen the gap. The Truth and Reconciliation Commission will fail if it only talks to the people in this room or to survivors, but to talk to every Canadian, every classroom. There are issues of complicity. What did band councils know about this issue of complicity, of silence and shame, of parents? People really want to know why. [There must be] support, with a hand around the survivor as they take statements. The perpetrator must come forward to confront their past. This is a wonderful opportunity. It is very difficult to value education in a community when there has been systematic abuse. We must lift this weight. We must rededicate ourselves. Every Canadian child deserves the very, very best education."

The next agenda item, "The International Experience of Truth Commissions: Lessons Learned and Best Practices," was chaired by Lisa Magarrell, Senior Associate, International Center for Transitional Justice, New York.

The first presenter was Professor Henry Steiner, Harvard University Law School, Director, Human Rights Center (Emeritus) whose topic was "Global Comparisons of Truth Commissions and Native American Comparisons." He said one of the aspects of this issue is the right to cultural survival. He stated, "This Truth and Reconciliation Commission looks to the dignity of Aboriginal people and the collective experience of a people with characteristics. [It is about] the importance of the inherent dignity of each individual. Truth commissions have always been part of a larger system. A truth commission has many different forms [and must be] considered in context in which it was born, example, the Argentine case following the Falklands War. Similarities are they are government created, endorsed, and run. Truth commissions were temporary bodies to the truth. There are variations like the Canadian experience and First Nations. Some truth commissions were confrontational. No victim is to be named in the Canadian Truth Commission. The Canadian Truth Commission will not have powers to subpoena nor will there be prosecution authorities. The involvement of First Nations [will raise questions like] 'What type of recommendations will the Truth and Reconciliation come up with and how will be success assessment [be made]?'"

The next session I attended was "What Can a Truth Commission Achieve in the Canadian Context?" chaired by Tamara Thermitus, Department of Justice and negotiator for Canada on the IRS Settlement Agreement.

The first presentation, "Rebuilding Relationships within Religious Communities," was made by Sister Gloria Keylor. Sister Keylor said, "There are fifty Catholic entities signatory to the Indian Residential School Settlement Agreement. Of these, twenty-three are of women religious communities who took for granted the views of their day. No one can blame the children. We want to see things happen, that we work with you, first of all that there will be no further harm."

The next presentation, "Building Relationships between Indigenous and Nonindigenous Peoples," was presented by Dr. Leroy Little Bear, University of Lethbridge. Dr. Little Bear referred to what he called "ideas." He related that in the spring of 1492, just before Columbus came over, the Spanish Inquisition was closing. He said the term "infidel" was central to the psyche of Western civilization. The idea of "infidels" started AD 350–AD 400 with St. Augustine. It was not a sin to conduct holy war against infidels. Six hundred years or so later, the Crusades began. In America, said Dr. Little Bear, "the British could not conquer the Indians through war. It culminated in imperialism and lies. They started assimilation, really was culminated imperialism, and all the dysfunctions we experienced is about that imperialism. Racist thinking is inherent in English thinking.

"Western thinking is in temporal times, example, Treaty was one hundred years ago. The referent is space or spatial thinking. In Blackfoot, Cree, the referent is place. Reconciliation is really like going on a diet. It really means we have to understand our situation. It's not about a magic formula. It's really about a change of lifestyle. Both sides have to bring about a change of lifestyle on both sides. In rebuilding relationship and dialogue, Canada has not been able to resolve the Quebec issue and the First Nations issues. Up to now, it's been all denial. If we are going to reconcile, we all have to stop playing the denial game."

The next presentation, "Helping Survivors to Tell Their Stories," was presented by Margaret Horn, Executive Director, Legacy of Hope Foundation. Ms. Horn said the purpose of the foundation is to educate the public and to create awareness of the legacy of residential schools. This education and awareness called "Sharing Circle" is done with video and audio-taping from willing survivors by gathering stories. The foundation has conducted four hundred interviews.

On Day 3—June 16, the topic "Truth Telling and Healing in the Community Truth Commission Process" was chaired by Kathleen Lickers, Seneca Six Nations, and counsel of the Indian Claims Commission.

The first panelist was Debra Hocking of Australia. Her topic, co presented with John Bond, Secretary of Stolen Generations Alliance, was "A Grassroots Apology Movement as a Form of Healing." Ms. Hocking said she was a member of the stolen generation circa 1959–60 in Tasmania, born of an Aboriginal mother. When she went to a foster home, she lost her identity. She said she was raised in a non-Aboriginal family. She noted the importance of understanding Aboriginality, healing, intercultural rejection, and the absence of formal apology from the Australian government.

Co panelist John Bond mentioned a news article of June 9 of the *Globe and Mail* that said Canada withdrew support of the Declaration of the Rights of Indigenous Peoples. He said, in Australia, nearly a million people signed Sorry Books in 1998. He referred to the *Canberra Times* front page of May 25, 2007, with a photo and script that said, "Aboriginal people still die in despair." He said stolen generations people live in every area and urban setting. Their removal to other locations was "because they were an embarrassment to Australian white society." Bond said, "One of the deepest pains is a child losing his mother." He highlighted the need for healing in a support environment. He mentioned the Sorry Day events and a journey of healing walks that were held in Australia.

The next presentation, "Healing Needs of Aboriginals," was delivered by Mike DeGagne, Executive Director, Aboriginal Healing Foundation (AHF). Degagne said the AHF received $350 million in 1998 for healing, earned $75 million in interest, $40 million given by the previous Liberal government, and will receive $125 million in the IRSSA. He said that the AHF funded fifteen hundred community projects, engaging two hundred fifty thousand people from a treatment center to small projects. He said the key was "Communities owned this process. It is not up to us to tell you what healing is about." Assessment is what community values, has the greatest impact, and uses traditional practices, elders, talking circles, culture, and traditions. Four important elements are listening, culture, inclusiveness, and balance.

Degagne said, "We held thirty-six national consultations in the last two years. There has to be an apology and asking for forgiveness. Any apology in this country has to come down from the highest level. [We] must educate the public and help them move closer to us. [With] reconciliation, [we] reach a situation of respectful mutual acknowledgment of each other, of 'a story from my heart,' not a legally confirmed story."

The next topic, "Community-Based Healing and Truth Telling: Engaging and Protecting Survivors," was presented by Chief Bobby Joseph, Residential School Survivors Council. Chief Joseph said, [We] "need the grace of God in the effort that is going to unfold, in cultural ways, in church ways. [In this] new destiny, there is fear of reliving our experiences of terror, of some of the shame. We [need] healing by telling our truth. Through reconciliation, survivors want to tell their stories. We and Canadians will be confronted by the magnitude of the experiences. There'll be movement. Be bold, courageous, and hold on the conviction that it is possible. You have a higher moral authority to bring about a true change in society [that] tells of the personal impact that results from residential school. If you can deal with this, then your family, friends, and others can do so. [We] need to empower ourselves.

I want the Truth and Reconciliation Commission that describes our unique situation, our needs, that will bring out true validation. In owning our experiences, we become empowered. Owning is a powerful instrument, and we engage the principles of the circle where equality is included. Truth telling is not a new phenomenon. It was done in talking circles. The Truth and Reconciliation Commission needs to be guided by a sense of spirit, the sense of time and spirit that started from the time of Genesis. Reconciliation is an ancient belief at the heart of our existence. Wise ones teach balance, that every part affects and is part of the whole. Reconciliation is not a magic wand. It is not an instant miracle. Reconciliation is a path, a journey. We need to start. Survivors, we can be free. You and I can be free! We don't need fame and riches."

The next agenda item, "Telling the Story—Teaching the Story," was chaired by Mary Simon, President, Inuit Tapiriit Kanatami (ITK). The first presentation, "States of Fear," was delivered by Mary Raftery as a short introductory documentary with testimonials. Ms. Raftery told of the Irish industrial schools that were church run and government funded. She said that these were built in almost every town. There was a need to publicize students' experience.

The next presentation, "The Truth Commission in Media: Blogs, Editorials, Letter, and News Coverage," was delivered by Allen Johnson, Editorial Page Editor of the *Greensboro News and Record,* Greensboro, North Carolina. Mr. Johnson related how, on "November 3, 1979, five people died in the one of the ugliest incidents that occurred in Greensboro. In three trials, no one was held criminally responsible. The Greensboro Truth Commission formed. Initially, there was indifference, then support for the Greensboro Truth Commission that produced a five-hundred-page report. Multimedia were used. There has been no apology to the people of the neighborhood."

At the discussion-and-question period, I expressed the need for attitudinal change in the mind-set of institutions, like chambers of commerce and learning institutions. We need to publicize and tell the non-Native society the Indian residential school experience.

The next agenda item was "Truth telling and healing," and chaired by Honorable Tony Mandamin, Justice of the Federal Court of Canada.

The first presentation, "Basic Requirements for Healing Survivors and their Families," was delivered by Cornelia Weiman, MD, Six Nations. Dr. Weiman is a psychiatrist. She gave a background of her delivery of mental health services. She said, "In helping, we had to consider social circumstances and economic status. Counseling included traditional counseling and listening. Healing takes a lot of time. It is like an onion. You take layers off the onion. Healing and resolving, taking your distress and pain when it doesn't bother you on a day-to-day basis, but once in a while, it surfaces. There is so much diversity in people's healing, in where people are at in their life. Consider family support, mental health, and truth and reconciliation support. People should not be retraumatized. Ensure individual, family, and communities are not stigmatized. Ensure that the truth and reconciliation be inclusive. Twenty-six percent of the homeless in Toronto are Native people according to a 2006 study."

The next presentation, "Working with Communities in Conflict—The Palestine and Israel Example," was delivered by Dr. Pam Steiner. Dr. Steiner referred to the Jewish and Arab Intercommunal Process (ICP). She said there are three processes of mediation. These are:

1. interactive problem solving—this is talking about community, needs, fears, concerns, and hopes
2. narrative—storytelling, and
3. decision making.

The reasons for the agreement between these two communities were that the Jews wanted to show respect for Palestinian pain. Dr. Steiner said the aforementioned processes could be intracommunal.

The next presentation, "Offender Accountability and Healing," was delivered by Rupert Ross, crown prosecutor and author. Mr. Ross talked on what truth is. He said, "It may well be how we experience it. In healing circles involving offenders, start thinking in relational terms. I hope that teaching about disturbing relationships will assist the truth and reconciliation process. I hope that real survivors' story will downstream [how] relational experiences were fractured."

The next presentation, "The Importance of Apologies to Healing and Reconciliation," was by delivered by Reverend James (Jamie) Scott of the United Church of Canada. Reverend Scott spoke of "How an apology can be the foundation of reconciliation." Reverend Scott said the steps of reconciliation involve:

1. approaching the other party
2. reconciliation, and
3. offering your gift after reconciliation.

He said, "Harmony with God is essential to harmony with those I live with. Reconciliation is coming back into balance with your brothers and sisters and with God, and the foundation is an apology." He described the features of an apology as:

1. must contain accountability, responsibility for harms done
2. impact awareness. Apology must demonstrate the impact. The wrongdoer becomes aware of the harm inflicted on the harmed, on their families, communities, cultures, and their nations

3. Remorse, sorrow, sincerity coming from the heart. Sharing some of the pain the offender has caused
4. Willingness to make reparation. Support efforts to language revival. Support implementation of treaty rights and settling land claims
5. commitment not to behave in the same way again, and
6. Asking for forgiveness. This cannot be commanded.

Last, Reverend Scott said that the United Church of Canada also urges the Canadian Government to apologize.

The next agenda item, "Community Involvement and Commemoration," was chaired by Ken Young, AFN Residential Schools Coordinator. He mentioned there is an elders' focus group, which held its second meeting in Calgary. The group drafted a resolution for participants to look at and consider.

Nelson Toulouse of Sakemok First Nation presented texts from the [AFN] Chiefs Committee on Languages that refer to the treaty right and revitalization of language. Mr. Toulouse said, "In 1998, the Assembly of First Nations declared a state of emergency as fifty languages were declining and facing extinction, and that only Cree, Ojibway, and Inuit would survive. Seneca and Tuscarora are now in extinction. First Nations data is needed. Start baseline data specific to languages. First Nation language and culture are linked."

In his presentation, "The Role of Culture and Ceremony," Chief Reg Crowshoe, Peigan First Nation mentioned the need for research. He said there are two kinds of thinkers on the Peigan Reserve—white man thinkers and traditional Indian thinkers.

The next agenda item, "Research, Evidence Gathering and Process: Getting it Right," was chaired by Lorena Fontaine, Saugeeng First Nation.

The first presentation, "Destruction of Documents and Getting at the Truth in Canada," was delivered by Ed Sadowski, Adjunct Professor, Department of Law and Politics, Algoma University College. He presented a PowerPoint with photos of the Shingwauk Residential School and of children, Mission World 1924. He spoke of the importance of dental treatment records/invoices. They made an inquiry into the destruction of government records. He said out of the Advance Payment program, 10 percent or 1,328 survivors (of 13,347 applicants) were denied due to records that were not found.

Sadowski said, "Government records, destruction of records began in 1930. In 1936 and in 1944, with Treasury Board approval through letters and minutes as proof, [there was] records destruction. In 1954, there was a Revised Records' Scheduling. In 1956, there were Indian Affairs Destruction Teams. Missing government records are Quarterly Returns, Admission/Discharge Forms, and Student Lists. Other sources of attendance are/could be student newspapers, annuity pay lists (by using these, you may be able to track school attendance), Department of Indian Affairs Annual Report, and Records of the Department of Indian Affairs."

The next presentation, "Research Challenges and Lessons Learned," was delivered by Emily Harwell, Research Director, Greensboro Truth Commission, North Carolina. Ms. Harwell referred to the racially inflamed shooting of November 3, 1979. She said the three trials resulted in acquittals. A truth commission was established and balancing two kinds of truth. There was individual narrative truth telling, statements collecting, and holding of hearings. The result was a public record that entailed rigorous treatment. One recommendation was being sensitive to people coming forward to make statements. Ms. Harwell said, "We had to ensure statement takers were funded. [We had to consider] trauma aftereffects of suffering and pain, as occurs after a hurricane, research findings, and encourage doing other kinds of a broader media accessibility."

On Sunday, Day 4—June 17, Bob Watts delivered the Reporter's Report. Mr. Watts said his, "Job is to summarize what was covered in the last two days." He gave an overview of his role as the Interim Executive Director of the T&RC. He said, "Schedule N gives us a tremendous guidance, is very broad, and gives us all kinds of room for us. The conference gives key concepts and challenges. There are important messages about deconstructing lies, myths, and replacing them with truth. There is need for documenting of the past.

"There is need to bring our best selves forward. There is children-focus [and that] on all those who attended residential school and those following deserve the best. There is need to educate Canadians and engage families, communities, and civility. There is need to bring forward the goodwill of society and mobilizing supporters for our efforts. How do we model reconciliation? Support each other in nation building, a Sorry Commission like in Australia. Communities must empower, not harm survivors. How do we reach out to non-Aboriginals in our areas, so they can understand and support us? Reconciliation is not magic. It is a journey or trip we must take together. We need each other and must reconcile our differences. We must not forget our women. The task before us, that is meaningful, the task is to create a process that will open hearts. The [Truth] Commission must be modest in its ability to do things."

On this the last day of the conference, National Chief Fontaine asked the delegates for direction. The delegates decided, by show of hands, that a discussion instead of workshops be held, along with a panel of facilitators and context experts to speak about their subjects. One of the panelists was Brian Calliou whose message is about educating future generations, our own communities, and Canada. Rolland Bellerose's, of the *Aboriginal Times* magazine, message was getting the story out. Charlene Belleau said, in the 1980s, in her community, "the churches did not want an inquiry." But her community went ahead with an inquiry. Cora Voyageur spoke of two types of benefits to the survivors and to their families. She expressed that resources must be available. She spoke of the multigenerational impacts of the IRS as key to understanding behavior. She was concerned about the impacts of monies coming to the communities as a result of the IRS settlement.

An Alkali Lake video produced by the CBC on the residential school trauma and called "Healing Circles" was presented by Charlene Belleau. She said this video was made to help "deal with the deep, deep work and that we have the resources and ceremonies."

In the open discussion, several IRS survivors spoke. Roy Littlechief spoke of the "curse of suicide" as an impact of the IRS. Another delegate spoke of the loss of parenting skills. Another elder wants unity, "so we can stop misunderstanding each other." A Siksika Blackfoot Nation frontline worker said, "Deep wounds will take time to heal. I am involved with Victims of Violence Program in my Reserve." Rosie Washie of the NWT, said, "We are geographically isolated. There are many former students. Use our own resources for the Truth and Reconciliation Commission. We can write. We can also read." I spoke of the need for the information flow to the survivors and families in the communities and the challenges of logistics, of distance, literacy, and of health-related disabilities of survivors. There needs to an appropriate outreach system. There must be preferential hiring of survivors needed for statement taking. Hire our own people who are educated, who have their BAs, MAs, BEds, and MEds.

Shirley Williams, of Algonquin Manitoulin Island, said, "All my family, except for one, went to residential school. I found that students today did not know about residential schools. [There must be education that] targets teachers, native education programs that will include residential school in the curriculum, also in nursing programs, tribal police, and mental health organizations. For commemoration projects, [that there be] perhaps a huge museum for Canada, cross-country museums, scrapbooks, reunions, and a healing journey. Churches have an obligation and responsibility to restore our languages and culture, and to help us protect and revitalize our languages."

National Chief Phil Fontaine said, "The resolution requesting sufficient resources for Bob Watts and the Truth and Reconciliation Commission is received by us, AFN, and will deal with it." A Councilor from Siksika Nation said survivors lost their language and that process and documentation be put in our schools and public schools. Barney Williams, a BC elder, said, "We must move on past the horrendous things we experienced. My elder's role and responsibility is to say these things to all of you. We need to love self. Listen to the voices of the past. We need to become visionary to paint our picture of ourselves, paint our picture, and not be afraid to acknowledge those that walked before us and walk with them, and extend our hands, so our journey becomes easier as we walk through life. We survivors need to be positive and move in a positive manner."

Ruby Dunston, elder from Litton, BC, said she spent five years in residential school. She advised, "Ask for more time for survivors about what is going to come after the settlement. We need to keep informed of what is happening especially in Ottawa. I had to relearn my language. I could not teach my daughter my language, as I did not want them to experience what I went through." Another delegate said, "I am first generation nonresidential school survivor. I did not know I was involved in the settlement agreement until now. There are twenty-two thousand five hundred to twenty-eight thousand First Nations children in Canada that are in care, three times more than non-First Nations children. Are you linking this with the residential school experience? I was told yesterday $96 million was being allocated to mental health services. How is Health Canada going to visit and sit with former residential school students and children like me? What are the Health Canada conditions for approving traditional healers? Make it easy access to First Nations communities. Make it easy for Native healing."

Gloria Morgan said, "I strongly believe in adequate resources. That is why I'm moving this resolution." Ms. Morgan presented the one-page resolution and said, "I so move." "I second that motion; my name is Rosie Young, OCN [Opasquayak Cree Nation]." National Chief Phil Fontaine acknowledged, "There is not anything here that prohibits this." He then asked for a vote. None of the delegates opposed or abstained. Ken Young commented, "Yesterday, I introduced a resolution. I am not going to ask for a vote on that.

We have an elders' group to advise the commission on what the components be. The group would want the majority of the [T&RC] Survivors Advisory Committee be First Nation and that at least one of the Commissioners be a First Nation person. The resolution I have will guide the work of the elders' advisory group and provide guidance to Bob Watts and government officials. National Chief Fontaine said, "We will take that resolution [Gloria Morgan's] to Ottawa. It will serve as a guide."

APPENDIX V

UNITED NATIONS INAUGURATION CEREMONY FOR THE YEAR OF INDIGENOUS PEOPLES, DECEMBER 10, 1992 NEW YORK CITY, NEW YORK—A BRIEF REPORT

CHIEF ERIC J. LARGE, SADDLE LAKE CREE NATION

The inauguration ceremony was held in the United Nations Building at the United Nations General Assembly opening session of the plenary meeting. The United Nations Secretary General made opening remarks. He talked of specific efforts to assist indigenous peoples. He encouraged State governments to work with indigenous peoples during the Year of Indigenous Peoples. The representative from the Government of Canada, Monique Landry, introduced a draft resolution to inaugurate the International Year of 1993 for Indigenous Peoples. She referred to the Canadian Government's policy of 1990 of speedy land claims and self-government efforts. The representative for New Zealand seconded the resolution and announced his country's contribution of fifteen thousand dollars for the International Year of Indigenous Peoples. Other representatives from various countries (Australia, Fiji, Nicaragua, Chile, etc.) made statements recognizing the International Year. The Nicaraguan representative said indigenous language is the maximum expression of the indigenous peoples. The representative for Chile called for:

1. recognition of the special identity of indigenous peoples and to disregard efforts for assimilation,
2. elimination of any form of racism or social discrimination,
3. explicit recognition of the role nongovernmental organizations (NGOs) can play.

The Norwegian representative announced that Rigoberta Menchu Tum has today received the Nobel Peace Prize. An expectation was raised that new initiatives for the International Year should involve action for long-term sustainable benefits for indigenous peoples. The ceremony ended.

Antoine Blanca, Undersecretary General for Human Rights and

Coordinator for the International Year for Indigenous People said the goal of the International Year is "to open a new chapter in the relations of indigenous peoples with the community of nations. I can assure you that United Nations efforts to help the indigenous people who live in the forests, deserts, etc. will reach them. One of the efforts is to give information on the indigenous people" with publications and educational material. He continued, "Everything will be done to inform the indigenous peoples of their rights." The General Assembly opened the floor to indigenous speakers. It was announced that the problem of indigenous people will be discussed at the World Council of Human Rights June 1993 meeting in Geneva, Switzerland.

The Chair of the Working Group on Indigenous Populations, Erica Irene Daes, next spoke of a new era of reconciliation of indigenous peoples and governments. She announced the names of indigenous speakers of various countries, for example, Ted Moses of the Grand Council of Crees in Quebec. She said the intent of the International Year is to promote the rights of the indigenous peoples and to complete the draft resolution of the Declaration of Indigenous Rights. She said the International Year "means bringing an end to racism, colonialism, and paternalism. Indigenous people anywhere have not been allowed to participate in the building of the States in which they live. They must be involved in partnership while keeping their unique identity in rebuilding the new States." She recommended to the United Nations agenda for 1993 the following perspectives of the indigenous peoples: (1) to assist them in sustainable development (2) establish more comprehensive data (3) adapt, assimilate, and adopt the Declaration of Indigenous Peoples that recognizes beliefs and that serves as a guide for priorities for action by governments and the United Nations system and (4) allow the mandate of the Working Group and increase its resources. Ms. Daes concluded by stating that "indigenous people have the most significant voice in politics. It is now time for the United Nations to listen to them."

The next indigenous speaker in the afternoon raised concerns, among others, over development projects on ancestral lands, for example, a telescope project financed by the Vatican ironically named Columbus. The speaker urged the recognition of indigenous territories with accurate demarcations, the ratification of Convention 159 of the International Labour Organization, repatriation of indigenous sacred objects to the societies to which they belong, the setting up by the United Nations Secretariat to set up a program to assure indigenous representation for their follow-up, and for the United Nations to approve the Declaration of Indigenous Rights.

The next speaker was a monk from Bangladesh. He said the common concern is lack of respect. He recommended that the Working Group for Indigenous Populations should be free to travel; the right to land with definite territories be drawn for indigenous peoples; and for the harmonious development of physical, mental, and emotional aspects of the person. He emphasized the rights of the child and said, "Our children are our only hope, most of them are deprived through lack of teachers. [We should] ask the United Nations Economic, Social, and Cultural Organization to preserve our culture and way of life. We must learn to renounce violence. Our common enemies are ignorance, fear, and violence."

The next speaker was the Secretary General of the International League of Indigenous Nations and Small Peoples of Russia. The speaker said this league is composed of thirty-four Small Peoples who have a natural growth of 16 percent per annum and live in tents. The Small Peoples' areas are rich in minerals and account for 6 percent of the gross domestic product and 30 percent of the currency produced.

The next speaker was the Premier of the Greenland Home Rule Government (Arctic) who said he worked closely with the nongovernment organizations (NGOs) and also worked in the Circumpolar Conference. He expressed the desire of people to be masters of their own destiny and urged that the door to racism be closed in the International Year.

The next speaker was the President of the Pacific Asia Council of Indigenous Peoples (Australia/Pacific). He advised people to "share in totally new ways of conduct based on respect." He expressed concern for health, the environment, and for indigenous people to have a strong culture.

The next speaker was William Means, Lakota Sioux, President of the International Indian Treaty Council, NGO Category II. He said the United States has bilateral treaty with the Lakota Sioux, as well as with more than three hundred other indigenous tribes in the United States. Means said he believed in the right to self-determination and added that the issue for the indigenous people is the land. He urged the United Nations General Assembly grant indigenous organizations observer status. Means urged support for the establishment of a Center for Indigenous Studies in the United Nations and stated that indigenous people have an absolute right to self-determination.

The next speaker was Ovide Mercredi, the Assembly of First Nations National Chief. He said, "We share the condition of colonized people. We were not involved in the statement made by Canada this morning regarding the Indigenous Year. The treaties have not been honored. We call upon the Canadian Government to honor our inherent right to self-government."

One of the other speakers was the First Director of the National Organizations of the Mapuche People of Chile.

On December 11, 1992, there was a meeting, referred to as "consultations," convened with representatives of indigenous peoples and United Nations agencies and departments. The following terms were discussed or references made to:

DPI—Department of Public Information (UN)
UNDP—United Nations Development Program working for technical cooperation at the nation level
World Bank—the major development bank in the world. Indigenous areas the bank deals with are (a) training bank staff with indigenous people as trainees, (b) poverty alleviation, (c) natural resources, and (d) efforts to increase participation through a small grants program, workshops, and conferences where issues of dialogue and development will be discussed.
Inter-American Development Bank
Transnational Corporations and Management Division—Department of Economic and Social Development
ILO—International Labour Organization
UNESCO—has set up a program called "Amerindian" in Canada for the whole region, planning for May 1993 in Mexico, discussing "Rights and Development," Inter-government and NGO with efforts to channel toward the World Conference in Vienna in December 1993
UNICEF—United Nations Children's Fund
UN Centre for Human Rights—(1) a series of meetings are taking place in 1993 to which indigenous people are invited. June 1993 in Vienna is the major one (2) there is a travel fund set up with the Working Group on Indigenous Populations, and there is a fund from the Secretary General for project funding for a clearing house for the UN system
FAO—Food and Agriculture Organization—land issues and activities in Latin America

On December 11, questions from the floor were directed to various departments, bodies, and agencies of the United Nations.

Question to the DPI—Will DPI publish information of demands from indigenous people in 1993? Answer: Yes.

Question to the agencies—Which agency can assist in grants to alleviate concerns/problems, such as suicides and racism, faced by our students in outside schools? The reply from the UNDP was that grant assistance has worked only in the countries classified as developing countries.

There was a question raised concerning communication. The response was that the numerous agencies need time to analyze what is available, which agency is doing what, and to realize that practical action is needed as well as strategic conferences to be held.

My comments and recommendation are, help must be available for indigenous people for training and skills development. We don't need any more intermediaries between indigenous people and the agencies. Indigenous people have advanced enough for them to be able to deal directly with the agencies. We can't allow third parties or groups to speak for us. At the same time, third parties cannot be excluded entirely, as they can still offer moral support. There must be a new partnership as called for with the inauguration of the new Indigenous Year.

There were concerns raised over the lack of access to the UN agencies through our home States. The Chair's response was that depending on the UN–nation agreement, access may not be available. The Peter Berger Centre for Human Rights is responsible for reviewing human rights violations and related questions.

There was a comment on the environmental assessments of large infrastructure projects and their impact on indigenous people and their culture.

The above brief report is only a summary of the purpose and activities related to the inauguration of the International Year of Indigenous People and is not meant to be a verbatim or extensive report.

RESUME

Eric John Large
P.O. Box 375
Saddle Lake, Alberta
T0A 3T0
Date of birth: November 19, 1945
Marital status: single   Hair color: black with gray

cell phone (780) 614-0064
office phone (780) 726-7615 ext. 2287
email: eric_j_large@hotmail.com

Place of birth: St. Paul, Alberta
Eye color: black
Weight: 71 kgs.

Descendancy: Great grandfather is Northern Plains Cree, Misih John Large who, according to my father Joseph Louis Large, was a cousin (either biological or adoptive) of Oneetahminahos (Chief Little Hunter) who signed Treaty No. 6 in 1876 at Fort Pitt, North West Territories. Maternal great, great grand father is Wood Cree, Tustukswes who signed Treaty No. 6 in 1876 at Fort Pitt.

EMPLOYMENT:
2007 to the present (2009) – Indian Residential School Coordinator/Resolution Health Support Worker 1 (IRS/RHSW1)
1995 – 2007 – Served as elected Councillor of Saddle Lake Cree Nation
1992 – 1995 – Served as elected Chief of Saddle Lake Cree Nation
1989 – 1992 – Served as elected Councillor or Saddle Lake Cree Nation
1983 – 1986 – Self-employed in retail product sales and some travel
1976 – 1982 – Employed briefly as a school and substitute teacher in northern and north east Central Alberta
1965 – 1971 – Employed with the Toronto Dominion Bank in three locations in north east Central Alberta

EDUCATION:
1987 – 1989 - Attended a management studies program at Blue Quills First Nations College
1978 – Completed the Bachelor of Education Degree Program at the University of Alberta. Granted degree on May 29, 1978
1973 – 1976 – Attended at the Faculty of Education, University of Alberta
1971 – 1972 – Attended at the Faculty of Education, University of Alberta

1961 – 1965 – Attended at Racette School in St. Paul, Alberta. Granted high school diploma.
1953 – 1961 – Attended at Blue Quills Residential School, near St. Paul, Alberta.

Hobbies: Golfing, reading, listening to music.

Past volunteering: St. Paul Junior Chamber of Commerce; Boy Scouts of Canada, Mannawanis Native Friendship Centre; Saddle Lake Red Wings Junior Hockey Club; Saddle Lake Rodeo Club; Custody and processing of wills and estates for Saddle Lake Cree Nation members; Confederacy of Treaty Six Skills Development Sub-Committee; McIvor vs. The Registrar, Indian and Northern Affairs Canada Treaty Six West Technical Committee; Senior Licence Holder 3 Registered Fur Management Areas; political elder for Saddle Lake with Confederacy of Treaty Six First Nations (Alberta); Elder/Advisor with the Health Careers Initiative of the Confederacy of Treaty Six First Nations; Commissioner for Oaths; judge at Saddle Lake Cree Nation Pow-wow; preparing and delivering of Christmas food hampers in Saddle Lake.

Life objective: I am interested in serving people where my experience in Native politics, engaged in responding to federal and provincial policies, federal legislation, and helping to provide a range of public services (education, social services, child welfare, policing, public works, health services, housing, employment procurement, and tribal enterprises) can be useful. I am specifically interested in the health and well-being of people. I am interested in advances made by medicine, social science, mental health, and writing. My values are: do no harm; respect all people regardless of their origin, heritage, and belief; I value history, tradition, and culture but also in the future and in the possibility of engaging confirmed knowledge with new findings that can be explored defined, processed, and validated for the benefit of people. I am especially interested in voicing health careers for Native people, in particular the youth. I would like to be associated with processes and persons, who operate with a minimum of specific governmental direction, are independent, forwarding looking, ethical, and responsible to society.